NÁYARI HISTORY, POLITICS, AND VIOLENCE

NÁYARI HISTORY, POLITICS, AND VIOLENCE

From Flowers to Ash

PHILIP E. COYLE

THE UNIVERSITY OF ARIZONA PRESS   TUCSON

FIRST PRINTING

The University of Arizona Press

© 2001 The Arizona Board of Regents

∞ This book is printed on acid-free, archival-quality paper.

Manufactured in the United States of America

06 05 04 03 02 01   6 5 4 3 2 1

Library of Congress Cataloging-in-Publication Data

Coyle, Philip E. (Philip Edward), 1961–

Náyari history, politics, and violence : from flowers to ash / Philip E. Coyle

p. cm.

Includes bibliographical references and index.

ISBN 0-8165-1908-0 (cloth : alk. paper)

1. Cora Indians—Rites and ceremonies.   2. Cora Indians—Politics and
government.   3. Cora Indians—Social conditions.   4. Rites and
ceremonies—Mexico—Santa Teresa (Nayarit)   5. Drug
traffic—Mexico—Santa Teresa (Nayarit)   6. Violence—Mexico—Santa
Teresa (Nayarit)   7. Santa Teresa (Nayarit, Mexico)—Social life and
customs.   8. Santa Teresa (Nayarit, Mexico)—Politics and government.

I. Title.

F1221.C6 C685 2001

972'.34—dc21   2001004104

British Library Cataloguing-in-Publication Data

A catalogue record for this book is available from the British Library.

Publication of this book is made possible in part by the proceeds of a
permanent endowment created with the assistance of a Challenge Grant
from the National Endowment for the Humanities, a federal agency.

Design and composition by Wilsted & Taylor Publishing Services

THIS BOOK IS DEDICATED TO SAN MIGUEL,
PROTECTOR OF THE NÁYARI PEOPLE

CONTENTS

FIGURES

This book concerns the history and politics of the Náyari (Cora) people of Santa Teresa in the Sierra del Nayar region of northwest Mexico. It charts the growing violence that engulfed that town as a result of a simmering conflict between contradictory political systems. As I write, it has been more than two years since my last visit to Santa Teresa and nearly five years since my last substantial fieldwork in the area. In that time, the Mexican government (with U.S. support) has increased its military presence in rural and indigenous areas around the country in order to curtail drug production and head off oppositional political movements. However, because this military strategy has not been linked to civil reforms, it seems unlikely to resolve the economic, political, and judicial crises at the root of rural instability in Mexico. On the contrary, such military responses to rural instability in Mexico contribute to spirals of violence and repression that threaten other sectors of society in Mexico and the United States, even as they fail to achieve their explicit objectives of controlling drug production and rural insurgencies. The lesson from Santa Teresa in this regard is that such interventions create more problems than they solve. Rural areas of Mexico are not isolated from cosmopolitan societies in either Mexico or the United States, and so political crises in the countryside have profound effects in the cities. Certainly this is the case in the Mexican and U.S. cities that I know, where drugs and violence have become as pervasive as they are in the mountains of Mexico and other Latin American countries.

It will come as no surprise to military planners of U.S.–Mexican anti-drug efforts that the isolated canyon lands around Santa Teresa and the other towns of the region were sites for growing marijuana and opium during the early 1990s. Soldiers have been patrolling the region against just such crops for at least the last two decades. For this reason I have not changed the names of any towns described in this book. I have, however, used pseudonyms for all individuals mentioned here, even altering some personal characteristics to hide identities. The primary purpose of this book is to describe the complicated but coherent symbolic world that underlies traditional political legitimacy in Santa Teresa, and by extension other indigenous areas of Mexico and Latin America. One point that I hope the reader will take from this book is that by failing to account for the deep local histories upon which such traditional legitimacy is based, aggressive but simple-minded governments and transnational organizations undermine their own standing in the indigenous areas they hope to claim. Hopefully, this book will contribute to a reappraisal of such aggressive military policies in these areas, which may in turn eliminate the need for pseudonyms in future research.

Although Santa Teresa is primarily an indigenous town occupied by native speakers of a Uto-Aztecan language, most of my fieldwork was carried out in Spanish. My lack of competence in the Náyari language created difficulties, but ironically it also allowed close collaboration with a number of local people, both men and women. These local people went out of their way to demonstrate and explain political and religious concepts in Spanish, a language that was equally foreign to all of us. We also worked together to transcribe and translate tape-recorded texts collected in the Náyari language, some of which are included in this book. To present these transcriptions of Náyari language, I employ a standard orthography that is widely used by scholars of Wixárika (Huichol), the language most similar to Náyari within the Uto-Aztecan language family. Paul Liffman describes this orthography in a co-authored article (Liffman and Coyle 2000: 5), which I slightly modified with alterations in brackets:

There are five vowels (a, e, i, +, u): /a/, /e/, /i/, and /u/ are pronounced as in Spanish; /+/ is halfway between /i/ and /u/ and unrounded like /i/. There are 16 consonants (the stops p, t, k, kw, '; the aspirate h; the liquid r; [. . .] the nasals m, n; the affricate[s] [s, x,] ts, [ch], [v]; and the glides w, y): /'/ is a glottal stop as in the Cockney English "'enry 'iggins"; /h/ is breathy and /r/ is retroflexed as in "hark" in Old Chicago English; /x/ is a trilled alveolar fricative like the /r/ in Czech "Dvorak" . . . ; [. . .]; /y/ is unpalatalized like in English. The rest can be pronounced as in Spanish. Vowel length is phonemic at times but not indicated here. All [. . .] syllables have the shape CV or CVV, so no word can begin with a vowel. [If not otherwise indicated, stress falls on the penultimate syllable.]

An alternative orthography using phonetic script is presented by the linguist Eugene Casad (1984) but has yet to be widely used in the region. Throughout the text key terms are translated in either Náyari or Spanish (which are occasionally difficult to disentangle etymologically), a reflection of the code switching that characterized my fieldwork (and, to a lesser extent, Tereseño speech patterns at that time).

In the years since I began this research, many people and institutions have helped me to complete the work upon which this book is based. In my undergraduate years at San Francisco State University, Steven Gabow, Mina Caulfield, Kathleen Zaretsky, and Philippe Bourgois all encouraged my interest in anthropology and offered friendly guidance. At the University of Arizona, the late Robert McC. Netting served as the chair of my dissertation committee until 1995. In the wake of Bob's untimely death, Thomas E. Sheridan graciously agreed to fill in, and has since proved himself an equal to Dr. Netting in both the breadth of his scholarship and the depth of his compassion. Jane Hill and Ellen Basso also served on my committee, and their comments greatly improved the dissertation upon which this book is based. Others at the University of Arizona that I would like to acknowledge include Alan Ferg, Marcia Inhorn (now at Emory University), Fritz Jandrey, and the late Daniel Nugent. At the Smithsonian Institution, William L. Merrill encouraged my research and offered concrete suggestions. This book also benefits from the large group of researchers in Mexico affiliated with Jesús Jáuregui and Johannes Neurath who have included me in an extremely valuable ongoing series of seminars and publications concerning the Gran Nayar region. Finally, at Western Carolina University, my department head, Anne Rogers, provided space and time for me to work on this book in an environment that encourages friendly interaction and collegiality. A number of students at Western also offered useful comments on earlier drafts, for which I am grateful. I take sole responsibility for errors that remain.

Family and friends have also helped me to complete this book. My parents and my brother shared with me their confidence in and enthusiasm for this project, and my sister her strength. My wife, Susan A. Martin, produced the maps and figures included here, and indulgently and lovingly lived with the research and writing of this book for many years. My friends Daniel Goldstein and Paul Liffman and my father-in-law, Ronald Martin, commented on ideas that have been incorporated here, and George Otis and his wife, Veshálica Castillo Guzmán, offered me a pleasant and engaging sanctuary in Tepic.

Field research was financed by a Fulbright–García Robles Fellowship and by a predoctoral grant from the Wenner-Gren Foundation for Anthropological Research. I also received grants from the University of Arizona Graduate Student Research Fund and from the Department of Anthropology at the University of Arizona. I appreciate their support.

Unfortunately, I cannot acknowledge by name the Tereseños who contributed so much to this research for fear of compromising their anonymity. Nonetheless, I recognize my debt to all those people who allowed me into their homes and welcomed me at their ceremonies, particularly those who also accompanied me to sacred sites and worked with me to record and translate texts and oratory. I would also like to acknowledge the young men who spared me any serious injury while I joined them in celebrating their Holy Week Festival. Equally, I thank the authorities and elders who gave me access to their old papers and who allowed me to sit with them in the church and courthouse. Finally, I would also like to acknowledge the many non-indigenous people of the region who offered generous hospitality to me through the years.

Cullowhee, North Carolina
September 29, 2000

xiv

I

Introduction

A civilization that proves incapable of solving
the problems it creates is a decadent civilization.

(CÉSAIRE 1972: 9)

IN THE EARLY MORNING HOURS of September 29, 1994—San Miguel's Day—the ceremonial dances that are performed in the indigenous town of Santa Teresa were interrupted by a killing. The victim's name was Antonio Morales Morales. He was a recently married young man who had coincidentally befriended me in the days before his death. His throat was cut in a dispute over money and he bled to death directly in front of the run-down, rural courthouse where the ceremonial dancing was in progress. It was the seventh violent death among many more assaults in the small town of Santa Teresa in only a four-month period.

As I waited to see what would become of Antonio's body on that day, a Náyari man standing near me gave voice to the question that had come up again and again during those months. He asked me, "Why are we always killing each other?" On that day, in that somber ceremonial plaza, I had no response to his question. Today the question still demands an answer —a solution—that no foreign anthropologist like myself could ever hope to provide. My written words will not ease the pain and dread caused by Antonio's death. Nor will they erase the memory of other instances of violence in the town. They will not convince people to respect local elders or the indigenous authorities, and they will not dissolve the hostility between local Náyari people and the non-indigenous Mexican outsiders who have largely usurped their town. Nor will they take back the shootings, the knifings, the drug dealing, and the selfish drunkenness that increasingly came to substitute for the careful completion of personal and ceremonial responsibilities during the time of my fieldwork in the town. Perhaps most importantly, they will not ameliorate the feeling among the indigenous people of Santa Teresa that "we are all dirty," as one Cora woman put it to me in the wake of Antonio's death.

But if the words of this book cannot take back the violence that seemed to overwhelm Santa Teresa during those years, they may at least be able to document some of the obliquely perceived processes that are implied by the question "Why?" They may also be able to place the "dirtiness" experienced by Náyari people in Santa Teresa during the time of my fieldwork within a more inclusive analytical and historical framework. After all, the tragic situation that I witnessed in Santa Teresa is far from unique. Not only Tereseños, but people throughout the Sierra Madre Occidental of Mexico have been deeply affected by violence associated with a pervasive drug trade that extends into and out of their mountain towns, connecting them to other damaged communities in Mexico, the United States, and beyond. Among the Tarahumaras and Tepehuans of Chihuahua and Durango, for example, human rights workers have been targeted for assassination, and indigenous people have been forced off their lands by non-indigenous drug traffickers (De Palma 1995). In Sinaloa, local people have for years been attacked and terrorized by corrupt army and police officials linked to regional narcotics bosses (Ellison 1989). In Nayarit, rumors circulated that entire towns near Acaponeta were depopulated by gunmen establishing drug plantations and safe routes in and through the mountains. In all of these regions of northwest Mexico, as in Santa Teresa, violence associated with the drug economy made a mockery of civilized life as it pitted cold-blooded killers and petty tyrants against the elders and ritual specialists who had previously led indigenous communities.

Experts have attributed this spread of drug cultivation by peasants in northwest Mexico to "Mexico's economic crisis and the continuous currency devaluations, in addition to low prices for and traditional difficulties in commercializing agricultural products" (Ruiz-Cabañas 1989: 58). From such an agronomic perspective the adoption of drug crops by farmers makes sense. Marijuana and opium poppies not only are lucrative cash crops, but they also nicely supplement traditional crops grown in the region. Marijuana is similar to corn, beans, and squash in that it grows in wet-season swiddens, and irrigated opium poppies can be cultivated during the coldest and driest part of the year when peasants have extra time to devote to side-line crops. From this perspective, peasants in northwest Mexico should also be better off as a result of their inclusion in the new drug economy, but unfortunately they are not. Instead, the pervasive and spreading violence that has accompanied drug cultivation and trafficking in northwest Mexico threatens to destroy indigenous communities. Thus, the successful expansion of the drug economy into the region requires a deeper explanation.

In this book I attempt such an explanation by focusing not on drug trafficking directly but rather on the politics of one town. My contention is that a weakening of the internal political structure of this town as a result of the formation of municipal and national government bureaucracies in the region left a community fragmented among antagonistic descent groups. The absence of any legitimate overarching community authority in turn presented an opportunity for particular individuals and households to involve themselves in drug cultivation and trafficking in hopes of earning money. But sporadic and unpredictable profits from this cultivation and trafficking were too often spent on beer and music in disorderly and unpoliced local festivals, resulting in violent disputes. In the absence of any legitimate local political or judicial authority, this violence then fed a spreading cycle of retaliation as the relatives of more and more disputants took revenge. At the same time, the violence of these local festivals further undermined the ability of community officials to carry out the traditional ceremonies—which are performed in the context of these festivals—through which they might derive the legitimacy needed to lead their town out of this dark period. The key point in this chain of violence, then, was not drug cultivation or trafficking itself, but rather the previous lack of legitimate political and judicial authority brought on by higher-level government intervention in the town. As one Tereseño put it, "Today there is both too much and too little government."

This book elaborates on this observation through a discussion of the history of the religious practices that, when performed properly, legitimate traditional authority in Santa Teresa. From this historical perspective, it is clear that neither violence nor struggles over local political authority are new in the history of Santa Teresa. Indeed, these long-term struggles point directly to a fundamental contradiction between ceremonially based forms of political authority and the bureaucratic and military modes of power that have been deployed by outside governments in their attempts to control and administer the town. During the time of my own fieldwork, this local political contradiction became a cultural conflict of international consequence as drugs and weapons crisscrossed the U.S.–Mexican border and Tereseños found themselves facing U.S.-supported military units at their doors.

FROM FIELDWORK TO METHOD AND THEORY

This book is based on my experiences in Santa Teresa over a ten-year period that began and ended during Holy Week. During those years of visits and longer stays, I attended many ceremonies and spent a great deal of time with people in day-to-day contexts, but my participation in Santa Teresa's Holy Week Festival became a touchstone for all of the rest of those experiences. Local people identified me with the festival and through it I identified with them. My participation in that festival also became a way to meet friends and to learn about their lives. In the end it even provided a method and theory for understanding the causes and effects of violence in the town. When I first arrived by small airplane for Santa Teresa's Holy Week Festival in 1989, however, these friendships and understandings were still far in the future. Much more immediate for me at the time was my own sense of failure as a young anthropologist.

Standing with my backpack on Santa Teresa's dirt landing strip, I reflected on my previous stay in the municipal capital of Jesús María. After visiting that town as a low-budget traveler with a bachelor's degree in cultural anthropology, I had hoped to begin an ethnographic research project there. My undergraduate professors had convinced me of the need for a collaborative relationship with consultants, and so in an attempt to be forthright and open I went straight to the town's traditional authorities to ask for their permission. Not surprisingly (in retrospect), I was turned down. Yet that same evening I was allowed to attend a public ceremony in the town and managed to stay awake all night, keeping vigil at a ritual fire with some of the town's elders. I decided to try again the following year, this time seeking "collaboration" not through hurried agreements, but rather through the ceremonies themselves. People in Jesús María told me that outsiders were welcome to participate in the grueling and hot Náyari Holy Week Festivals, and that the mountain town of Santa Teresa had a cooler climate than Jesús María's, so I went there. This time, I thought, I would let myself get carried along by people and events.

Almost immediately after I got off the airplane that following year I was taken under the wing of Pedro Medina Morales, a strong-willed nonindigenous man who, it turned out, had a long history of disputes in the town. Pedro had recently been deported from his job at an amusement park in the United States, and my presence reminded him of the good times that he had enjoyed while working there. That year he participated with me in Santa Teresa's violent and disorderly Holy Week Festival, pointing out that by "eating the banana" on Thursday afternoon I would obligate myself to a five-year term as a low-level *tyaru* (devil) in the festival organization. Shortly thereafter he was attacked as a result of a feud that I did not understand, and I got drunk on unfamiliar liquor and passed out dramatically. But since my vow to continue in the festival was welcomed by the Náyari people of the town, I returned. By the fifth year, now a graduate student in anthropology, I thought I had finished my career as a Holy Week participant and looked forward to more systematic fieldwork. When I returned with camera and notebook the following year, however, community elders invited me to continue as a participant in the Holy Week Festival, this time as an Apostle—a five-year, upper-level position—and so my association with Santa Teresa's Holy Week Festival continued.

That year the indigenous authorities of Santa Teresa also gave me the explicit permission that I had long before sought to undertake a more focused research project, which I began in September 1993. Despite this support, however, I was forced to face the fact that many other Tereseños refused to accept my work or even my presence in their town. Some people told a story about the *saura*, a type of vulture. This is how I remember it:

> There was once a vulture that was flying in circles over a Cora man's ranch. The vulture kept asking the man if he could land, but the man would not let him. The Cora man, however, was not as smart as the vulture, and after five years the vulture tricked the man into letting him come down to earth. As soon as he was in the ranch, he ate the Cora man and his children and then had the man's wife and all of his possessions for himself. He started having children with his wife, and these children are the *gabachos* [Spanish: North Americans] today.

This story hit me particularly hard because, like the saura, I had "circled around," showing up intermittently for five years before asking permission of the local authorities to undertake my "study."

But beyond making me feel uncomfortable at times, the attitude revealed by this story also made it impossible for me to collect the type of quantifiable data that I had hoped to use as part of a scientific "experimental method" (Bernard 1988: 62). Indeed, most types of measuring, tape-recording, photographing, or note-taking that I attempted during my stays in Santa Teresa were seen as a threat. Even questions concerning "mundane, petty facts about residence, kinship, and crops that individuals can tell the interviewer with reasonable accuracy" (Netting 1993: 5) brought on recriminations. Some accused me of being in the employment of the U.S. government (which was in a sense true, due to my status as a Fulbright award recipient whose funds are administered by the United

States Information Agency) and of surveying lands that the outgoing President Carlos Salinas de Gortari had secretly sold to the gabachos. *Corridos* (Spanish: folk ballads) about the murder of United States Drug Enforcement Agency agent Enrique Camarena were popular in Santa Teresa during the period of my fieldwork, and so some people took me to be a drug-enforcement agent like him. Even when I stuck to participation in ceremonies, as most people preferred, some individuals remained suspicious. After one ceremony, for example, a ritual healer divined that someone had cursed me with an invisible arrow, but that it had glanced off my lower back ("but who knows next time . . .").

As I spent more time in Santa Teresa, however, I came to realize that I was not alone in my apprehensions and fears, and that these fears would not soon be resolved. Worries about my position in the town, or my inability to become fluent in the Náyari language, or ever finishing the work that I had begun years before paled in comparison to the apprehensions and fears of the people among whom I was living. If people distrusted me, they also distrusted each other, and at night most braced their flimsy wooden doors and listened for the sound of gunfire. This realization did not make it any easier to do scientific research, but it did ease my concerns about being forever isolated from "the community." Instead, in Santa Teresa research became a matter of picking sides, and in my case, as an outsider interested in knowing Náyari people, this side was already picked for me.

Nearly all of the people who worked with me came from a few large families, most of whom have long been open to contact with outsiders. Not coincidentally, the principal ranches controlled by these families are located on the edges of Santa Teresa's lands, bordering the lands of neighboring non-indigenous towns. The non-indigenous (Spanish: *vecino*) people of these towns (many of whom are related through blood and marriage to the Vecinos of Santa Teresa) have long been merchants and cattle traders in the indigenous towns that surround them, and Vecino men still make the trip overland to Santa Teresa to purchase cattle. Amadeo Flores Rojas, for example, was explicit in stating his positive attitude towards outsiders. He said that his own grandfather had taught him to be friendly to Vecinos and other strangers who came through town and encouraged him to learn Spanish in order to facilitate these interactions. Amadeo Flores passed on this friendly attitude towards outsiders to his own grandchildren, including his granddaughter Teresa Morales Flores, with whom I took most of my meals while living in Santa Teresa. She described to me the negative attitude towards outsiders that some other Tereseños held: "You'll never know those people over on the other side," she said. "They don't speak Spanish and so they are afraid of you. But what does it get them?" From Teresa's perspective, her family's openness to me and to other outsiders was a long-term social and economic strategy that had served her family well since before she was born. Unfortunately, however, her pessimistic estimation of my chances for winning the confidence of those other Náyari people also proved to be correct.

But despite my limited circle of close friends and consultants in Santa Teresa, a larger number of Náyari people in Santa Teresa did at least grudgingly accept my presence in town. Not surprisingly, their motivations were focused less on my foggy research proposals than on the concrete instances when I proved useful. In some cases these benefits centered on the manufactured goods that I brought from the city, or on the posed photographs that I took of their families. Many more, however, were less interested in material goods than in information. They wanted to hear about the world beyond their experiences, to turn the tables and to interview me in order to be able to make better decisions: What was AIDS? Was it true that the United States was at war with Iraq? Did the war cause AIDS? Had President Salinas de Gortari really sold the country to the gabachos? Why was the Mexican government sending troops and paramilitary police into the Sierra del Nayar to torture Coras, and what could anyone do to stop it? In the end, the informal relationships that developed through these discussions provided me with the opportunity to attend and participate in Santa Teresa's Holy Week Festival, as well as the other public ceremonies from which I derived much of the data upon which this book is based.

Between 1989 and 1998 I lived in Santa Teresa for about two years (fourteen months between September 1993 and February 1995), and over that period I witnessed all of the major public ceremonies at ranches and in the town center. I also visited most of the settlements and sacred sites located in and around Santa Teresa and spent time in neighboring towns and regional cities. Clearly, this type of fieldwork is not based on the "quantitative methods of practical reason" (Netting 1993: 6), but neither is my discussion of the experiences that comprised this fieldwork meant to win over the reader by creating a rhetorical sense of "ethnographic authority" (Clifford 1988: 35). Rather, as I argue in the remainder of this chapter, the reliability and validity of this work is based on an interpretive methodological and theoretical approach (cf. Geertz 1973) grounded in my own fieldwork experiences.

Methodologically, this interpretive approach emerges from my personal but also public experiences as a participant-observer in Náyari ceremonial performances. It begins with the assumption that such public performances can be interpreted by observing and describing explicit symbols and the creation of meaningful tropes that their placement into particular juxtapositions creates. Theoretically, I link the interpretation of this symbolism with a cultural-historical perspective in order to show how struggles over the legitimacy of political authority in Santa Teresa have been intimately tied to the meanings of the ceremonies in which I participated.

LEGITIMATION, PERFORMANCE, AND CULTURE HISTORY

Max Weber (1961b: 229) argued that legitimacy provides a motivation to follow the rules of a particular social order not out of either fear or simple expediency but because of "a belief" in the correctness of those rules. Weber also argued that traditional (as contrasted with bureaucratic or charismatic) authorities, like those in Santa Teresa, depend on a belief in "the sanctity of immemorial traditions" (Weber 1961a: 628) to support this type of legitimacy. But Weber did not explain how such beliefs might be sustained or lost, which is crucial for any historical understanding of traditional authority. In Sally Falk Moore's words (1978: 13–14), he as-

9

sumed that beliefs in the sanctity of traditions and thus the legitimacy of traditional authorities "arose from the opinions and practices of 'the people' 'like mists from a marsh.'" Most anthropologists who have worked in northwest Mexico or Mesoamerica have also taken the legitimacy of traditional authorities for granted. Such authorities have simply been assumed by these scholars to be legitimate in the eyes of villagers because of their association with ancestral ceremonial traditions. As a result of this assumption, the symbolism of the traditional ceremonies of these regions has been either documented as folklore or bypassed entirely as researchers instead focused on the ultimate "functions" of traditional political institutions (for a review of these approaches, see Greenberg 1981).

But the fragile legitimacy of traditional authorities in the indigenous communities of northwest Mexico and Mesoamerica is not based on timeless beliefs. On the contrary, in the case of Santa Teresa during the period of my fieldwork, local officials found such beliefs challenged because the meanings of their ceremonial performances were contradicted by other performances required of them as members of municipal and national bureaucracies. The traditional legitimacy of these local officials was eroded as a result of these performative contradictions, which allowed disputes that emerged in the town's large, collective festivals to go unmediated by community-level authorities. Resulting escalations in turn again undermined the ability of people to properly perform the town's ceremonial festivals, which further eroded the ceremonial foundation of traditional legitimacy in Santa Teresa. Thus, at each step participation in ceremonies was fundamental to the construction or erosion of traditional political legitimacy in this indigenous community.

A method and theory that draws on both performance-centered and cultural-historical approaches is useful for understanding this tension between political order and fragmentation because these complementary approaches can connect the interpretation of contingent, ceremonially produced meanings to larger-scale social processes through time. Performance-centered approaches focus on the small spaces of time between the "opening and closing" of a particular performance (Bauman 1977; Briggs 1988: 9; Goffman 1974). However, during these small moments traditional performers may occupy very important places in cultural history. They take responsibility for invoking traditional genres even as they innovate, attempting to convey a uniquely creative and artful performance that will hold the attention of an audience (cf. Basso 1985: 1–2; Bauman 1977: 11; Briggs 1988: 8). As Beverly Stoeltje writes, "Cultural performances build themselves out of tradition, the known and the familiar linking the present and the past; yet the new and the different must be integrated as well to ensure fascination and excitement" (Stoeltje and Bauman 1988: 592). Performers of tradition do not simply repeat old rituals and stories, nor, if their performances are to be accepted as meaningful, are they entirely free to improvise. Rather, "the individual and the creative are brought into parity with tradition in a dialectic played out within the context of situated action" (Stoeltje and Bauman 1988: 588). In other words, through "traditional" ceremonies in northwest Mexico and Mesoamerica, struggles for political authority become lived as history.

Just as performance-centered approaches attempt to understand the relation of creative performers to pre-existing culture at a particular moment, a cultural-historical approach is also interested in exploring the relation of active individuals to their culture, but over a longer period of time. Such a perspective links large-scale historical changes with the "actors" or "agents" who shape culture. Indeed, Richard Fox argues that early cultural-historical anthropologists like Boas, Kroeber, Sapir, Radin, and Wissler all pointed out ways that "individuals creatively interact with existing cultural patterns" (Fox 1992: 104). Like performance theorists, such cultural historians would agree that culture becomes meaningful in its enactment, that meaning is "emergent in performance" (Stoeltje and Bauman 1988: 588), but contemporary cultural-historical approaches also take a longer view. A technique advocated by Fox (1992: 110–111) "starts with a cultural practice or belief and traces its history—with emphasis on its creation by specific authors, its diffusion by actual individuals or institutions, and its acceptance, rejection, or modification in particular new environments." This approach sees certain institutions as being constituted through moments of performance, but then also attempts to trace the longer histories of those institutions. Such an approach is particularly useful for analyzing the construction of "belief" in Santa Teresa because it allows a participant-observer like myself to apprehend the complicated meanings that emerge during ceremonial performances. Moreover, it also provides an avenue for exploring the larger political relevance of changing, performatively constituted institutions.

The difficulty of apprehending such performance-based meaning in Santa Teresa, however, was pointed out to me by Calixtro Noriega, a disaffected former political authority. As he put it, "Look, we are born and the *costumbre* [Spanish: custom] was already here. Who knows what it means?" As Mr. Noriega points out, ceremonies do have a certain preexisting coherence, but no participant or observer can say exactly what they might signify to someone else. Each person receives a uniquely personal understanding of collective meanings as he or she is guided by the ceremonies. Because of this implicit, unspoken relationship between individuals and the unifying symbolic force of ceremonial performances, the rare interpretations of ceremonies provided by Tereseños themselves are far from complete summaries of the meanings that these people might actually derive from their costumbre (cf. Turner 1967). Instead, by far the most common response to direct questions about the meanings of ceremonies is to hunch shoulders and reply, "Who knows?" If pressed, a Náyari person in Santa Teresa might respond, "Well, I don't know what these things mean, but people do tell this story . . ." Such stories, however, are less likely to offer clear meanings than they are to build on the symbolism mobilized in ceremonies. They introduce allied characters and scenes that add to the complexity of the meanings. In this way, rather than nailing down the specific meaning of their ritual practices, Tereseños expect and encourage the "deferring" of meaning (Derrida 1973: 145, cited in Leitch 1983: 42). This "dissemination" (Leitch 1983: 105), however, is not meant to be random, but is instead constrained within a semantic field (Eco 1976: 75) whose boundedness is determined by the "semiosis" (Peirce 1931: 5.488, cited in Eco 1976: 15) produced by the performance of the ceremonial customs themselves.

Research on the "play of tropes" (Fernandez 1986) can help scholars to document such slippery, emergent meanings. This research moves beyond the symbolic anthropology of Victor Turner, particularly in his emphasis on the "dominant symbols" (in ritual practice) and "root metaphors" (in spoken discourse) that for him lie at the heart of culture (Turner 1967: 27; 1974: 26). Instead, it analyzes the range of figures of speech and ritual action used in creative performances. Fernandez, for example, argues that an emphasis on any single trope in cultural analysis—such as his own previous use of the notion of "organizing metaphors" (Fernandez 1972, cited in Fernandez 1991: 5)—will always be incomplete. He notes that anthropology's unique perspective on the study of metaphors is to understand them as they are actively deployed, "in dynamic relation to all the other tropes" (Fernandez 1991: 9–10). It is through such a dynamic relation that ritual symbols become meaningful in Náyari ceremonies, and so it is important to be able to follow these distinct tropes as they are used to give meaning to objects (and people) in different ceremonial contexts. Through these tropes, ceremonial performances "bring things into meaning" (Schieffelin 1976: 2).

Specifically, two types of "contiguity tropes" (Freidrich 1991: 34) appear again and again in Náyari ceremonies. The first of these contiguity tropes is metonymy. As David Sapir (1977: 4, cited in Durham and Fernandez 1991: 193) defines the term, "Metonymy replaces or juxtaposes continuous terms that occupy a distinct and separate place within what is considered a single semantic or perceptual domain." In Náyari ceremonies, this metonymic contiguity is produced by the spatial juxtaposing of distinct signs or symbols. During Santa Teresa's Holy Week Festival, for example, bananas were tossed to painted "devils" who wore colorful crepe-paper decorated hats and held wooden swords. Such a series of referents made up the "inner storehouse" of symbols (Durham and Fernandez 1991: 195) that helped to define the contents of the particular semantic field of Santa Teresa's Holy Week Festival.

Freidrich refers to the second contiguity trope as "pointers" because they act to point something out. Pointers (like Peircian "indexes") locate things in space or time, or refer to particular people. In Náyari ceremonies, this type of symbolic pointing indicates meaningful metonyms, which emerge and circulate, for example, when a tyaru "eats the banana" on Holy Thursday. In doing so, the young man embodying the tyaru points out a meaningful metonymic signification (in this case, the meaningful relationship of the devils with traditional political authorities, who are also associated with bananas when they take their offices by sitting in banana-decorated thrones). In the end, this kind of "pointing" or indexing also reproduces the metonyms that constitute a particular semantic field by re-emphasizing their significance and thus replenishing the meaningful content of a field.

As in all performances, the artful use of such closely linked tropes in Tereseño ceremonies is directed to an audience, but for Tereseños this audience is not composed of living people only. Instead, these ceremonial performances are also directed to the deceased ancestors of living ceremonial performers, and to other more remote deities. These ancestors are considered to be active agents in the world of their living descendants, particularly in their manifestation as the seasonal rains, so ceremonies are oriented to them in the hope that they will continue to work for the benefit of living people. In order for these deceased ancestors to work properly, however, the elders who direct ceremonial life attempt to closely reproduce the performances that they learned from their own fathers, who have since been transformed into the rains. From the perspective of senior Tereseño ceremonial performers, too much innovation in ceremonial performance would be ineffective for the desired ends of bringing back (and seeing off) the rains because the ceremony would be incomprehensible to the seasonal rains themselves. In assuming a "responsibility to an audience for a display of communicative competence" (Bauman 1977: 1), then, these elders also guard an ancient ceremonial institution—the costumbre—that resists modification.

Despite the cultural conservatism inherent to Tereseño costumbre, however, documentary accounts suggest that this performatively constituted institution has nonetheless changed in important ways over time. Here performance-centered and cultural-historical approaches diverge. Unlike performance-centered approaches to culture, which examine history as it is represented in myth or ritual (Hill 1988), culture history maintains a chronological focus in order to document the transformation of culturally constituted institutions over time. It seeks to discover the "intentions, contingencies, and relationships" (Fox 1992: 95) that are involved in this historical change. Similarly, in this book I show how changing ceremonial performances have been tied to the shifting fate of local political authorities in Santa Teresa. To do this, I provide an ethnohistorical account that discusses documented events of the past through the perspective gained by direct study of contemporary people (Spicer 1980: xiii). In alternating sections of the book, I write in the present and past tenses to emphasize this ethnohistorical perspective. I use the (ethnographic) present tense to describe the rough shape of some ceremonially produced semantic fields. I then use the past tense to contextualize this description historically in order to understand the relationship of Santa Teresa's changing ceremonial practices to recent waves of violence in the town. My purpose is to show how the legitimacy of traditional authorities is renewed or undermined through the performance of ceremonies, and how the ongoing construction of this legitimacy is related to the world outside of Santa Teresa. I argue that this legitimacy is based on the ceremonial positioning of traditional authorities within a bounded and hierarchical religious cosmology. However, Tereseños do not blindly accept the ceremonies that reproduce this cosmology as a necessarily valid basis of traditional political authority. Rather, their potential sanctity derives from careful and sincere ceremonial practice. As a result, this sanctity is threatened both from within by Náyari individuals, households, and larger descent groups who remove themselves from participation in community-level ceremonies, and from without by disruptions linked to non-indigenous settlers, municipal and national governments, and international agencies and organizations.

2

People, Land, and Livelihood in Santa Teresa

THE INDIGENOUS PEOPLE OF SANTA TERESA call themselves Náyari Kweimarútsana, after the sacred mountain Kweimarutse that rises near their ceremonial plaza. However, I sometimes refer to them as Tereseños or Coras; both are common terms of address that they recognize as referring to themselves when coming from outsiders like myself. Tereseños trace an ancestral connection to all of the other Náyari peoples who live in the Sierra del Nayar, which they consider to be the homeland of the Náyari peoples. The Cora people from Santa Teresa and Dolores speak the same dialect of the Náyari language. This dialect differs from those spoken in the areas in and between both Mesa del Nayar–San Pedro Ixcatán and Jesús María-Gavilanes, as well as from the two different dialects of the Náyari language spoken in San Francisco and San Juan Corapán. Linguists classify the Náyari language as part of the Corachol branch of the Southern Uto-Aztecan language family, which includes the language of the neighboring Huichol (*Wixáritari*) people (Casad 1984). This classification agrees with the linguistic and ethnic classification of Tereseños themselves, who feel that they share an ancestry with Huichols that is much closer than that with the other indigenous people of the region—the Mexicaneros (*Nahua*) and Tepehuans (*Odan*).

In addition to sharing a dialect, the people of Santa Teresa and Dolores also wear a similar style of dress, which is quite distinct from that of other Coras. During the time of my fieldwork, many men still wore a *cotense*, a

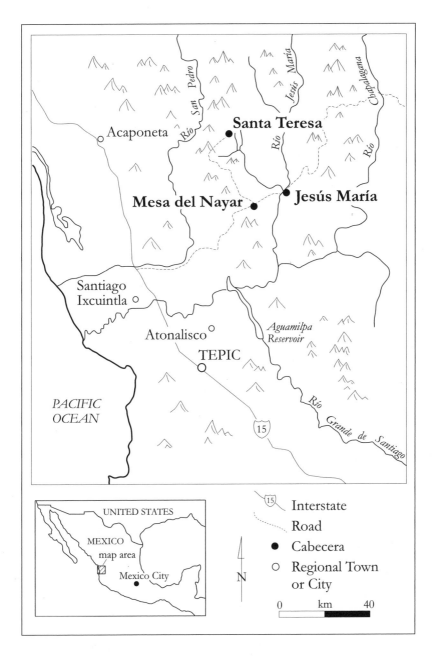

FIGURE I The Sierra del Nayar in Mexico

triangular piece of cloth embroidered at the lower edge with black and red piping. It was worn tied around their hips and over their baggy white *calzón* trousers. This cotense provided a layer of cloth in which to tuck a leather sheath holding a multipurpose short-bladed machete. Other men bought pants from local stores, but these tended to be more expensive than cloth calzones. Those men who did not buy their clothes ready-made also wore brightly colored shirts that were sometimes appliquéd by their female relatives with flower designs in contrasting colors. Younger Tereseño men were also likely to wear plastic flowers in their white cowboy hats, and nearly all Cora men tended to prefer these cheaper store-bought hats over the *zoyate* (Spanish: sotol) hats that were popular in neighboring non-Cora towns.

Like all Cora men in the Sierra del Nayar, including those who had come to rely on store-bought clothes for their wardrobe, Tereseño men rarely left the house without taking along a brightly colored hand-woven or embroidered shoulder bag. Beyond their usefulness for carrying things, these bags were a marker of pan-Cora ethnicity in the Sierra del Nayar. In Santa Teresa a distinctive "old-fashioned" style of multicolored embroidered shoulder bag that complemented the black and red piping of the cotense was still sometimes worn. In recent years, however, the women who made these bags had begun to embroider designs reminiscent of those found on woven bags, but with more colors than a backstrap weaver could hope to achieve.

Women wore long, heavy skirts that provided them with extra protection against the mountain cold. These skirts, like the women's blouses, were also edged at the bottom with rows of black and red embroidered piping. This piping created a common style between women's attire and the clothing of their husbands, brothers, and sons who continued to wear cotenses. These long skirts were quite different from the lightweight calf-length skirts of Cora women from the lowlands. Like these other Náyari women, however, the women of Santa Teresa tended to prefer the brightest and most contrasting colors that they could afford. Magenta (the color of the Santa Teresa flower) and lime green (the color of fresh grass) were very popular. Women were also drawn to floral patterns and shiny or

FIGURE 2 A Tereseño family

fluorescent fabrics that they highlighted with appliqués of flowers, deer, and abstract geometrical designs. Very few Cora women in Santa Teresa (if any) wore store-bought dresses during the period of my fieldwork.

Women in Santa Teresa also distinguished themselves by the quantity of colorful plastic bead necklaces that they wore each day. Some hung a small bell in their necklaces in reference to a similar bell that was rung during festivals for the female saints Teresa and Dolores. The gold color of these bells harmonized with the gold hoop earrings that most women wore. Additionally, women used their necklaces to display unusual collectibles—anything from small plastic goats to Swiss army knives to New Orleans Mardi Gras coins.

Both men and women in Santa Teresa were regionally well known during the period of my fieldwork for the quality of their *huarache* sandals. Just as many women in Santa Teresa were expert seamstresses, many Tereseño men were excellent leatherworkers, and they spent much of their free time making huaraches for themselves and members of their families. Fancy huaraches featured cut-out designs of deer or geometrical figures over the toes through which leather strips were threaded to make the sandal. Even everyday sandals might contain twelve or fourteen rows of locally cured leather thong.

All households in Santa Teresa also owned a number of black wool blankets, which constituted their only bedding. At night or during particularly cold weather, men and women wrapped these blankets around their shoulders when they left their houses. Only women with access to wool wove these blankets, and they were as highly valued for their warmth as for their durability. Like all Cora women, women in Santa Teresa also wore a multipurpose store-bought black *rebozo* scarf. These scarves were used for extra warmth, or to wrap around their heads as a hat or veil, or to carry children on their backs as they went to work or on a visit.

In general, the clothing of Tereseños was more expensive and demanded more time on the part of women to weave and sew than did the clothing of Náyari people in the warmer (and poorer) regions of the Sierra del Nayar. Indeed, women in Santa Teresa normally spent four to six hours each day weaving and sewing. However, the elaboration of clothing styles among Tereseños and the dramatic differences between Tereseño and other styles of Cora dress are a recent innovation. Old photographs confirm the reminiscences of Tereseños who told me that their clothing styles were once very simple. In earlier days both men and women wore clothes made entirely of inexpensive *manta*, white muslin cloth. The only decoration was a thin stripe of red and a thin stripe of black piping at the base of women's blouses and skirts and at the base of men's cotenses. This decoration continues today, but it is now overwhelmed by brilliantly colorful recent styles of "traditional" Tereseño dress. Necklaces were also very simple—a single strand of beads—and people went barefoot or wore simpler huaraches. These changes in clothing styles have occurred over the same period of time as the building of the modern town of Santa Teresa on the ancestral lands of the Náyari Kweimarútsana.

Within the memory of many Cora people living today, the main ceremonial plaza (where the Holy Week Festival takes place) and a number of dispersed homesteads were all that comprised the "town" of Santa Teresa. The buildings on the plaza were made of stone and had thatched roofs. On the east side of this plaza stood the church, whose thick walls were used as a mausoleum to inter deceased infants. Wooden crosses and mounds of dirt covering the graves of the dead surrounded the church. Just north of it was a smaller building—"the governor's house"—used to store ceremonial paraphernalia and to house the governor and his family during his year-long term of office. On the west side of the plaza stood the courthouse or *juzgado*, where local authorities heard disputes and supervised annual ceremonial cycles. Just north of the courthouse was a smaller two-room building, one room used as a jail and the other used by women to cook communal meals for community ceremonies like the Holy Week Festival. On the north side of the plaza was the impressive ruin of a church left from the Jesuits' period of missionary work in town during the 1700s, along with a few other smaller buildings that housed the occasional priest or teacher sent from the lowlands. On the south side

of the plaza a rail fence kept out livestock, and in the center was a framework of four tall posts within which Santa Teresa, the female patron saint
of the town, was raised during her feast day.

Like the red and black piping that still trims the Tereseños' elaborate
new clothing, the old buildings that mark the ceremonial plaza were still
present during the period of my fieldwork, but they were increasingly
overwhelmed by the recent buildings that make up the modern Mexican
town of Santa Teresa. Furthermore, the people who increasingly defined
the terms of social interaction in this town were no longer Náyari, but
non-indigenous shopkeepers who were building their homes just outside
of the plaza in the center of this new town. Most of these shopkeepers
were related to each other by blood or marriage and traced their descent
to families in Jalisco and Durango. Indeed, although sometimes referred
to as *mestizos*—mixed-blooded Mexicans (called Vecinos locally)—many
of them denied any Indian ancestry whatsoever. Instead, they took pride
in connecting their ancestry to nearby Spanish-speaking towns. Like the
"military settlement colonies" of colonial northern Mexico (cf. Katz
1976), these towns were derived from bellicose communities of soldier-
farmers who defined their racial identities in opposition to the enemy Indian groups that once surrounded them (cf. Nugent 1993).

Still, most of these Vecino shopkeepers were not newcomers to Santa
Teresa. Many could trace at least three generations of relatives who had
resided continuously in or around the town, a deeper local descent than
some local Náyari people (who traced their descent to other towns).
However, prior to the completion of the federally funded Zacatecas-Ruiz
road in 1987, these Vecinos lived on dispersed homesteads among local
Tereseños as ranchers, small-time *arrieros* (Spanish: muleteer-traders), or
cattle buyers. The small business enterprises of the parents of these local
Vecinos came and went depending on the luck and fortitude of the individual merchants. The new road, however, allowed more substantial
businesses to flourish, and these local Vecino families used their profits to
build up a town center where not long before there was only a ceremonial
plaza edged with a few old buildings.

In addition to the shops and homes of these local Vecinos, the Mexican

FIGURE 3 Santa Teresa in 1993

government and the Catholic Church also constructed a number of newer buildings in and around the plaza of Santa Teresa. Following the clearing of an airstrip in the 1960s, outside government officials decided to build a grammar school, a clinic, a basketball court, and a "cultural mission" along the main trail—then widened to a dusty (or muddy, depending on the season) dirt road—on the south side of the plaza. A government-subsidized food store was also built on the north side of the plaza. Next to the old courthouse, the jail and women's cook house was torn down to make way for a modern brick building, which was supposed to house the agrarian commissioner's office and a refurbished jail (still incomplete at the end of my fieldwork). Later, the former site of a one-room school, on the north side of the plaza, was converted to a military base for the soldiers who occupied the town between 1987 and 1990. A Franciscan mission was also built in the northeast corner of the plaza beginning in 1965, and at that time a new cemetery was established away from the church on the outskirts of town.

Most of these new buildings were staffed by lowland Mexicans who chose to live near the shops of local Vecinos close to the plaza. By and large these outsiders spent as little time as possible in town before seeking out better-paying and less-isolated posts elsewhere. Others, however, took up more permanent residence. Priests and mission workers were known to stay for more than five years at a time. Some soldiers married into a local Vecino family and opened their own successful shops near the plaza. Several Náyari teachers also took up permanent residence in town, but these bilingual teachers were from the municipal capital of Jesús María, and their Spanish-speaking children preferred to associate with the children of local Vecinos.

As the town of Santa Teresa grew and the influence and power of local Vecinos spread, Tereseños continued to work their lands. These lands were isolated, rugged, and of poor quality, but when compared to other Náyari communities, the land base controlled by Tereseños was envied. At the time of my fieldwork, Tereseños claimed 166,000 hectares as their patrimony and had ratified government title to 104,000 hectares,* larger than any other Cora *comunidad indígena* (Spanish: indigenous community) in the Sierra del Nayar. Santa Teresa's lands included whole watersheds that extended from the semi-tropical river bottoms through brushland and oak woodlands and on up to the prairies and highest pine-covered peaks of the region—an elevation gain of 2,000 meters. These different land types gave Tereseños options for diversifying their agrarian livelihood that other Coras did not possess, and it was this relatively ample land base that accounted for the long-held impressions of other indigenous people in the region that Tereseños were a wealthy people.

But although Tereseños have long been envied for their relative personal wealth and the size and productivity of their agricultural lands and pastures, government bureaucrats and industrial capitalists in Guadalajara and Durango coveted a still more lucrative prize. Into the 1990s,

---

*Presidential Resolution, April 20, 1967, published in the *Diario Oficial* on May 30 of that year. This land title is also published in *Agrario Nacional*, volume 631, page 232, November 17, 1975.

Santa Teresa contained one of the largest stands of virgin pine forest in the Sierra Madre Occidental (Sanchez O. 1980). Throughout the mountainous areas of Sonora, Chihuahua, and Durango, large-scale forestry operations had been cutting logs for decades, and Santa Teresa had received offers to buy their timber for more than fifty years. During the time of my fieldwork, however, these offers had still not been accepted, and wildcat loggers—both Náyari and Vecino—were shut down.

In the absence of a timber (or drug) economy, then, Tereseños remained agropastoralists. This complicated livelihood combined swidden farming, small-scale plow agriculture, kitchen gardening, tropical and highland orchard-keeping, and the gathering of wild foods with the herding of diverse livestock. Those Tereseños who could not make a living in Santa Teresa as agropastoralists were forced to work as wage laborers on the coast (very few Tereseños had managed to find work in the United States). Two types of day labor were open to short-term migrant workers from Santa Teresa at that time—picking coffee in the plantations around Compostela or picking beans and tobacco on the farms around Acaponeta. But in either Compostela or Acaponeta the work was hot and tiring, and the ordeal of trekking back and forth was dangerous and sometimes—if no work was contracted—futile. Except for an occasional group of teenage boys looking for adventure, Tereseños worked as laborers on the coast only when they were forced to do so by dire economic need.

Beyond the harsh working conditions, Tereseños also disliked going to the coast to work because of the difficulties involved in maintaining their orchards, gardens, and herds while they were away. Work in Compostela weeding, pruning, fencing, and picking coffee went on year-round, and so wage labor there necessarily tended to conflict with agropastoral production in Santa Teresa. But even work in the tobacco and bean fields near Acaponeta, which occurred during the dry season, could lead to problems back home: fences might be breached, animals might be lost, or property might be stolen. Even the poorest Tereseños, with little property to lose, feared returning to find themselves abandoned by their spouse or having missed out on some short-term opportunity.

Wage labor outside Santa Teresa, like the formation of an agropastoral livelihood inside the town, involved a number of trade-offs and balancing acts, and labor to pursue these diverse agricultural and economic enterprises was mobilized from within allied households connected through ties of kinship. In this agropastoral adaptation, the ability of these related households to control resources within the common-property lands of Santa Teresa and to overcome the conflicting responsibilities involved in pursuing wage labor and other diverse agrarian enterprises determined in large measure the wealth of individuals, households, and descent groups. In the following section of this chapter I discuss in more detail the social organization of this agrarian livelihood in Santa Teresa.

TERESEÑO CULTURAL ECOLOGY

Today seven Cora towns (Jesús María, San Francisco, Mesa del Nayar, Dolores, Sánta Teresa, San Juan Corapán, and San Pedro Ixcatán) are divided into two municipalities (El Nayar and Ruiz). Unlike the ethnographically more well-known *municipios* (Spanish: municipalities) of Guatemala and southern Mexico, each of these towns supports a separate civil-religious hierarchy or "cargo system" of traditional political and religious authorities. Only Jesús María is a municipal capital. It is also the only Náyari town divided into *barrios* (Spanish: districts), a fact that led Arturo Monzón (1945) to argue long ago that the four Cora barrios of Jesús María represent a survival of exogamous (out-marrying) patrilineal clans similar to the type that made up the *calpulli* residential compounds of the pre-conquest Aztec capital of Tenochtitlán. As will be discussed below, Monzón was on the right track regarding exogamous descent groups among the Cora, but, ironically, for the wrong reasons.

The only other ethnographer to provide in-depth descriptions of Cora social organization was the U.S. anthropologist Thomas Hinton. He differed from Monzón (who based his article on information from one Cora consultant in Mexico City) in arguing that not patrilineages but the village community as a whole was the most important level of social integration above the household (Hinton 1981: 1). For Hinton the basis of this village community was the local cargo system. He described Jesús María's traditional system of political and religious offices in some detail (Hinton 1964), arguing that participation in that system was the principal source of cohesiveness among distinct nuclear family households in each of the different Cora towns (Hinton 1970: 18). Indeed, in at least one article he is explicit in arguing that for the Coras, "primary identity is with the *pueblo*" (Hinton 1970: 20). At the same time, however, he also briefly mentioned the pervasiveness of dispersed settlements, or *ranchos*, where most Coras were said to spend their time. But, beyond mentioning that these Cora ranches were less formalized than Huichol ranches, and that "virilocality [a.k.a. patrilocality (living with your father after marriage)] predominates slightly" (Grimes and Hinton 1969: 803), he did not pursue the topic.

In Santa Teresa during the time of my fieldwork, community-level political and religious officials were important. Their work focused on the courthouse, the church, and the centrally located ceremonial plaza where inclusive ceremonies like the Holy Week Festival were celebrated. But I also gradually came to see that ranches represented an even more fundamental level of social organization through which people adapted themselves to an agropastoral livelihood. Census data gathered from 150 households in Santa Teresa (an approximately 50 percent "snowball" sample [Bernard 1988: 98] of total households, excluding the areas "on the other side" around Rancho Viejo, Cabezas, Linda Vista, and Dolores) suggests the importance of these ranches for understanding Tereseño cultural ecology (Table 1). At first glance such census data seems only to show, as Hinton suggested, that patrilocal (or virilocal) households slightly predominated among non-nuclear households in Santa Teresa. However, such data can be misleading because it ignores just the kind of loose clustering of households through which ranches of allied households are formed in the Sierra del Nayar.

Closer analysis of this data based on information gathered during fieldwork shows that although only 26.7 percent of these households (the patrilocal and fraternal households) demonstrated a clear tendency towards the localization of patrilateral kin within the same household, the

TABLE I *Tereseño Household Morphology*

Neolocal	92
Patrilocal	33
Uxorilocal	8
Fraternal	7
Uxoripaternal	5
Other	5
TOTAL	150

heads of 65 percent of the total households in this sample were immediately neighbored by the households of other male patrilateral kin. Another 6.4 percent of households were themselves geographically isolated patrilocal households, and an additional 4.2 percent were headed by widows who were once part of such patrilocal households. Finally, another 3.5 percent of household heads lived near a maternal uncle or grandfather, and so participated more closely in their maternal, rather than paternal, descent group (see Figure 5). This means that the members of 79.1 percent of households in this sample were consanguinally related (through blood, or rather "maize"; see below) to the localized descent-group segments within which they lived. In contrast, 7.1 percent of household heads lived within affinally related (through marriage) descent-group segments; they were in-marrying son-in-laws of a localized descent group to which they did not belong. The remaining households in the sample consisted mostly of isolated nuclear families, with the occasional isolated female-headed or dual-sister (uxorilocal) household. This data shows that ranches—in Santa Teresa at least—were not simply random aggregations of households, but instead tended to consist of particular localized descent-group segments, especially patrilateral descent-group segments.

Correspondingly, in Santa Teresa primary identification during the period of my fieldwork was not with the pueblo and its community-level officials and ceremonies, but with these localized descent-group ranchos. These descent-group segments were in turn linked to other descent

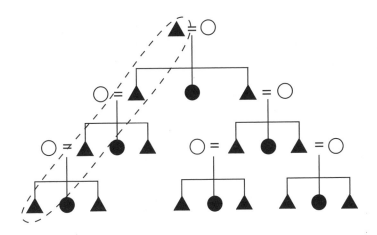

FIGURE 4 Idealized Kinship Diagram
of Leading Descent-Group Segments

groups within a complicated and extensive cognatic system (cf. Fox
1967: 146). This cognatic descent system—based on the tracing of descent to more than one ancestral group—was formed and sustained
through participation in cycles of ceremonies called in Náyari the *yi'irá* or
"custom" of each descent group. In Spanish the ceremonies that comprised these cycles were called *mitotes* (Náyari: *nyera*, "dance") and were
carried out at the homes of each of the elders of the distinct descent
groups. These elders were referred to in Náyari with the kinship term *ta-
watsi* (*tawátsimwa*, pl.), "our ceremonial elder." These ceremonial elders
were all men, and with noted exceptions they were the eldest sons of deceased ceremonial elders; they had an inheritance of ceremonial responsibilities that tended to form ranked segments within distinct descent
groups (see Figure 4). They had responsibilities to all their descendants
that took part in their mitote ceremonies.

Mitote ceremonies constructed descent-group affiliation through the
ritual association of descent-group members with bundled ears of white
maize. Thus their consanguineous relation is not based on a notion of
shared blood but of shared maize. For this reason I subsequently refer to
the people who trace their descent to a particular mitote ceremony as a

"maize-bundle group." Typically, descent-group members (those sharing the same yi'irá) become associated with bundles of maize in their early childhood, during their first mitotes. After completing their baptism ritual (discussed in the following chapter), young people born of descent-group members receive their first ear of white maize during that year's mitote ceremonies. Each year an additional ear of maize is given to them. A girl receives only four of these ears in four consecutive years to complete her bundle. In contrast, a boy receives the full complement of five ears in five consecutive years, at which point his soul is considered to be fully integrated into the maize-bundle group, of which the descent group's ancient variety of white maize is a powerful symbol. Friends commented to me that this variety of white maize originated during the time that sacred rocks and mountain peaks still walked the earth as the ancestors of these descent groups. For this reason, the ongoing cultivation of this maize was taken as concrete proof of the connection of each member of each maize-bundle group with the originators of that group during the distant ancestral time. Indeed, descent-group affiliation through mitote participation was spoken of as much stronger and more deeply abiding than an unconsecrated birth relationship to relatives outside of an individual's immediate household. A child who did not participate in mitotes because he or she moved away, or had a Vecino parent, or simply never attended the mitotes of a particular maize-bundle group for whatever reason was lost to that descent group. Thus, for Tereseños, "blood" was a necessary but not sufficient indication of consanguinity.

But kinship among the Cora was reckoned bilaterally, and so individuals might "have their maize" at the house of the ceremonial elder of each grandparent's maize-bundle group. In this way a cognatic descent system was elaborated through continued attendance at distinct mitote ceremonies linked to distinct descent groups. By continuing to attend descent-group mitotes, some people actively traced their descent back to the ceremonial elders of their great-grandparents, or even great-great-grandparents. There was no fixed limit to the number of maize-bundle groups to which an individual might pertain. Unlike unilineal descent systems, then, in this cognatic descent system an individual might be a

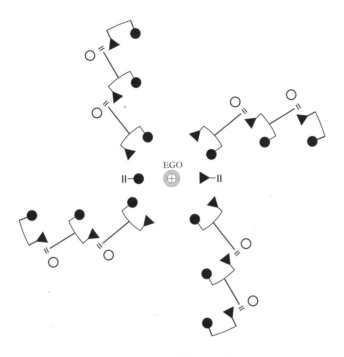

FIGURE 5 Idealized Kinship Diagram
of Tereseño Cognatic Descent System

member of many different descent groups. In practice, however, distant kin relations almost always faded away in favor of continued affiliation with closer, particularly patrilateral, mitotes.

As was demonstrated through the census data presented above, these exogamous patrilateral segments were localized in ranchos of the type that Hinton also described as existing in Jesús María. In Santa Teresa, these groups of related households also controlled grazing and agricultural lands in the vicinity of their houses. Indeed, descent groups claimed very large expanses of land as their de facto territories. Commonly this land would include highland prairie and lowland scrub forest that provided forage for large and small livestock, especially cattle—for many years a primary source of wealth in Santa Teresa. But the broken and unevenly watered terrain that makes up this region, along with the ongoing labor requirements of subsistence farming, meant that successful live-stock herding necessitated sustained cooperation among individuals and households. Cattle must be brought down to the lowlands in order to sur-vive winter and then back up in the summer (the wet season) as soon as fresh grass sprouted. Cows were constantly wandering off, getting lost, or being stolen. Most difficult of all the tasks involved in maintaining a herd in Santa Teresa, however, was simply obtaining and defending common-property pastureland over time. Because rights to land were based on customary use, others quickly usurped underused pasture as expanding herds sought adjacent areas. In order to defend pastureland, then, a cattle owner needed to mobilize a constant presence on the land he claimed. Those who could not establish such a presence lost land, live-stock, and wealth.

In Santa Teresa, labor for these never-ending tasks was mobilized from within localized descent-group segment ranchos. Consider the plight of a sixteen-year-old herder's son in Santa Teresa. He would like to find a wife, but has no wealth of his own to convince his girlfriend or her family that he is worthy. His alternatives are to go to the coast and work in order to earn money, which would anger his father and mother who would lose his talents as a rancher, or to take an early inheritance—a cow—from his father. His bride might then move in with the rest of his family until he could build a house of their own. Assuming that he chooses to remain with his father, it would be foolish to separate his cow from the rest of the herd, and so this boy must work for his father to maintain the herd as a whole. Eventually this boy and his wife may build a house to one side of his father's house, and the process then repeats itself, daughters marrying out, some brothers being pushed out, but a core of patrilaterally related relatives tending to remain as long as the pasture and the cattle survive.

Importantly, if this teenage boy happens also to be the oldest son of his father (and his father was himself the eldest son of his father, and so on), then he would not only inherit cows from his father, but would also even-tually inherit his father's obligations as ceremonial elder. The most fre-quent of these obligations would be the maize-oriented mitote ceremo-nies that should be performed three times each year by every descent group in Santa Teresa. Because the families of male relatives living nearby would also be expected to help, a small group of closely related people who shared a particular territory would work together to carry out ceremonies for more distantly related participants. Equally, this same group of localized patrilateral relatives would also separate in order to attend mitote ceremonies at distant homesteads where they had matrilateral ties through descent or marriage (or both).

In this way, mitote ceremonies tied descent groups together in localized patrilateral segments during the period of my fieldwork even as they also linked these maize-bundle group segments to other geographically distant maize-bundle groups. A result of this ranch-based social organization was the division of Santa Teresa's common property into a patchwork of localized descent-group lands. These isolated groups and lands were tied to one another through women who had married into these localized patrilineages and who transferred matrilateral ceremonial possibilities to their offspring, both male and female. In many cases these localized descent-group territories have been associated with particular maize-bundle groups for many years. The Zepeda family, the Flores family, the Noriega and Ortiz families, and the Pacheco family (among many other localized descent groups in Santa Teresa) all traced several generations of patrilateral maize-bundle group relatives who had lived at a particular ranch. In many cases, the abandoned ruins of the house of a deceased patrilateral descent-group ancestor could be observed to one side of the house then in use by his or her living descendant. Often these homesteads were fringed with century plants, each of them marking the point where the umbilical cords of long-deceased descent-group members were buried.

A result of this settlement pattern is that cognatically related families of particular maize-bundle group elders must walk back and forth through the canyons, forests, and prairies of Santa Teresa to participate in the different mitote ceremonies at which "their maize" is kept. This ceremonial participation creates a web of cognatically related maize-bundle groups that are linked together by out-married women. In Santa Teresa these linked ranch-based maize-bundle group segments were an integral

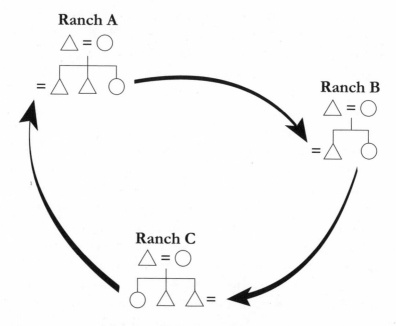

FIGURE 6 Idealized Diagram of Out-Marrying Women
Linking Localized Descent-Group Segments

feature of Cora social organization during the period of my fieldwork. For this reason, although the community as a whole might ideally be thought to have ultimate jurisdiction over these ranchlands, there was little practical sense of them "belonging to the pueblo," as Hinton (1970: 18) states was the case for such ranchlands in Jesús María.

Hinton's emphasis on village-level rather than ranch-level social organization among the Cora is most likely based on a characteristic of Jesús María itself—the tendency there to elaborate village ceremonial festivities at the expense of maize-bundle group ceremonies. In discussing mitote ceremonies, Grimes and Hinton (1969: 806) only discuss those held by community-level political and religious officials in Jesús María, although they briefly mention that the ceremonies were also held at ranches. In Santa Teresa (and in other Cora towns like Dolores and Mesa del Nayar), cargo-system authorities also carried out both mitote ceremonies and church-and-courthouse-oriented ceremonies like the annual Holy Week Festival during the period of my fieldwork, but these cargo-system mitotes did not substitute for ranch-based mitotes. Clearly, the subject of Jesús María's manner of celebrating (or at least emphasizing) only cargo-system mitotes at the expense of ranch mitotes requires further research, but based on the information presented here, Hinton's simple model of community integration cannot be generalized to Santa Teresa. Indeed, in the following chapter I discuss how the symbolism through which maize-bundle groups are constructed in Santa Teresa is crucially related to the positioning of these descent groups within a local hierarchy of traditional authority. The preliminary discussion of Tereseño descent groups outlined above, then, is not meant to account for all of the diverse ways that individuals and households might strategically use kinship to mobilize labor as they adapt themselves socially and ecologically to the land (cf. Netting 1986: 57). Rather, it is meant to set the stage for a more nuanced approach for understanding Tereseño struggles over the legitimacy of traditional authority.

3

"On Top of the Earth"

THE SYMBOLISM OF DESCENT-GROUP
MITOTE CEREMONIES IN SANTA TERESA

You think all of these customs are the same? No. At the ranches
those customs are just for the people who have their maize there.

CALIXTRO NORIEGA RIVERA

ALTHOUGH DESCENT-GROUP and community-level mitote ceremonies are performed separately, the mitote ceremonies carried out by community-level cargo-system officials draw on a number of symbols and
symbolic connotations that are most profoundly established for Tereseños
at descent-group mitotes. These descent-group mitotes provide meaningful ceremonial contexts within which children are positioned as descent-group members in relation to specific ritual symbols. These symbols include maize, stairways, sacred water, beads, tobacco, and locally
distilled century-plant liquor. Taken together, these symbols form sets of
connotations that link these children not only with their contemporary
living kin in a particular descent group, but also with the deceased ancestors of that maize-bundle group.

At the same time that these symbols link maize-bundle group members with their deceased ancestors, another allied set of ritual symbols maps out a sacred space onto the physical geography that surrounds the mitote ceremonial ground of each maize-bundle group in Santa Teresa. These symbols include gourd bowls, mountains, caves, and prayer arrows. Mitote ceremonies, then, position maize-bundle group members both temporally (in relation to their ancestors) and spatially (in relation to the surrounding geography) within a symbolically constituted world. The symbols and connotations deployed in these descent-group mitote ceremonies in turn create a sense of natural affiliation that is later drawn upon as children become adults and begin to participate in community-level ceremonies. These community-level ceremonies are sponsored by the traditional authorities of the town and include both mitote ceremonies and a church-and-courthouse-based ceremonial cycle that includes the Holy Week Festival that first drew me to Santa Teresa.

The political legitimacy of traditional authorities in Santa Teresa is based in two ways on this relationship between descent-group and community-level ceremonial cycles. First, by symbolically incorporating simpler descent-group mitote ceremonies into more elaborate and inclusive community-level mitotes, a naturalized hierarchy of sacred affiliation is constructed in ritual. Second, the agricultural season, to which both descent-group and community-level mitotes refer, is opposed in complicated ways to a dry-season-oriented church-and-courthouse-based ceremonial cycle sponsored by cargo-system officials.

In this chapter I set the stage for a discussion of the first of these relations (between descent-group and community-level mitote ceremonies) through an interpretation of the symbolism of descent-group mitotes. I postpone discussion of the Catholic-derived church-and-courthouse-based ceremonial cycle until after the following chapter, which deals with the history of mitote ceremonialism in the region. I begin the present chapter by describing the general ceremonial structure shared among descent-group mitotes (a ceremonial structure that is also followed by cargo-system officers as they celebrate their more elaborate community-level mitote ceremonies). This ceremonial structure provides a common symbolic context for the three different mitote ceremonies of the year, which in turn provide distinctive symbolic contexts for a series of life-cycle rituals performed in the context of descent-group mitotes. These life-cycle rituals are powerful emotional events that are meant to ritually incorporate the bodies and souls of children into their maize-bundle groups. The symbolism of these rituals, however, is also evoked in ceremonies led by the town's traditional authorities. As a result, through the relation of descent-group and community-level ceremonies, the legitimacy of these authorities is based less on Weberian "belief" than on the successful reproduction of a hierarchy of embodied ritual symbols with its roots sunk into the heart of each Tereseño.

In the Cora language, both descent-group and community mitotes are referred to using the same verb stem, -nye-, meaning "dance." Maize-oriented mitote ceremonies—through which the yi'irá ("custom") of a maize-bundle group is continued—are clearly distinguished in the Cora language from church-and-courthouse-based community festivals, which are referred to with the verb stem -ye'estya, "make festival." Each of the three annual mitotes commonly celebrated by a maize-bundle group in Santa Teresa takes place at a ceremonial ground located adjacent to the house of the ceremonial elder of the maize-bundle group. The central focus of the ceremonial ground is a hearth. In addition to this ceremonial fire, the mitote ground also minimally consists of a wooden platform (Spanish: tapanco) placed between the fire and the rising sun. This platform serves as an altar, but the ceremonial ground around the fire is also entered by passing underneath it. The shape of the mitote ceremonial ground, then, is circular, with an opening under the platform to the east serving as a door.

If a singer is present, he sits with his back to the fire on a special chair ('ɨpwari) facing the tapanco to the east, sometimes with an apprentice to his right. With hardwood sticks that look like arrows, he plays a droning rhythm on a musical bow (túnamu) that rests on the ground in front of him. Men and women usually dance to this music separately, but groups of two or more people may embrace each other across the shoulders as they skip-step a counterclockwise dance around the fire. Singing begins during the evening, after the light of the sun has completely faded from the sky. Five sets of music and dancing are divided by equally long breaks, so that the dancing continues through the night. The last set of dancing and bow-drum music ends sometime before the first light of sunrise. The music of the dance is accompanied by songs that are sung in what seems to participants to be an archaic register of the Náyari language that refers to the ancestral deities of the Náyari people (examples of these songs are transcribed in Preuss 1912).

Even when no dancing occurs, as is the case during the cicada mitote, or when no ritual singer is available to perform, the ceremonial elder should stay awake "fasting from dreams" (Spanish: *ayunando de sueños*) during the final night of the ceremony. This final night of "fasting" from sleep is the culmination of the five nights of fasting and prayer that serve as the basis of all mitote ceremonies. The rigor of these fasts differs among ceremonial elders, but at no time during the five-day fast should a ceremonial elder have sexual relations. Most also deny themselves liquor, food, salt, and water during the daylight hours for five consecutive days. Weaker men fast only until midday. The strongest elders have no liquor, food, salt, water, or sex for five days and nights, eating only on the morning of the sixth day, after a full night of wakefulness has sealed their five-day fast. Even those who break their fasts at midday eat no salt with their food for the entire five-day period.

Like the differing rigor of fasts among ceremonial elders, the specific practice of each descent group's mitote ceremony varies depending on the particular "custom" passed on to that ceremonial elder by his father. During the time of my fieldwork, however, I was a guest at about thirty different descent-group mitote ceremonies, and based on these experiences several general features can be outlined. In these mitotes, fasting from food and sex begins just after sunset on the date each descent group customarily begins its six-day-long mitote ceremony. At this time the ceremonial elder stands within the circular ceremonial ground facing east to pray. In this direction the morning star—*Xúrave* (a manifestation of *Tahatsi*, "Our Elder Brother")—may shine on the horizon prior to the appearance of the sun—*X+ká* (a manifestation of *Tayáu*, "Our Father").

However, prayers are not addressed directly to Our Elder Brother, the Morning Star or to Our Father Sun. Instead they are directed to a small gourd bowl (*tuxa*) that is filled with a special kind of ground raw maize (*tz+wí*, raw) often referred to as *Tanana* (Our Mother).

This tz+wí maize is of the same variety that is bundled to represent descent-group members, and in praying to this maize the ceremonial elder of each descent group establishes himself as the voice of the descent-group members who are affiliated with him. Tereseños say that the prayers uttered during mitotes are refined and purified by the ground maize; they are made sensible to the deceased ancestors who in turn transmit them upward to the realms occupied by Tahatsi and Tayáu. As one ceremonial elder put it, "She speaks for us." This maize is cultivated from the same variety of white maize that once sustained descent-group ancestors when they served as ceremonial elders, and so it is also a concrete indexical link (a "pointer") between separate cosmological realms occupied by living and deceased elders of a common descent group.

A number of ritual practices within the mitote ceremonies symbolize this link as a kind of stairway between living people, deceased ancestors, and the deities of all Náyari people. For example, prior to the uttering of ritual prayers directed to the descent group's mother-maize, each member of the group takes a turn pouring sacred water and then ground raw descent-group maize into a gourd bowl. The ceremonial elder then recites prayers to this maize while it rests in the gourd bowl on a woven mat on the ground. The maize-filled gourd bowl sitting on the earth (*hapwán chánaka*, "on top of the earth") represents the first step. Once the prayers are completed, the bowl is then raised to the next step—the tapanco platform on the east edge of the circular mitote ceremonial ground—and flowers are placed around the bowl by the ceremonial elder and other descent-group members. This is the second step. The third step is occupied by the rain clouds (*tawáusimwa*, "Our Deceased Elders"). The fourth and fifth steps are in "heaven" (*tahapwa*, "zenith") and are occupied by "Our Elder Brother" and "Our Father," respectively.

The ability of prayers to ascend this step-like cosmos, however, is said to depend on the purity of the first steps. For this reason, a successful mitote ceremony also depends on the ability of a ceremonial elder to complete five consecutive days of fasting and prayer, which are themselves said to be like a stairway, with each day representing a step upward. As one ceremonial elder in Santa Teresa is reported to have said, "During the first day of fasting, the prayers rise up a little bit, and a then a little more each day, until on the sixth day [after the five days of fasting have been completed], they go by themselves to heaven and the clouds" (Amaro Romero 1993: 57). But before fasting for a mitote ceremony can begin, the ceremonial elder or his relatives must collect the different materials that are needed to hold the ceremony itself. Of these materials, perhaps the most symbolically significant is sacred water (wáw+).

Sacred water is collected from springs (haihsa) that border the lands within which descent-group members live. Long and difficult pilgrimages to "join the waters" (Spanish: juntar las aguas) act as a kind of preparatory ritual forming symbolic connotations that link mitote ceremonies with the geographical territory taken to be the homeland of each maize-bundle group in Santa Teresa. Descent groups differ in the springs from which they retrieve sacred water, but members of each of these groups collect water from five distinct sites that represent a cross-shaped map of the world that encircles their lands. At each of the five points of this medicine wheel–like map of the world is a mountain peak (h+rí) named for a distant ancestor: for example, "Our Grandfather," "Our Grandmother," or "Our Elder Brother." Also associated with each of the springs is a cave (tásta'a) leading into the earth. Emerging from these firmaments at the edges and center of the descent group's world are the sources of sacred water. This water is distinguished from regular water (háhti) precisely because of its emergence from these special springs whose location at the five corners of the world suggests their connection to some common subterranean aquifer.

These sites for collecting sacred water establish the edges and center of a cross-shaped map of the descent group's world; but each site also has its own cross-shaped symbolism that forms a miniature version of that larger world. As a descent-group member gathers water at all of these isolated and remote springs—a task that takes a week or more to complete—the

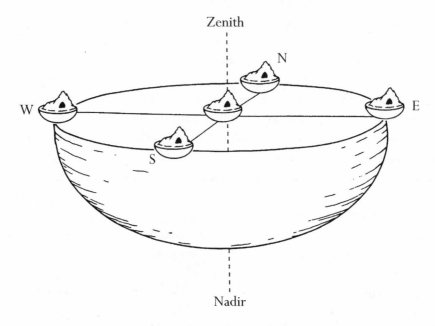

FIGURE 7 Ideal Conception of Cosmology
Reproduced Through Pilgrimages to "Join the Waters"

characteristics of each of these springs reinforce and elaborate on the larger image while also opening other symbolic possibilities. The cross-shaped image, for example, can be collapsed down to the level of a circular-shaped mitote ceremonial ground, or even to the level of a similarly shaped gourd bowl containing the ancestral tz+wí maize through which prayers are spoken. While the patrons of the sacred sites for collecting water are said to watch over the whole world from their positions at the five cardinal points, each of these sites is also a representation of the world as a whole. The result is the image of a nested series of smaller and smaller gourd bowl–like bisected hemispheres whose hard shells encircle and protect the sacred maize at the heart of each maize-bundle group.

Because descent groups differ in the sites from which they collect water, in the following section I will describe only one of these sites—the lake that lies east of the town of Santa Teresa. This is perhaps the most important sacred site for all Tereseño descent groups, and many of the symbolic characteristics of other sacred sites are clearly found here.

THE LAKE AND THE WORLD

The sacred lake of Santa Teresa (*Nákuta*) is set in a steep and inaccessible gorge between one-thousand-foot escarpments on the east and west. From the north it is fed by a stream that passes over a high waterfall, blocking access from that direction. To the south a trail leads to the lakeshore over hills of boulders that attest to the origin of the lake in a dramatic cataclysm: rather than carving out a canyon to form the lake, the stream was obviously dammed by rocks falling from the canyon's walls.

The cataclysm that formed this lake is an ongoing preoccupation for Náyari people. Folk tales link the formation of the lake with the end of a previous world, and so, implicitly, with the repeated renewal of the world through mitote ceremonies:

> Where the lake is today was once a flat prairie. Some people were dancing in a mitote when a huge rock near their ceremonial grounds began to vibrate. Out of the rock emerged a giant snake. It rose in the air over the frightened people, threatening to kill them all. Just then, however, the snake was pierced by an arrow, a shooting star shot by Tahatsi Xúrave the Morning Star who protects all the Cora people. The snake slammed to earth, causing the ground to give way, which formed the hollow that today contains the lake. The head of the snake broke into pieces when it landed and formed into a few huge boulders that can still be found here and there.*

People occasionally claim to see the form of this snake just beneath the murky water of the lake. They say that it is still curled up on the bottom

---

*Amadeo Flores Rojas recounted this frequently told story in an informal interview. Other versions have been published by Amaro Romero (1993) and Preuss (1998a: 109).

of the lake, and that if it ever rises again it will cause a devastating flood of the Cora towns downstream. Others say that it already left during the earlier flood that destroyed the last world, carving out present-day canyons in the region before plunging into the sea.

It is nearly impossible when approaching this lake not to recall these apocalyptic stories. Indeed, to reach the lake one passes a place called in Spanish *Las Víboras*—"The Snakes"—a streambed that has basins in the shapes of snake heads eroded into the rock. Then, arriving at the edge of the escarpment and looking down on the lake from above, one sees the lake's overflow outlet (which only carries water during the rainy season) curving around huge piles of boulders that form the shape of a slithering snake. On the east side of the lake, seemingly aligned with the rising morning star, is a rock called Tahatsi Xúrave, the slayer of the serpent turned to stone. Most dramatically of all, in the vicinity of the lake is a cave that contains a place for a single person to sit. Next to that sitting place, a tunnel-shaped cave goes into the bowels of the earth, and seemingly to the blackest part of the underworld itself. Along with the mythical serpent, wealth and power are said to reside in the cave if one can withstand five nights of fasting there. For pilgrims to this site, then, stories of the world destroyed by a snake seem to be preserved in the physical characteristics of the place itself. As at other sacred sites in Santa Teresa, the distinction between ritual symbol and natural feature is hopelessly blurred.

Arriving at the lakeshore, a person collecting water is confronted by more ritual symbols. Indeed, it is said that all of the plants and animals known to the Náyari people can be found at this place. Among these plants and animals is a stand of white *carrizo* reeds (*haká*) used by Tereseños (and other Náyari and even Wixárika peoples) to make prayer arrows (*'+r+*). Once feathers have been fixed to these prayer arrows at the home of a ceremonial elder, they are in turn taken to sites (like Nákuta itself) where sacred water is collected as part of pilgrimages to "join the waters." In this way, the transportation of these prayer arrows from the mitote ceremonial ground to the five sacred springs is like the transport of water back to the mitote ground from the sacred sites; it maps out a cross-shaped sacred territory. Furthermore, the use of these special reeds to make prayer arrows, like the ritual act of joining the waters, "points" to the unique features of the sacred site from which the reeds (and water) are collected.

One of the evocative features of Nákuta to which these reeds "point" is the island in the middle of the lake. On the very summit of this island is a huge *chalate* fig tree (*xapwá*), the *xapwá ví'ihatana* (fig-tree-at-the-place-of-the-rains), or sacred tree of life. Its roots weave downward through the serpent's cave and its upward spreading branches and leaves arch over the entire island. This island surrounded by the water of the lake, then, is itself another model of the world at the eastern point of a larger cross-shaped map. Both sacred water and reeds point back to the fig tree that forms a central pole linking heaven and the underworld along a single axis, just as each descent-group mitote ceremonial ground links heaven and earth at the center of its larger cross-shaped territory.

But despite the cosmological significance of their pilgrimages to collect water and reeds, Cora people are primarily motivated to make the long walk to sacred sites like Nákuta to be "bathed" (-'+ǥ-) at the source. People are ritually "bathed" in two ways. First, using a *tsuwá* (tree-growing iris) flower, sacred water may be flung from a gourd bowl on each person's forehead, neck, nape, stomach, lower back, legs, and feet. Second, the senior male descent-group member may simply take sacred water from a gourd bowl into his mouth and then spray each person in attendance from head to toe. In either case, people react to the shock of the water on their skin as if they had plunged in a cold pool, gasping, shivering, and commenting on the cold temperature. Bathing is perhaps the most common ritual act practiced by Cora people. It is said to maintain good health by keeping the "dirt" (*cháumwariste*) that wind blows into people out of their bodies. This act is part of every mitote ceremony (as well as the church-and-courthouse-oriented ceremonial festivals), and many people are motivated to attend these ceremonies (just as they are motivated to walk to distant sources of sacred water) in order to receive this blessing. Indeed, the traditional style of Cora dress, which features flared blouse-bottoms on both men's and women's shirts, facilitates this ritual.

Once the pilgrims have been bathed, more sacred water is poured into a gourd bowl in the same way that will later be repeated "on top of the earth" back at the mitote ceremonial ground. Each of the descent-group members who have come to collect water first pours the water in thin streams at each of the four corners of the gourd, and then into the center. Once each of these people has added water, each in turn then adds ground raw white descent-group maize (tz+wí) to the water in the gourd bowl. This maize is also sprinkled at each of the corners of the bowl, and then into the center. The result is another model of the world: an island—the earth (chánaka)—made of maize, called "Our Mother." The maize island floats in the gourd bowl, just as the island with its snakes and tree-of-life seems to float in the lake to one side. At an even larger scale, the earth as a whole might then itself be thought of as floating on the vast (Pacific) Ocean that can be seen from certain mountains on the western edge of Santa Teresa's lands. The cataclysmic flood that destroyed the last world and created Nákuta, then, was just a rising of those seas; the Náyari's fragile earth-island was covered with water, with only the five highest mountains (the most ancient ancestors, now turned to stone) remaining above the sea-snake floodwaters.

In actual practice, following the rituals undertaken at this spring, representatives of the maize-bundle group would then move from Nákuta to the northern, western, southern, and central springs that form a cross-shaped world centered at the mitote ceremonial grounds of that maize-bundle group. At each of these sites, rituals involved in the collection of water would be repeated. However, the symbols reproduced through these rituals would also then resonate with the specific characteristics of that site, producing distinct connotations. Nákuta is perhaps the most dramatic sacred site in Santa Teresa, but each site has unique characteristics that emerge in the course of the pilgrimage. By "joining the waters," the particular characteristics of each of these sites—a tree growing out of a cliff here, sacred water dropping into a bowl-shaped rock there—are collapsed and, as it were, physically transported (through indexical connotation) back to the mitote grounds. There the complex sets of symbols that make up the sacred sites seem to inhabit the water itself. In the course of the mitote ceremonies, these symbols emerge and resonate with other symbols that are mobilized in the ceremonial context of the particular mitote ceremony. Taken together, these symbols position maize-bundle group members both temporally (in relation to ongoing lineages of ancestors and descendants) and spatially (in relation to a sacred geographic territory) within a meaningful world.

THE THREE MITOTE CEREMONIES

For descriptive purposes, descent-group mitote ceremonialism can be divided between the three annual mitotes (cicada, roasted maize, and parched maize mitotes) and three additional rituals (baptism, liquor-drinking, and deer-dancing rituals) that are each added to a particular descent-group mitote every five years or so. The mitotes that include these additional rituals follow the same format and include all the symbolism that occurs during the particular annual mitote ceremony of which they are a part. However, even more than the thrice-yearly mitote ceremonies, these special rituals are said to form a deep emotional connection between particular individuals and the ceremonies that constitute their descent groups. They open a social position for individuals as descent-group members at a particular life juncture, and so they position these individuals within the small social hierarchy of a descent group's world.

At the same time, and like the pilgrimages to join the waters, these rituals provide a symbolic content that is just off stage even when not explicitly celebrated at the regular annual mitote ceremonies. Ritual movements and paraphernalia used during the annual mitotes make reference to these special rituals and so repeatedly renew the sense of a stepped series of social positions that these special rituals help to produce. I discuss the mitote ceremonies with their associated life-cycle rituals in turn.

Ancestry, Age, and Gender in the Cicada Mitote Ceremony

The cicada (*tzicurí*) mitote—referred to by Tereseños in Spanish as "burning [or 'eating'] the cicada"—is named after an insect that appears in the thorny scrub around Santa Teresa in the hottest and driest days prior to the beginning of the rains. This insect produces a loud and high-pitched buzzing that is the pervasive sound heard while cutting down brush in order to plant a swidden garden (Spanish: *coamil*; Náyari: *ví'ira*). Each descent-group elder holds his cicada mitote at an established date during the month of May. The buzzing of the cicada, however, along with the appearance of tsuwá orchids and a kind of magnolia flower called in Náyari '*+chwe* (Spanish: *corpus*), is also thought to signal the onset of these ceremonies.

The distinctive rituals of the cicada mitote begin exactly at noon on the sixth and last day of the ceremony (after the five-day fast has been completed), "the time that those who have already died come down to eat" (Amaro Romero 1993: 39). At this time a number of men in attendance—men who are not themselves members of the maize-bundle group, but who attend the ceremony as visitors—are selected to "burn the cicada." Like the rains, these men are temporarily passing through, helping the living representatives of a sponsoring descent group complete the ceremonial work needed to renew themselves for another year. The principal task of these men is to burn a pile of brush representing a Náyari slash-and-burn coamil. To do this, the second oldest of the visiting men is handed a spherical dried gourd and the oldest is handed a clay jug. Both containers are filled with sacred water, but the clay jug also contains pieces of roasted century plant. The rest of the men are each given a prayer arrow and a flower-decorated bundle of pitchwood. All then walk in a counterclockwise circle before heading to the pile of brush a few dozen meters from the ceremonial plaza.

The men circle the brush in a counterclockwise direction five times. They then take the flowers from their bundles of pitchwood, light the wood, and plunge it into the pile of brush. The smoke of the brush pile looks like clouds of tobacco smoke, and indeed the clay jug (*xá'ari*) of the eldest cicada-burner closely resembles a similarly named ritual tobacco pipe (*xáuxa'ari*).

While these men are waiting for the brush to burn, the members of the sponsoring maize-bundle group are "bathed" in the same manner as at the sacred sites where they earlier collected water, and the culminating prayers of the mitote ceremony are uttered. After the brush turns to ash, the cicada-burners again circle the pile five times. The elders among them pour water at the four cardinal points of the pile and the rest of the men follow by placing the tsuwá and '+chwe flowers from their bundles of pitchwood at those same points. These men then return in rank order to the front of the tapanco where they are blessed with sacred water. At this point the ceremonial work of the cicada-burners is over and these visitors relax.

Two large oak-leaf-wrapped tamales—the "cicadas"—that had been resting on top of the tapanco are then cut up into trays, and pieces are distributed to everyone in attendance. These are treated with sacramental reverence, especially by parents, who make sure that all of their children receive a taste. After the cicada-tamales are distributed, gourd bowls filled with pinole—a blend of ground toasted corn and tiny chia seeds—along with pieces of roasted century plant are given to the rest of the people in attendance. This communal meal is followed by the giving away of other foods that members of the sponsoring descent group may have brought.

Like all of the annual mitotes, the cicada mitote draws on and elaborates symbols and symbolic juxtapositions earlier produced in preparing for the ceremony. Specifically, it links a number of references to geographic territory with maize and century plants, and so to descent-group ancestry. The burned brush pile, for example, is an image of a slash-and-burn maize field prior to planting. But the counterclockwise procession around this brush pile (like the earlier pilgrimage to each of the sacred springs) also connotes the geographic boundaries of the descent group's world. The pouring of sacred water onto each of the cardinal points immediately surrounding the ashes left from the burning of the brush pile strengthens this connotation, and also associates rain with the deceased ancestors of the descent group.

This association of rain with the deceased ancestors, however, depends on symbolism mobilized within particular life-cycle rituals that are periodically celebrated within the context of these cicada mitote ceremonies. Specifically, the use of a clay jug to pour century-plant-infused sacred water refers to tobacco and a kind of locally distilled century-plant liquor, substances that are associated with the baptism and liquor-drinking rituals, respectively. I now turn to a discussion of those rituals.

BAPTISM RITUALS Maize-bundle group mitotes are periodically supplemented with a series of important life-cycle rituals. During these rituals, children or adolescents are singled out for focused attention. They are provided special roles from which they are meant to apprehend densely resonant and compelling symbolic images and connotations that give meaning to their particular positioning within each of the maize-bundle groups of which they are a part. They constitute another stepped pathway, here leading to adulthoods characterized by systematic gender and age inequalities within the descent group.

Baptism rituals (*titi'irátini*, "taking little ones out") are the first ritual, and indeed the first custom, in which children (and/or infants) participate. They set the stage for the subsequent liquor-drinking ritual, after which children then begin to receive the ears of maize that will make up the maize bundle that will be with them for as long as they continue to attend the mitotes of a particular maize-bundle-group elder. During the baptism ritual, children also become associated with the *mwátsuvi* beads that link them with their descent-group ancestors.

Children receive these beads on bracelets that are tied to their right wrists during the baptism ritual itself. As a child is baptized at the mitote ceremony of each of his or her four (or more) maize-bundle groups, the number of beads that he or she receives grows, and the bracelets are expanded to necklaces. The result is a necklace of many different colored beads. Each of the beads is an heirloom from a direct ancestor in one of the maize-bundle groups. This necklace, then, is a concrete indication of cognatic affiliation; like "having their maize" at the home of different ceremonial elders, it points to a number of different maize-bundle groups. But although during their lifetimes Tereseños trace descent cognatically (to different descent groups), their necklaces are bequeathed to the ceremonial elder of their patrilateral maize-bundle group alone. These necklaces are then broken down into bracelets and are redistributed to the young children who enter that maize-bundle group during the subsequent baptism ritual. As in the inheritance of the mitote ceremony from the ceremonial elder to his eldest son, these inheritances of mwátsuvi beads provide distinct patrilateral centers of gravity within an overarching cognatic descent system.

Tied onto the bracelets with these beads are tiny canine-shaped pouches of black dog hairs (*chíkate*, "dogs") along with other tiny pouches containing a potent variety of tobacco (*yaná*). Both are meant to protect the child who wears them. The dog-shaped pouches relate to the mythical origin of Náyari people as the offspring of a black dog:

> After the flood the ground was firm but there were still no people. God said, "Where am I going to get people?" Pine trees started to grow where God planted them, and among the pines a man appeared along with a house and some tortillas. A black female dog was running around trying to get at the tortillas and eventually it got into the kitchen as the man was watching. He kept on watching and a woman came out of the house and went for water. The man went into his house to explore the situation and saw the dog's skin lying there. When the woman came back she asked him to hand over her "shirt," but he refused. For this reason women are still unable to return to their true form as dogs.*

Black dogs are also said to accompany the souls of the dead. One Náyari man in Santa Teresa is reported to have described it this way: "The little woven dog has hairs from a dog so that when you die, the dog, with his

*Felipe Morales Morales told me this version of the story in an informal interview.

51

sense of smell, takes care of you on the road and guides you to the other side" (Amaro Romero 1993: 47). The "dogs," then, are allies or helpers received by children at their baptism ritual that allow them (hopefully) to pass unharmed through the world of the living and on to the world of the dead.

Similarly, the pouches of tobacco that are hung on these necklaces are also meant to help the children who receive them. Ritual curers are able to use these pouches to divine the location of any illness that may have invaded the body of their wearer. The tobacco smoke from their pipes and the tobacco-filled pouches attached to mwátsuvi necklaces are said to have a natural affinity. The necklace as a whole is also said to represent the embodied soul of its wearer. Stiffness of its cotton string or any kind of damage to the beads are signs used by ritual curers to locate illness.

Children are meant to sense the bodily connection between themselves, their descent-group kin, and the ancestors who came before them through the beads, the "dogs," and the tobacco that make up their necklaces. Each of the beads that they wear once lay against the skin of an ancestor. Who were they? How did they live? The dogs provide a clue, a signpost pointing toward the stories and ceremonies that their contemporary descent-group relatives learned from their own parents. The tobacco, like the ears of ceremonial maize that the children will later receive, makes it clear that these same ancestors, the ones who have passed on pieces of themselves as beads, are somehow integral to the healthy constitution of their own bodies. Then, in mitote pilgrimages and ceremonies, this sense of the body's link with an upwardly growing ancestral trunk or stalk is reproduced through ritual bathing with the sacred water out of which that tree grows. For Tereseños, the children who enter the baptism ritual are thus represented more as manifestations of this ancestral lineage, like ears of maize growing off a single ancestral maize plant, than as autonomous individuals. Indeed, even as the baptism ritual ties all children to their ancestors, destinies of lifelong gender and age-ranked inequalities among these children are also forged.

The baptism ritual begins during the afternoon preceding the "fast from dreams" of the fifth night of the mitote ceremony. At this time all of the necklaces of the participating descent-group members, which are normally kept hidden in their different houses, are hung together on a crossbeam of the ceremonial tapanco altar. After a communal meal, each of the girls to be baptized is brought into the room at the ceremonial elder's house where the descent-group maize is stored and a flower-decorated altar has been set up on the east wall. Each girl faces this altar as she is hugged to the chest of a standing female relative, just as these same relatives will later embrace maize bundles to their chests during mitote ceremonies.

While so embraced by her female relative, each girl receives a string of beads tied to her right wrist. After the girls receive these bracelets, the ceremonial elder blows tobacco smoke on each of them, symbolically linking the tobacco of their bracelets to the protecting and curing power of the tobacco of the ancestors who have come before them. A green feather of the *perico* bird (Spanish: a small green parrot) is then stuck to each girl's hair with a tiny ball of wax, and she is given a tsuwá-decorated prayer arrow also hung with perico feathers. Each girl is then given a wooden spindle (wound with black and white yarn) of the type that is used by Tereseño women to spin wool for weaving. Importantly, this spindle is the same shape as the large pole—called chánaka, "the earth"—that is brought out during the community-wide parched maize mitote (to be discussed in Chapter Five). As such it is meant not only to emphasize the proper role of women as weavers, but also to associate them—like Tanana—with the earthly world of human beings.

Having received these items, the girls are "brought out" of their ceremonial elder's house, which accounts for the name of this ceremony. While still embracing these girls to their chests, their female relatives carry them four times around the house in the counterclockwise direction of a mitote dance. The women holding their descent-group daughters then form a line facing east outside the eastern wall of the house. The line is formed in a rank order from youngest to oldest. Their relatives, also lined up from youngest to oldest, then pass in front of the little girls with containers of sacred water, "bathing" each of the girls over their entire bodies with water sprayed from their mouths.

FIGURE 8 A Náyari girl
after her baptism ritual

Boys are carried into the house of the ceremonial elder by their male relatives after the girls have completed their baptism ritual. The same pattern is followed for boys as for girls, but with some important exceptions. Rather than a pretty green perico feather for their hair, boys each receive the feather of a high-flying hawk (*chwix+*). Their prayer arrow is hung with another hawk feather, and it is marked with five black chevrons rather than the four chevrons of the girl's prayer arrow. These five chevrons refer to the five times that boys are later taken around their ceremonial elder's house, and to the fact that boys receive five ears of maize in their maize bundles, compared to the four ears that girls receive. The markings of these arrows are also thought to convey a message to the heavens, and so the five chevrons on a boy's prayer arrow represent the full five steps upward that a girl can never successfully complete. Likewise, the hawk feather, unlike the perico feather, is used by curers, who draw on its power to fast for five full days, and in this way communicate with male ancestral rain deities (like those represented as the visiting "burners" in the cicada mitote) in order to heal the sick. The position of women is represented as being lower than that of men. They are portrayed as never being able to fully reach the upper heights of heaven, and so they remain dependent on men for their own good health.

Additionally, rather than spindle whorls, boys receive tiny bows. The most obvious association of this bow is to the musical bow played during some mitote ceremonies. However, it also signifies the type of bow that was used in the not-too-distant past to hunt deer, a reference to the deer-dancing ritual also associated with some mitote ceremonies (discussed below). In both of these cases, the bow refers to a type of rugged spirituality, the ability of a hunter to get close to deceased ancestors and ancestral deities through self-sacrifice and bodily suffering.

After taking these boys out of the ceremonial elder's house and circling it five times in a counterclockwise direction, the boys are "bathed" in age-ranked order, as were their descent-group sisters previously. This age ranking is referred to repeatedly during a Náyari person's life. Its importance is also reflected in the kinship terminology used by the Náyari people of Santa Teresa. Here again the position of men within such systems of age ranking is of more consequence than that of women. Coras distinguish only generational—and not collateral—distance among women, so that the female relatives who hug girls to their chests will refer to each other as "daughter" (-yau), "sister" (-iwara), "mother" (-nana), and "grandmother" (-yákwari). More commonly, however, a wide variety of women are referred to simply as "female relative" (-tyí), a linguistic token that tends to diminish overt kinship-based social differentiation among women. The exception here is affinal relationships: terms for "sister-in-law" (-híta) or "mother (or father, son, or daughter)-in-law" (-mu'u) are clearly distinguished from "sister" or "mother."

55

In contrast to the situation for girls and women, Coras distinguish both generational and collateral relations among males outside of one's own generation: "son" (-yau), "father" (-táta), "uncle" or "nephew" (-sí), "grandfather" (-yaxú), "great-grandfather" (-tu'rú), and even "great-great-grandfather" (-wák+sa) are all distinguished. As with girls, among the males of one's own generation no collateral distinction is made, so collateral siblings of either gender are called (-iwara). However, both younger (-hu) and older brothers (-ha), and younger and older cousins, are distinguished. Moreover, as Grimes and Hinton (1969: 803, emphasis in original) point out, "Cora cousin terminology is reckoned by seniority, the relative ages of the siblings from whom a cousin pair descended, not the relative ages of the cousins themselves" (for a more recent discussion of kinship terminology in Jesús María, see Magriña 1999). In Santa Teresa, this type of terminology for distinguishing seniority is commonly used only among boys and men, and so it corresponds directly to the emphasis in making distinctions within descent groups based on gender, birth order, and generation. Thus, elder brothers tend to lead maize-bundle groups.

LIQUOR-DRINKING RITUALS Unlike baptism rituals, which are celebrated as part of either cicada or parched maize mitotes, liquor-drinking rituals occur only as part of cicada mitotes.* As in the cicada mitote itself, the deceased ancestors of a maize-bundle group are strongly evoked. Here a sense of connection with male maize-bundle-group ancestors is produced not only through the association of this ritual with the cicada mitote as a whole, but more specifically through the association of distilled century-plant liquor (nawá) with deceased maize-bundle-group ancestors, who are also represented as the rains. This liquor forms another

---

*The descent-group liquor-drinking ritual that I was to witness in 1994 was called off after the sudden death of the sister of that maize-bundle group's ceremonial elder. The following account comes from a description of this ritual provided by Amadeo Flores (the ceremonial elder of that descent group) and by observations of similar community-level liquor-drinking rituals.

link between the deceased ancestors and the children who drink it. They internalize it, literally taking it inside their bodies where it changes their sensual relation to the world. Like the mwátsuvi necklaces with their tobacco and dogs, it is also meant to form a deeply embodied emotional connection with those ancestors, and thus with the ceremonial customs that those ancestors have passed down.

As is the case with pilgrimages to collect sacred water prior to mitote ceremonies, preparations for the liquor-drinking ritual add important significance to the ritual as a whole. Specifically, the type of century plant (*mweh*) used to make liquor is another model of the world. These wild flowering century plants closely resemble the chánaka pole brought out once a year during the community-level parched maize mitote. Although I will discuss this pole in greater detail later, it is sufficient here to point out that its basic shape is exactly the same as the spindles earlier received by girls during their baptism rituals. The eight-foot pole is like the shaft of the spindle with a "wheel" at the top of the pole like the disk-like spindle itself. In the case of the chánaka pole (recall that "chánaka" means "the earth"), the disk is decorated with flowers and feathers. Similarly, before a wild century plant is ready to be harvested, it shoots up a tall shaft (*harí*; cf. *haríkame*, "soul") that is topped with spreading flowers, making it look very similar to the chánaka pole. As with the shaft of a chánaka pole, or the shaft of the spindle whorl, or even the trunks of trees-of-life that are found at sites from which sacred water is collected, this wild century-plant shaft represents a connection of nadir and zenith—earth and heaven—along a single pathway from the future to the past. As the fifth cardinal point, it ties the four corners of this world with the watery world below, as well as with the levels of deceased ancestors and ancestral deities above. This set of meanings is strengthened during the ritual harvesting of these century plants.

During this harvesting, a single leaf is cut off each of the four sides of the circular plant and passed around the plant in a counterclockwise direction, the direction of the mitote dance. Each leaf is then placed on the ground at the side from which it was cut and is sprinkled with sacred water, a symbolic connection of the geographical boundaries of the descent-group world with a single century plant. Once each of the four corners has been blessed in this way, the shaft of the plant is cut down and roasted in a fire. This roasting is reminiscent of both the preparation of the reed shaft of a prayer arrow and the roasting of fresh ears of maize during the subsequent roasted maize mitote. In both cases the fire stands for Our Father, the Sun, and thus the roasting of reeds, maize, or century-plant flower spikes is a type of offering to this ancestral deity aimed at securing good fortune in the ritual requests to come.

After the first two century plants are prepared in this way, all but two of the rest of the leaves of both of these plants are then removed, and the remaining leaves are notched to look like antlers. This variety of wild century plant is referred to as *xápwa*, a word that people compare to the word meaning "deer" (*mwaxá*). Like cooked deer meat, the raw material for this liquor is a prototypical offering to the ancestors. Indeed, roasted century plant (like the human body itself) is referred to simply as *wéira* ("meat" or "flesh").

Besides *mweh xápwa*, two other ceremonially important kinds of "mweh" are distinguished by the Náyari. These varieties are fundamental not only to the manifestation of the seasonal rains as the deceased ancestors, but also to the subjective identification of children with those deceased ancestors. The symbolism of this identification begins when parents receive a live cutting of a century plant from the ceremonial elder sponsoring the ritual. The parents of girls receive a kind of sotol called *mweh t+mwéhxati* (Spanish: *ixtle*) and parents of boys receive *mweh t+hímwehwaka* (Spanish: *maguey*). Both varieties are also referred to simply as *Tawátsimwa*, "Our Ceremonial Elders." Parents bring these cuttings back from the home of their ceremonial elder to plant at their own homes. The carefully saved dried umbilical cord (*sipú*) of the child to which this cutting pertains is then "planted" beneath the respective century plants. Of these, the magueys tend to flourish, each of them pertaining to long-forgotten male ancestors. Older households may have dozens of these magueys forming the edges of their house compound. The rising shafts of these century plants serve as a reminder of the organic, now umbilical cord–like link between descent-group members on earth and deceased ancestors in heaven. At the same time, the emergence of the shafts from these century plants (particularly mweh t+hímweh-waka) is a signal to begin the preparations for the cicada mitotes, where pieces of this type of century plant are served roasted in gourd bowls filled with pinole.

Moreover, this distinctive dish of pinole served with sweet roasted century plant is itself a representation of the cosmos in a sexual embrace. The essentially male roasted century plant is placed *into* the female pinole. Use of sweet banana (*xána*) to substitute for roasted century plant in this context strengthens the connotation. The phallic shape of the banana is not lost on Tereseños, who use its name as the basis of their term for "sin" (*xának+re*). The pinole is made of both ground maize, a prototypical "mother," and chia seeds ('*+ka*; cf. '*uka*, "women"). Of these chia seeds, one Tereseño man is reported to have said that they are "like fertilizer found in the soil" (Amaro Romero 1993: 47). The smaller tamale that is served along with roasted century plant in the pinole is wrapped to resemble the larger "cicadas," for which the mitote is named. The same Tereseño man continues:

> The cicada is the one who sings when it gets hot. It is the patron of those that will be born in the soil, of everything that is going to be born. She has the seed that is going to be planted, the whole seed. The sun is the husband of the earth, because the earth is pregnant, and when the seasonal rains get to her it is like he is having sex with her. Later all the things of the world are born from her as if they were her babies. (Amaro Romero 1993: 47)

This "seed" in the pinole, then, is like an unfertilized egg in a mother's womb. It is fertilized by the roasted century plant whose semen-like liquor also represents the rains.

This connection of liquor with the rains is formed through the process of roasting, fermentation, and distillation. The roasting of century plants prior to their fermentation takes place in an earthen pit that is the shape of a huge gourd bowl. Once these plants are roasted, the "meat" is then carried to another pit, this one wood-lined and decorated with flowers.

This pit is the exact image of an open grave. Water is added to this pit, and as the plants ferment, the water is covered with foam that resembles clouds. The resulting century-plant mash is then transferred to a pan in a rock-and-mud distillery (which looks like a miniature mountain) where it is heated by a fire, turning it into vapor that precipitates as precious drops of rain-like liquor. Through this process, then, the meaty "bodies" of the century plants are placed in the ground (like the umbilical cords of long-deceased people who were "planted" under such agaves), and the disembodied human souls once lodged within them emerge upward—like foam or vapor—where as clouds they rain liquor.

This connection of liquor with the rains and so with the deceased ancestors is taken for granted by local people (recall that both the rains and deceased ancestors are called "Tawáusimwa"). Moreover, liquor is thought to be very attractive to the deceased ancestors who return as the rains. "After all," a Náyari man once commented to me as he carried roasted century-plant hearts to a grave-shaped fermentation pit, "if they liked to drink liquor while they were alive, they probably still like it." Like the "joining of waters," then, preparations for the liquor-drinking ritual add important symbolic content to the liquor itself. This content finds specific meaning in the periodic liquor-drinking rituals, adding further levels of meaning to annually celebrated cicada mitotes.

The ritual drinking of liquor occurs at sunrise, on the day following the prototypical rituals of the cicada mitote. After everyone in attendance has been "bathed" as a group by the ceremonial elder, each of the children (first girls, then boys) sits in turn on a small stool, of the type used by musical-bow singers, under the inner edge of the tapanco-altar. The sponsoring female or male relative sits on a larger stool next to the incoming child. A tsuwá-decorated prayer arrow of the type given during the earlier baptism ritual (again hung with green perico feathers for girls and women and hawk feathers for boys and men) is tied upright to the back of the child's head with a colorful handkerchief. The handkerchief is then tied again with a colorful ribbon, making the regal feather-topped prayer arrow sticking up behind the child's head look like an ancient crown. In this position, sitting under the tapanco on the special throne with the sun rising behind, the child seems to momentarily embody the ancestors whose ancient descent group he or he is joining.

After a prayer arrow has been tied to the head of the initiate and his or her sponsor, small gourd bowls are placed at the feet of both individuals—four bowls for girls and women and five bowls for boys and men. These bowls are filled with liquor, and helpers hold each of these bowls to the special ceremonial pressure points of the seated initiate and his or her sponsor (the points where people are "bathed") before offering the contents of the bowls to be drunk. The ceremony concludes after all of the children have finished off their gourd bowls of century-plant liquor, and then again join together facing east in front of the tapanco to be bathed.

Everyone should be at least tipsy following this ritual, and all sway together. The scene would surely be disorderly on the surface, but through this drinking of special century-plant liquor an inclusive unity of mind among the intoxicated ritual participants is also hoped for. Moreover, the placing of gourd bowls at the pressure points of the body, and then the drinking of the liquor that they contain, continues a "semiosis" (Eco 1976: 15)—a complicated and extensively ramifying signification—that links a child's body with particular substances and ceremonial practices (century plants, ground tz+wí maize, the making of liquor, etc.), as well as with fellow descent-group members, the deceased ancestors of that descent group, and a specifically marked and meaningful landscape within which those children will spend most of their lives. As a result, cicada mitotes serve to not only help the cicada "call the rains"—their explicit purpose—but also remind living maize-bundle group members of their position in relation to an ancestral tradition that seems to reproduce life itself.

The Femaleness of Maize and the Symbolic Domestication of Women in the Roasted and Parched Maize Mitotes

Whereas the distinctive signification of the cicada mitote (with its life-cycle rituals) reproduces the representation of seasonal rains as deceased ancestors, the roasted and parched maize mitotes focus less on rain than on the descent-group maize that is ripening and drying at the time of these ceremonies. Specifically, these mitotes mobilize a number of symbols that consolidate the sense of maize as a sacred mother. The coordination of roasted and parched maize mitote ceremonies with the fruitful period of the growth cycle of descent-group maize easily leads to linking ritual symbols like flowers, arches, bells, and the color white with maize as intrinsic aspects of its (but really "her") character. Indeed, for most Náyari people the association of maize with a type of undirtied femaleness—like the association of rain with deceased ancestors—is so close as to seem entirely natural and inevitable.

The construction of this association through the performance of roasted and parched maize mitotes begins with the different manner of preparing the ceremonial tapanco at these mitotes. Perhaps most distinctive is the flower arch tied to the west side of the tapanco facing the ceremonial plaza. This arch (*túnamu*) carries a number of connotations. First, the arch's name and shape connote the musical bow commonly played by singers during these mitotes (and not during cicada mitotes). Second, it is the shape and color of a rainbow, which is said to be like a door opening onto a stairway to the gods. Most importantly, the arch also closely resembles the flowered arches that are renewed each week (except during Lent) by traditional officers of the church of Santa Teresa. As such, it is also related to two female saints of Santa Teresa—Santa Teresa and Guadalupe—whose church-and-courthouse-oriented festivals are celebrated during the same time of the year as the roasted and parched maize mitotes, respectively. Santa Teresa's Day is celebrated October 15, when maize ears are green on the stalk, and Guadalupe's Day is celebrated on December 12, after the dried ears have been harvested. Both of these saints, like the maize itself, are referred to as Tanana, "Our Mother."

Arches at both descent-group roasted maize mitotes and at the community-oriented Santa Teresa's Day Festival are decorated with pink-petaled cosmo flowers called *xuxu santaterésaxa* ("Santa Teresa's flower"). Later, during the parched maize mitotes that occur near the time of the Guadalupe's Day Festival, the arches are decorated with a red honeysuckle called *xuxu guadalupexa* ("Guadalupe's flower"). Arches in both of these festivals also include the white tsuwá orchids that are used during the roasted and parched maize mitotes.

Each arch is decorated the same way. To begin, handfuls of flowers are tied with their stems together to form crosses, with flowers marking each of the four points of the cross. These flower crosses again index the sacred sites at which flowers are left when collecting water, as well as the four corners of the mitote ground where these flowers are later placed during both the roasted and parched maize mitotes. The decoration of the arch then begins with the attachment of the largest flowered cross at the apex of the arch. This cross of flowers includes a single white bell-shaped flower (Spanish: *campanilla*). The white campanilla flower refers to the bells that hang in the ruins of the colonial-era church on the north side of the town's plaza, and to the bells that most women wear each day as decoration in their beaded necklaces. After the first flower cross with its campanilla flower is attached, more flower crosses are then tied down on either side to completely cover the arch.

The position of the arch tied to the inside (west) edge of the tapanco also evokes the position of the flowered arch that is placed in the church of Santa Teresa during the two female-saint-day festivals. This arch defines a sacred enclosure within the church; people take pains to walk under it when "visiting" with the saints, and they crowd to the inside of the arch during church-based ceremonies. The placement of a similar arch on the inside edge of the tapanco associates the surface of this tapanco with the church's sacred enclosure and with the female saints whose festivals are also celebrated during that time of year.

THE ROASTED MAIZE MITOTE The distinctive ritual actions of the roasted maize mitote begin at midnight during the dancing of the fifth evening of the ceremony. At that time, the arch is unfastened from the tapanco by senior male members of the maize-bundle group while the bow-drummer plays and sings. Two more senior descent-group members pick up prayer arrows from beneath the tapanco and carry them behind the men holding either end of the arch. Another two men light and smoke clay pipes of tobacco and follow the men holding the prayer arrows. The most senior elder takes up a feathered wand called the *náru* and stands under the apex of the arch next to a younger man holding a smoking branch pulled from the fire. Once all of these men have taken their places, each of the descent-group members—both men and women—picks up a bundle of maize and hugs it to his or her chest.

This dramatic action refers to the baptism ritual, when children are clutched to the breasts of their descent-group relatives in the same way. It also refers to a particular folk tale that accounts for the origin of maize among the Náyari people:

> This happened long ago, when Our Elder Brother wanted a wife. His new mother-in-law called him lazy and rejected him. Then he became sad. He no longer spoke to his wife. Then she said to her husband: "Why do you no longer speak?" Then he said to his wife, "Your mother is speaking of me in this way: That he is lazy, as if he were lying down inside, he's just very lazy." Then San Miguel went inside a corn-crib, with his wife as well. In that way she hugged her husband. Then he said to his wife: "Alright, then. Take these clay pots. I am leaving." Then his wife hugged her husband there inside of the corn-crib. Then the husband said to his wife: "You are going to do it, you will plant the maize." In that way his wife was hugging him when maize leaf appeared in her arms and she remained standing there with his maize ears. So she planted it. Then maize was born there. It was born and matured. Then she gave the ears for seed to other people. Then everywhere all around maize was planted as it is today. In this way it came to be that he appeared long ago, that one San Miguel, the big star [Xúrave].*

In this story San Miguel Xúrave is rejected as a son-in-law and in his sadness disappears from the standing embrace of his wife to be replaced by maize plants that she hugs to her breast, just as children and maize bundles are hugged in contemporary mitote ceremonies.

Because of these connotations, embracing bundles of maize during the roasted maize mitote evokes complex feelings. The maize bundle represents each participant's soul in its connection with an ancient line of an-

*Diego Flores provided this story.

cestors going back to the origin of people on the earth. But, at the same time, it evokes a lack of connection with those ancestors, a distancing from heavenly grace while living in human bodies on earth. Hugging these bundles also evokes the children that each person has similarly hugged during baptism rituals. Thus, it also represents a commitment to care for generations to come, to continue a set of customs through which people in this world can sustain (and be sustained by) deceased ancestors in the next.

The descent-group members, each of them embracing a bundle of maize, bunch together behind the unfastened arch and its smoking and prayer-arrow-carrying elders. All dance in this formation five times around the fire, detouring to make additional counterclockwise circuits at each of the four corners of the mitote ground. In effect, the pattern of the world with its sacred sites is danced around the fire—one circle for each step-like day of fasting leading up to the dancing itself. As descent-group members dance, hugging their maize bundles, I have seen people cry to themselves, letting the tears run down their faces. Others clutch the maize bundle tightly to their hearts, seeming to draw strength from its purity. To me it seemed that in embracing their maize bundles the "dirtiness" of daily life was momentarily deferred as everyone danced as a group around the fire. The maize provided a link with the world of the ancestral past that for each individual also seemed to represent at that moment a desire to continue their traditions into the heavenly world of the future.

After the final dance of the night, the bundles are unpacked and the maize is roasted on the fire until the kernels of the descent-group maize pop. This popping is said to be a kind of pure speech that has the ability to transfer contemplative thoughts and spoken prayers directly to deceased ancestors and on to the rest of the deities who watch over the world. Once the kernels in all of the maize ears have spoken in this way, the ears are replaced on the tapanco until sunrise.

As the sun rises, its light streams over the tapanco and through the arch in what seems to be a purposeful act on the part of the sun, an act of eating the steaming maize that was earlier placed there. After the sun has been up for an hour or so, the ceremonial elder of the sponsoring maize-bundle group directs other men of his descent group to again unfasten the arch from the tapanco. The prayer arrows, tobacco pipes, and náru feathered wand with its smoldering piece of firewood are all again picked up and danced around the fire another five times as the roasted maize rests on the tapanco. Smoke (k+tsí) from the ceremonial fire drifts upward like smoke from the tobacco pipes. The prayer arrows and wand are waved in a cross-ing and topping-over motion at the four corners in order to "cover over the badness [sickness]" (Spanish: *tapan lo malo*), as local patriarch and cer-emonial specialist Juventino Flores Cabrero put it.

While these men circle the fire, the ceremonial elder and his helpers stop at each of the cardinal directions and unfasten flowers from the arch. They drop these flowers at each of the four points corresponding to the sacred sites from which water was collected until only the last cross of flowers with its campanilla bell remains on the arch. At this point, the arch is then again refastened to the tapanco, but now on the outside or eastern edge, symbolically moving the roasted maize ears and other foods on top of the tapanco to within the space of the mitote ceremonial ground occupied by the ritual participants. "Our Father has finished eating," I was once told at this moment during a roasted maize mitote. The roasted ears are distributed to ceremonial participants, and after this fresh maize is eaten, more food is distributed as at other mitotes.

Through these ritual acts, the roasted maize mitote elaborates on a number of symbolic connotations that are referred to only indirectly dur-ing the cicada mitote. Rather than the seasonal rains, the focus here is on maize, which in this context strongly connotes a pure mother (who gives birth to the maize ears that also connote San Miguel Xúrave). From this perspective, the representation of the seasonal rains as men, especially old men, has increased significance. Although these "deceased ances-tors" are prayed to by both male and female members of a maize-bundle group, it becomes apparent that only the men, and perhaps only the se-nior men or ceremonial elders, actually continue as active agents in the lives of living descent-group members (as the seasonal rains) after their deaths. Conversely, women as maize are of the earth. Like the tree-of-life represented by the xapwá ví'ihatana at the lake, maize joins the worlds. It literally grows out of the past, from the times of the ancestors who once carried out the mitote ceremonies through which a land-race of maize has been perpetuated. These ancestors then passed that maize and its associated mitote ceremonies *down* (a felicitous double entendre) to living ceremonial elders. After their deaths, these ceremonial elders then in turn rise up to the heavens, a stepwise passage to the past.

But living and deceased ceremonial elders are also connected *through* maize (another useful double entendre). Firstborn males who will become ceremonial elders emerge onto the bounded Tereseño earth through their mothers' bodies, and there find connection with a previous generation of descent-group ancestors by means of the common white descent-group maize—"Our Mother." As these ceremonial elders die and move up a cosmic stairway to become the rains, the organic white maize is left behind. Thus, maize and women serve as vehicles through which related male ceremonial elders are connected across the generations. This complex set of connotations linking maize with women is elaborated in the subsequent parched maize mitote.

THE PARCHED MAIZE MITOTE Although the roasted and parched maize mitotes have nearly identical ritual structures, the few differences between them elaborate on the symbolic connection of maize with women that appears in the roasted maize mitote, while also depicting women as wild animals that are domesticated by men. A pair of special deer-tail prayer wands is used toward the conclusion of the parched maize mitote to make this connotation. Still, maize is again the focus. Instead of getting roasted, however, this maize is ritually parched on a circular *comal* griddle that is placed on the ceremonial fire.

To begin the parching, the ceremonial elder whisks a handful of maize kernels around the hot griddle with a brush made from the leaf of a century plant. These kernels are then tossed to each of the four directions. One or more elderly women are then specially selected to complete the parching of the remaining maize. These women seem to be living representations of Our Mother, and their presence creates another symbolic connection to maize. Both the maize and the elderly women who parch it are old (*wachi*, "old," "thin," "dried") and at the end of their reproductive cycles. In this sense these old women also seem to represent *Tayá-kwari*, "Our Grandmother," who in such ritual contexts is suggested to be another deceased ancestor serving with the much more numerous old men in heaven.

The parched maize mitote ends differently from the roasted maize mitote. To end the parched maize mitote, the men who earlier danced the flowered arch around the fire pick up the deer-tail prayer wands, push the singer off of his chair, and grab the musical bow. Having stolen the bow, these "deer" jump around the mitote circle, running through the smoldering fire and scattering ashes to the four directions. This wild display is referred to as the *mwaxárika* ("what the deer always do"). It is a reference to a deer-dance ritual, a drama periodically performed within the parched maize mitote in which rebellious and wild women are domesticated by men.

DEER-DANCING RITUALS   Both boys and girls go through baptism and liquor-drinking rituals, and both receive the maize bundles that represent their embodied connection to each of their maize-bundle groups. Girls, however, are represented as never being as completely and complexly connected to their descent groups as are boys. At each stage in the progression of these life-cycle rituals, they are depicted as one step lower. In the deer-dancing ritual, girls and women, many attending as visitors from other maize-bundle groups (and so as prospective brides), are symbolically domesticated by boys and men. They are literally dragged kicking and fighting out of the forest and are tied to the tapanco of the sponsoring ceremonial elder. The ritual symbolism that constitutes descent groups, then, does not position descent-group members in the same way. Rather, in rituals such as this one, it becomes clear that women are considered to be not only lower than men, but also peripheral to the central line of male descent-group ancestors.

Deer-dancing rituals are added to the parched maize mitote of which they are a part every five years or so. Preparations for the ritual again add important signification that is later drawn upon in the ceremonial context of the mitote itself. In this case, a deer is hunted. Like the pilgrimage to gather water, this hunt takes men who represent the descent group to the edges of the geographical territory within which members of the descent group live. Furthermore, it also involves the type of fasting and bodily deprivation through which ceremonial elders later make prayers to their deceased ancestors prior to mitote ceremonies themselves. Perhaps most importantly, this experience also links the young hunters of the sponsoring maize-bundle group with a particular story that is associated with the deer-dancing ritual:

A poor hunter dressed in rags went out to look for a deer to eat. He looked a long time and finally found some deer that he was going to kill, but they instead told him to wait by the side of a pool of water, and that there he would find his wife. He waited and a series of women came to the pool to bathe. Each took off her clothes and bathed. He managed to grab the fifth one before she could put her clothes back on. As she put her shirt over his hands she promised to come with him. The parents of the girl said that she could go with him, but that he would need to draw the shapes of a house, and a corral, and all of the things that they would need in the dirt. They promised that these things would be his on the firm condition that he not get drunk as long as he was with her. He agreed, and went to draw. When he woke up after doing this he found himself at a nice ranch, clothed in new pants with a new hat and a gun and a strong saddle mule—everything he could want. Eventually, however, he went to a festival and got drunk. When he woke up in the morning the mule was bones and all of his things were old and useless. His wife was gone. He went through five doors to get back to his in-laws and asked, "What happened?" They told him that because he had gotten drunk he had lost everything. However, the man managed to grab his wife, and with the help of a deer they exited back through the five doors. They escaped and returned to the ruined ranch, but when they arrived the wife told the man that he would have to go and work for the things that they would have from then onward, and they were always poor and struggling for enough to eat after that.*

*Felipe Morales Morales told me this version of the story in an informal interview.

In preparing for the deer-dancing ritual, then, these young hunters become associated with a particular ritual role in which an explicit connection is made between the hunt for a deer and the hunt for a wife.

The deer-dancing ritual (*mwaxati*, "deer" [pl.])—referred to by Coras in Spanish as *"jugando los venados"* ("deer playing")—is an extension of the night-long dancing that occurs during parched maize mitotes. During years in which the deer-dancing ritual is included as part of the parched maize mitote ceremony, the fifth and final dance of the night ends when the dancing women flee into the forest, whooping and hollering as they run. Young men follow close on their heels, and as the sun rises, the shouts and howls of women and men off in the woods echo in the air. As the young people chase each other, old women of the sponsoring maize-bundle group parch the maize. Meanwhile, the young men slowly manage to move the women closer to the mitote grounds, and the shape of this mostly female "herd" becomes clearer. Each of the women carries antlers that she uses to fight off the men who try to rope her with their lariats, and these women are also accompanied by at least one male "buck" who carries the deer skull or hide from a recently hunted deer.

As the deer are rounded into a group, their resistance grows stronger. The buck tries to defend "his" deer, using the deer skull to pummel the young men who surround them or the hide to whip the young men's feet out from under them. The women fight savagely, slashing at young men with the antlers of the deer skulls that they hold in front of them. Several men in Santa Teresa have been scarred for life as a result of "playing" in this manner. The young men alternately pretend to hold out food to the women and sneak up behind them in order to lasso their antlers. They laugh and yell out, *"Hoo, xa! hoo, xa!"* as if it were a cattle roundup. As the women are corralled, they back into a tight circle to defend themselves collectively with the deer antlers that they hold in front of them. The young men taunt particularly pretty young women, trying to anger them into leaving the tight circle of their "female relatives." Men gang up on these isolated women, lassoing them and fondling their bodies as other (especially older) women try to defend them. Eventually, however, each of the women is lassoed. Once the antlers have been roped, the deer skull becomes the center of a tug-of-war between the woman and the young man who tries to drag her toward the mitote ceremonial grounds. During this struggle, women may jump in the air or dig their heels into the ground as they are dragged closer to the tapanco. Eventually, however, each woman is pulled through the "door" underneath the tapanco to the mitote grounds. But then they manage to get away, and flee into the forest again.

The same roundup is repeated four more times, the women each time growing more lethargic as their fatigue betrays them. The fifth time that each woman is brought into the mitote grounds, her struggle weakens as she is finally tied to an inside post of the tapanco. The buck becomes increasingly irrelevant to the proceedings as his herd diminishes, and he is also brought in without struggle. Once all the deer have been captured, the singer again begins to play his bow drum. The buck and his deer join the young male relatives of the sponsoring ceremonial elder, who have carried deer-tail prayer wands in previous dancing through the night. Together all dance five counterclockwise circles with members of the sponsoring maize-bundle group. After dancing the parched maize around the fire, and then taking it into the house, both descent-group members and the visiting women with their "buck" are "bathed" together in front of the tapanco. The mitote ends as gourd bowls of pinole and roasted century plant are distributed to all.

Unlike baptism and liquor-drinking rituals, the deer-dancing ritual positions individuals not only in relation to their descent-group kin, ancestors, and geographical territory, but also in relation to other descent groups. These descent groups are characterized particularly in terms of the women who live away from their own descent-group kin as the "captured" wife of an unrelated man. Indeed, men explain the problems that they have in holding their marriages together by pointing to the wild and uncontrollable behavior of their wives. Many men have earnestly informed me that a husband is like the buck of a herd who periodically needs to "work" sexually in order to keep the female from running away. Men say that women go into heat like animals and that this "hotness" is dangerous because it can cause men to fail in their religious fasts from sex. As a result, men sometimes speak of their in-marrying wives as more like domesticated animals than people: their fecundity is the practical measure of the efficacy of a maize-bundle group's ritual life, but they are unpredictable and may wander off to be captured by another "owner." Despite the chauvinism that this view may seem to imply, women are also drawn to this image of themselves as wild and undomesticated deer. One of the most common decorations they add to their clothing are the appliquéd figures of deer running along the fronts of their blouses or the embroidered hems of their skirts. Moreover, during the deer-dancing ritual itself, a drunk or obnoxious man will occasionally attempt to grope a woman portraying a deer, and such men are gored mercilessly, particularly by the older women who clearly delight in such brief rebellions.

The deer-dancing ritual, like the rest of the life-cycle rituals, offers infants, children, and adolescents compelling images and connotations with which they are meant to identify. Specifically, it aims to produce an embodied connection with deceased ancestors and geographical territory that is shared among maize-bundle group kin. Maize-bundle group members, however, are positioned differently as adults based on both their gender and their relative age. As children grow up and move through the life-cycle rituals, it is made clear to them that certain descent-group members are more central than others to the effective performance of mitote ceremonies, and thus to the reproduction of the maize-bundle group as a whole. These different social positions, among other meaningful connotations, are evoked and renewed in the annual mitotes. Just as a gourd bowl filled with water, for example, "points" to Nákuta, a mwaxá prayer wand used in an annual parched maize mitote carries the deer-dancing ritual with it in the years that the "deer" do not actually "play." The old women that parch the maize in those years may appear hardworking and quiescent but are still not fully subservient to the male-dominated maize-bundle group within which they live. In community-level ceremonies, the use of such symbols also "points" to the deeply embodied hierarchical structure of the descent group as a whole, which is in turn represented as only one part of the even larger, hierarchically organized community.

However, before moving on to a discussion of the symbolic relationships between descent-group and community-level ceremonies, in the next chapter I begin to contextualize these ceremonial traditions historically. I show that mitote ceremonialism, which seems to have ancient roots in the region, was only integrated with Catholic-derived ceremonialism in the nineteenth century. At that time the complementary ceremonies of this integrated costumbre began to produce the sets of hierarchical symbolic relationships between descent-group and community ceremonies that might position cargo-system officials as the legitimate authorities of Santa Teresa.

4

The Politics of Tereseño Ceremonialism
in Historical Perspective (PART I)

These things come from very far back.

GREGORIO CAMPOS

HISTORIES OF THE SIERRA DEL NAYAR have tended to focus on a single event: the conquest of the Mesa del Tonatí (now called the Mesa del Nayar) by forces under the Spanish in 1722, more than two hundred years after the conquest of Tenochtitlán in central Mexico. By all accounts the capture of the Mesa del Tonatí was a very dramatic assault that culminated decades of back-and-forth raiding and set the stage for the establishment of Spanish missions and a presidio in the Sierra del Nayar, which in turn had profound effects upon the Náyari people of this region. Moreover, many primary documents were produced and archived during this period, and these documents have been gleaned by generations of historians. For these reasons, if *Náyarite* (Coras) are mentioned at all in more general histories, they are mentioned in terms of the relatively late and dramatic Spanish conquest and missionization that these documents discuss (e.g., Borah 1970: 709).

It is not surprising, then, that anthropologists and ethnohistorians interested in the history of the Sierra del Nayar have also identified the late colonial period of Spanish history as the most important for the development of contemporary Náyari culture. As Grimes and Hinton (1969: 795) put it, "Modern Cora culture took form in the eighteenth century, and has since proved resistant to change." This view of the emergence of Náyari culture in the eighteenth century also jibes with the work of Phil C. Weigand (1992: 184). He argues that the people who came to be identified as Coras in the eighteenth century were previously a "contestatory composite society" made up of former mission Indians, escaped slaves, and other ethnically diverse peoples who all fled into the Sierra del Nayar to avoid Spanish domination. Because this composite rebel society nonetheless had trading relationships with surrounding Spanish towns, Hinton argues that a period of "pre-conquest acculturation" set the stage for the creation of "Cora" culture following the conquest of 1722 in the late colonial period of Spanish history. For Hinton, this acculturation helps to explain what he sees as the sudden acquiescence of Náyari people to passive mission communities following the Spanish capture of the Mesa del Tonatí. "The fact is," he writes, "that there was no great and disastrous confrontation of cultures . . . [because] the Indians were already half acculturated and knew what to expect" (Hinton 1972: 166). From this perspective, the distinctive features of a syncretic or blended Cora culture were established in the late Spanish colonial period and remained resistant to change into contemporary times (cf. Hinton 1970).

This interpretation, however, cannot account for documentary evidence more recently cited by Marie-Areti Hers (1992), Richard Warner (1998), Johannes Neurath (1998), and Jesús Jáuregui (1997). Hers shows that although a number of Coras do seem to have been "readily missionized," as Hinton (1972: 166) suggests, others offered stubborn resistance to the Spanish. Warner takes up this theme, pointing out that the Náyarite were never truly "conquered" or "converted." Instead, they continued to secretly practice mitote ceremonies, despite the establishment of Spanish mission communities in the Sierra del Nayar. Nonetheless, Neurath argues that the Catholic community-level ceremonialism of these mission communities did have profound effects in that it replaced a region-wide preconquest chiefdom with community-level political and religious authorities. Building on Neurath's and my own (Coyle 1997) work, Jáuregui then argues that mitote ceremonies were brought out of hiding in the nineteenth century—after the collapse of the Spanish colony but prior to the establishment of Mexican control of the region—and were combined with community-level ceremonies.

In short, Náyari history cannot be reduced to a single event or period. Instead, ranch-level maize-bundle groups with their mitote ceremonies are an enduring political structure in the region whose relation to higher-level political hierarchies changed in important ways through both the Spanish and the Mexican periods of Náyari history. In this regard, Neurath's (1998: 25–34) comparison of Cora history with the history of the Kachin of Burma (Leach 1965) and the Merina of Madagascar (Bloch 1986) is particularly apt. As in these ethnographic cases, historical change among the Coras is best understood as a series of struggles over political and religious integration rather than as the acculturation of new political or religious ideas. From this perspective, Spain's failed attempts to create a coherently integrated society in the Sierra del Nayar during the eighteenth and early nineteenth centuries foreshadowed Mexico's own failed initiatives of the late twentieth century. In both cases "too much and too little government" created unintended local legitimation crises with national and international ramifications.

THE CONQUEST OF THE MESA DEL TONATÍ AND PUBLIC CEREMONIALISM IN THE SIERRA DEL NAYAR

According to Spanish colonial documents, maize-bundle group mitote ceremonies seem to have been performed in the Sierra del Nayar long before the Spanish conquest of the Mesa del Tonatí in 1722. Reports of "tlatoles" or "mitotes," for example, are common in sixteenth-century colonial documents from the northern frontier of New Spain. They usually refer to the war councils or dances of rebellious Amerindians. Documents concerning the Sierra del Nayar also make general mention of the prevalence of such "mitote dances" during the sixteenth and seventeenth centuries (e.g., Arias de Saavedra, in McCarty and Matson 1975: 203). José Ortega (1754: 22–24) provides a detailed description of one of these ceremonies based on his observations around the time of the conquest of the Sierra del Nayar in 1722. When combined with earlier reports, it shows that mitote ceremonies very similar to those described in the previous chapter have a deep history in the region: "When the maize had formed ears in the month of September they did not eat them, despite their need, until they were blessed by their priests in the temples of their gods, which they did in these ceremonies. With all of their families together the Indians would put the fruits that each had brought on top of a log. . . . A little way from that log was seated the one who would play the bow which was tied to a deep tray that was played with a little stick from which resulted a type of harmony that could be heard without annoyance, if the disagreeable mumblings of the singers did not confuse it."

The dancing at these ceremonies was also similar to the dancing at contemporary mitote ceremonies: "They would form in a circle of men and women, as many as could be fit in the space of earth that had been swept for this end. One after the other would go dancing or slapping their feet on the ground with the musician in the center." Also like contemporary mitote ceremonies, the dances described by Ortega concluded at sunrise with the blessing of the maize and of the other foods brought by participants and by the ceremonial elder: "They danced from five o'clock in the afternoon to seven o'clock [in the morning] without stopping or leaving the circle. At the end of the dance, all would stand that could stay on their feet, because with the peyote and liquor that they drank some were incapable of using their legs, or even to pay attention to the benediction that the high priest tossed over the fruits, spraying them with fresh water from a deer tail that served as an aspergillum with certain entreaties that they would say between their teeth so that no one could hear them." In another continuity with contemporary mitote ceremonies, the most senior male elders seem to have had central roles: "Later they would signal for one of their old men who seemed the most suited for the job to give a sermon of thanks to their God for having given them life, and for letting them see and taste those new fruits. And I am aware of some that did it with such ardor that it was necessary for their tear-filled eyes to help them say that which their voices could no longer speak." All of these descriptions clearly suggest that ceremonies very similar to the mitote ceremonies that are practiced in the Sierra del Nayar today were also practiced in that region well before the Spanish attack on the Mesa del Tonatí.

Moreover, the mitotes that Ortega describes seem to have served as a vehicle for producing cognatic descent much as they do in contemporary Santa Teresa. For example, Ortega explains how relations of what he thought of as godparenthood (Spanish: *compadrazgo*) were established within the context of mitote ceremonies. When a baby was born, he writes, "his parents looked for one of their uncles or aunts, and to no other that was not in the ascending unequal transversal lineage [Spanish: *ascendiente en la línea transversal desigual*], and they said to him: 'Look here at our son, we want that he should be your name-mate'" (Ortega 1754: 26). By "ascending unequal transversal lineage," Ortega is presumably referring to the way that ranked descent-group segments are formed through the hereditary recruitment of the eldest son of previous ceremonial elders to serve as the ceremonial elder of that descent group. This practice creates a hierarchical division between leading descent-group segments and secondary segments or dispersed households who attend, but do not sponsor, mitotes. Perhaps lost on Ortega was the notion that parents did not recruit only one "uncle or aunt," but rather the ceremonial elder of each of their grandparents' descent groups. Instead of describing random ties of compadrazgo, then, Ortega seems to be precisely noting the formation of maize-bundle group affiliation within an overarching cognatic descent system.

In several places Ortega also writes of elders speaking for and having possession of particular "rancherías" (e.g., Ortega 1754: 209). For example, elders named Alonso and Capulín, among several other *viejos* (Spanish: old men) and *caciques* (Spanish: chiefs), negotiated on behalf of the people of their ranches with the Spaniards at San Juan Peyotán (e.g., Ortega 1754: 138, 146). These elders seem to have acted much like present-day maize-bundle-group elders, each of whom manages a piece of land adjacent to other related households. If this is so, then Alonso, the head of the ranch of Cangrejo, whom Ortega (1754: 138) describes as "very capable and astute," was himself the ceremonial elder of a localized Náyari descent group, similar to the elders who lead mitote ceremonies in Santa Teresa today.

As a Jesuit missionary, Ortega worked to stop these mitote ceremonies, and in his history he writes of them in the past tense, but documentary sources collected by Marie-Areti Hers and Jean Meyer make it clear that these ceremonies continued after the conquest of 1722. For example, dispatches written by the Spanish captain Antonio Serratos in 1755 report on the confessions of religious backsliding that he was able to obtain from many of the residents of the town of Dolores. One of these dispatches reports the case of a man who fled that town to solicit the help of an old woman named Ysabel to carry out a mitote ceremony to baptize her newborn baby: "And having himself a boy child he availed himself of the old woman named Ysabel as a sponsor so that she would bless him, and to that end he went down to the river that runs between one and the other town. Right there he made a bit of liquor and a ramada . . . and there they were dancing until sunrise . . . and later that old woman took a gourd bowl of water from the same river and taking that water in her mouth she commenced to spray the child, his parents and a small century plant . . ." (Meyer 1989: 137–138). As in some other reports of religious idolatry during this period, a woman is portrayed as the leader of this indigenous ceremony, but aside from this difference the specific ceremonial practices described here are very similar to those of contemporary mitote ceremonies.*

The missionaries who were assigned to the Sierra del Nayar after the conquest of the Mesa del Tonatí were spread too thin to stop these secret mitote ceremonies. Moreover, the few soldiers and presidial officers who

---

*Although women led many clandestine mitote ceremonies during this time, only men served as bow-drum singers: "They would put a hollow gourd in the middle that they played and arranged in such a manner that it would make a great deal of noise, but only men, because women were prohibited from playing it . . ." (Ponce de Leon Cañaveral, cited in Hers 1992: 192).

manned the newly established Presidio de San Xavier de Valero in the town of Mesa del Nayar were of little help. Of these soldiers, the Jesuit Cristobál Lauria wrote in 1727: "those soldiers are composed of many who are guilty of the crime of murder from assaults or outright homicide and are the most inexpert in the military arts" (Meyer 1989: 49). But although these soldiers were reported to be "very prejudicial to the Indians because of their scandals and bad habits," their commanding officers caused even more trouble for the mission program of the Jesuits. The most notorious of these officers was a presidial commander named Manuel de Oca who was accused by the Jesuits of failing to prosecute religious criminals in exchange for peace agreements with local Cora leaders.

Meyer also points out that Náyarite took advantage of administrative divisions between the Jesuit missions of Nueva Galicia and the even-more-understaffed Franciscan mission communities that surrounded the Sierra del Nayar in Nueva Vizcaya to continue their mitote ceremonies. In 1733, for example, the Jesuit missionary in Santa Teresa reported that fugitives from that town named Martin Surabet (i.e., Xúrave, "Morning Star") and Baptisto Zeucat (i.e., X+ká, "Sun") had fled into Franciscan territory, where a town of Amerindians lived "like some kind of libertines and gentiles" (Meyer 1989: 77). Reports like this one document the continuing practice of mitote ceremonies and the presence of small groups of people who lived beyond the day-to-day control of their Jesuit missionaries, even after the conquest of the Mesa del Tonatí.

But despite the inability of the Spanish to stop mitote ceremonialism, historical accounts make it clear that the Spanish did manage to control another, more centralized, form of public ceremonialism in the region —namely, human sacrifice–oriented ceremonialism. These accounts describe human-sacrifice ceremonialism as an integral aspect of the "strange pagan state" (as Thomas Hinton [1972: 166] put it), centered in the preconquest Sierra del Nayar. A personage referred to as "Tonatí" or "Nayari," whom Hinton (1972: 161) describes as a "priest-king," supervised these ceremonies. A number of documents provide breathless accounts of the human sacrifices that were supposed to have been carried out in this town. The Franciscan Antonio Arias de Saavedra, for example, described the cave where blood offerings were made prior to the conquest of the Mesa del Tonatí: "[In it is] a well or cistern whose mouth is carefully oriented to the south where they offer the blood that is brought in vessels from every ranchería. Usually they offer blood when they have killed some Huaina Motteco Indian. They cut off his head and collect the blood in a jar and pour it into this cistern as an offering to the sun" (McCarty and Matson 1975: 205). The historian Antonio Tello presents an even more fantastic version of the human sacrifices that were offered at the Mesa del Tonatí's shrine to the sun prior to the conquest of the Sierra del Nayar:

> In ancient times there had been much devotion to this cave. The sacrifices that they made were to each month slash the throat of five of the most beautiful maidens. The Indians would take the lives of these maidens on top of a rock in front of their temple and they then took out the hearts of these maidens and hung them up outside so they would dry. They saved them for the festivals when they would cook the hearts, grinding them and mixing them with the blood of maidens and young men that on that day had been sacrificed. They gave the hearts to be drunk in gruel by the mothers of those maidens so that they would live forever grateful that they had given their daughters to be sacrificed. They did the same for the fathers of those maidens. (Tello 1891: 30)

Although these accounts of human sacrifice seem exaggerated, an eyewitness description of the shrine written by the Jesuit Antonio Arias Ibarra (who accompanied the Spanish conquest of the Mesa del Tonatí) supports the idea that human sacrifice was integral to a centralized form of preconquest ceremonialism in the region:

> On said day of Saturday in the afternoon the [Spanish] governor and I made our way to the *güeicalli* [Nahuatl: "shrine-house"] and removed the cadaver of the Great Nayari and his ornaments in order to remit them to his excellency . . . and also the statue to the sun, which is a stone that looks like a *tecalli* [Nahuatl: "altar-piece"]. We put a torch to the thatched house and the shrine and also to another thatched house next to it where they had their dances. Also burned were a blood-stained hide on which they sacrificed children, killing a child each

month in order to feed the sun, as well as a hollow tree that was next to it in which we found a great quantity of small bones with the skulls of infants. (Meyer 1989: 36)

These documents show that prior to the conquest of the Sierra del Nayar, widespread mitote ceremonialism was practiced in relation to a more centralized political and religious tradition under a single "priest-king" at the town of the Mesa del Tonatí.

Following the conquest, however, this centralized ceremonial tradition was effectively suppressed by the Spanish, even as Náyari people continued mitote ceremonies in the canyons surrounding the new mission communities. An elaborately carved stone figure that served as the main altar piece associated with the Coras' priest-king was smashed. Mummified skeletons that were venerated in a cave near this town were sent to Mexico City to be burned in the plaza of San Diego (Meyer 1989: 39). The Tonatí was himself baptized and became the *compadre* (Spanish: ritual kinsman) of a Spanish presidial officer, and a number of other important Cora leaders also sought baptism.

The Spanish success in gaining converts from among the political and religious leadership of the Náyarite was surprising even to Catholic missionaries. Writing only three years after the conquest of the Mesa del Tonatí, Ortega could report that "the Nayeres, who before were a disorderly multitude of savages separated by the canyons and caverns of these mountains, are now congregated in eleven towns . . . none of them leaves without the express permission of their missionaries, indicating up to the day the length of their absence" (1754: 267–268). Based on this account, the sudden acquiescence of these Náyari people to Spanish missionaries does not seem to be the result of simple military coercion. Indeed, Ortega boasts that many Coras even went beyond the requirements of their missionaries: "Everyone knows the orations and doctrine. They pray the Rosary in most towns every day, even when the fathers advise them upon seeing their continuous attendance that there is no obligation to do so. Despite this notice, all who are in town do not cease to pray in the church at sunset" (Ortega 1754: 275). Moreover, although groups of Náyari people living in the canyonlands beyond Spanish control attacked a number of underdefended mission communities immediately after the conquest, other Náyarite worked without military supervision to rebuild the churches that had been burned by the rebels (Ortega 1754: 266).

The historian Jean Meyer (1989) has downplayed the glowing reports of widespread religious conversions that are present in the documentary record (and that helped convince Hinton of the "pre-conquest acculturation" of the Coras), especially in light of the anti-missionary rebellions and religious backsliding that followed. Nonetheless, a number of Cora people were clearly quite faithful to their missionaries following the conquest. "My Indians," Ortega wrote in the midst of a potential uprising in neighboring communities, "are the best of this land" (Meyer 1988: 75). Even in Santa Teresa, where a number of violent rebellions occurred, missionaries had a good deal of success involving Coras in Spanish religious customs. By 1739, for example, Father Jacome Doye wrote of the Náyarite of Santa Teresa, "These neophytes of mine are so subject to laws of Christianity that they even confess their sins" (Meyer 1989: 94). This, despite the fact that on at least one other occasion Doye was forced to retreat from Santa Teresa in the face of death threats from other local Náyarite (Meyer 1989: 75). Indeed, the establishment of Catholic-derived ceremonialism in Santa Teresa seems to date precisely to the period in which this one Jesuit missionary worked there.

Jacome Doye worked in Santa Teresa from 1729 until his death in 1749, longer than any other missionary in the history of Santa Teresa. He seems to have organized the labor to begin the massive stone church that remains today unfinished on the north side of the plaza of Santa Teresa, and his name lives in several descent groups with the name "Dué." He also seems to have established many of the Catholic ceremonial practices that are continued today as part of the Tereseño community-level ceremonialism that is discussed in the following chapter. In a report submitted in 1745, for example, he writes of the town's *chirimía* (a simple clarinet) player accompanying lines of horsemen (Meyer 1989: 89) in a manner similar to that followed by the Moorish horsemen of contemporary community-level ceremonial festivals in Santa Teresa. He also trained groups of singers similar to those that today perform during the Festival of the Deceased and Holy Week (Meyer 1989: 93). In those years he also emphasized the importance of the Festival of San Miguel, calling this saint "Our Celestial Captain" (Meyer 1989: 87), a reference that would be recognizable to Náyari today as their own San Miguel Xúrave, the Morning Star. Doye also reported that he had managed to establish the processions of Holy Week, and that these processions had, "in an exemplary fashion, continued in the subsequent years" (Meyer 1989: 94). Doye described these Holy Week processions as having become important events in the town and as having involved enthusiastic Náyari followers who whipped themselves as penance until they passed out (Meyer 1988: 95).

This Jesuit, however, also noted some unusual occurrences in Santa Teresa. He describes, for example, the "old vices of idolatry and drunkenness" (Meyer 1989: 86) and tells of the ridicule that he faced while trying to celebrate mass during Holy Week. During the very first Holy Week that he celebrated in Santa Teresa in 1730, for example, he writes: "The old men were so perverse that they were even drinking in a house next to the road where the procession of Holy Friday passed, a temerity that they repeated on Easter Sunday, without respect to my presence" (Meyer 1989: 87). This type of ridicule continued during the mass itself: "Those Nayaritas were so far from the things of God that it happened again and again that some of them would make fun of the Holy Sacrifice, instead hanging behind me, at the elevation of the Sacred Host, another one made of straw" (Meyer 1989: 87). Based on these documents, then, it seems that the missionary work of Jacome Doye not only established many of the Catholic-derived ceremonial practices of Santa Teresa but also spurred the burlesque of these practices that continues in contemporary Santa Teresa Holy Week festivities.

Doye later had those who made fun of his Holy Week masses punished, but this type of burlesque—like the continued performance of mitote ceremonies in the canyons outside of town—nonetheless points to a cultural struggle that Jesuits like Jacome Doye could not permanently dominate. Indeed, almost immediately after the Jesuits were removed from the Sierra del Nayar (and the rest of the Americas) in 1767, a new region-wide indigenous priest-king emerged.

According to documents cited by Marie Hers, this indigenous leader—named Granito—sent notices from the Mesa del Nayar to the other Cora towns announcing that the departure of the Jesuits signified that the king of Spain had allowed them to return to their indigenous ceremonial practices. He ordered that each of these towns should immediately begin the performance of large-scale public mitote ceremonies "because the world was coming to an end" (Cañaveral Ponce de León, cited in Hers 1992: 182). Moreover, in each of the Náyari towns a shrine to the sun was built under the authority of a single Cora ceremonial specialist named by a council of elders led by Granito. Based on a report by the Spanish commandant Cañaveral Ponce de León, Hers (1992: 191) writes that only Granito and his helpers—like the Tonatí before him—had access to the main shrine in the Mesa del Nayar. However, she also notes that "in the mitote ceremonies all of the members of each town came together," and that other mitotes "directed toward family idols" persisted (ibid.).

By 1769—only two years after it had begun—the Spanish put down this political and religious revival and Franciscan missionaries replaced Jesuits in the missions of the Sierra del Nayar. However, a report written in 1777 by Franciscan missionary José Antonio Navarro again documents the ongoing practice of mitote ceremonies in the canyons near Santa Teresa: "The native priest sat in the center of the circle, and near the fire, where he put a gourd bowl of water with a deer tail right next to it. Taking up a long bow and a small thin cane in his hands the native priest began to play, and at the sound of that music to sing a little song that was composed in honor of the sun and spoke of the happenings of their ancestors. Two Indians then began to dance by jumping with their legs together to this music and song. . . . in this way these two continued dancing and the native priest singing from sunset until the sun rose the next day" (Meyer 1989: 237). Like the Jesuits, the Franciscans who moved into the missions of the Sierra del Nayar for what would become the final years of Spanish colonialism in the region managed only to keep their Catholic ceremonial traditions alive in each of the town centers, while mitote ceremonialism continued in the inaccessible canyons. Indeed, the ability of Franciscans to control and direct community life in these towns seems never to have matched the previous success of the Jesuits, who were themselves faced with many setbacks.

In Santa Teresa, for example, construction on the large stone church that was started under the direction of the Jesuits stopped after their departure, its walls crumbling by the time the Franciscans arrived in the town (Meyer 1989: 275). The inability of the new Franciscan missionaries to continue this construction also seems to have reflected their generally marginal position in colonial society. In contrast to the Jesuits, the Franciscans in the Sierra del Nayar were seen by colonial authorities as simple placeholders, and soon after their arrival the viceroy of New Spain pushed to secularize their missions in order to decrease costs to the royal treasury (Meyer 1989: 241). Hers (1993: 198) also points out that during this period Spanish settlers were clamoring to "populate the Sierra del Nayar with *gente de razón* [Spanish: non-Indians]." Meyer (1989: 160) argues that compared to the Jesuits, the Franciscans "did not have the same power to resist the government, the Spanish and the mestizos who coveted the labor and territory of Nayarit." For these reasons, after the initial prosecution of rebels following the transfer of missions from the Jesuits to the Franciscans, the poverty and inaccessibility of the region isolated the new missionaries. As a result, the old division between the Spanish town and the Náyari countryside—between, on the one hand, the Catholic missionaries who oversaw the ceremonies pertaining to saints and civil and religious offices, and, on the other, those Náyari people who continued to attend outlawed mitote ceremonies in the surrounding areas—again asserted itself: "The Indians dance their gentile mitotes in the canyons . . . while the Father Missionary is there, alone, in town" (Polo, cited in Meyer 1989: 173).

THE WAR OF INDEPENDENCE, THE LOZADA REBELLION, AND THE FORMATION OF CORA COSTUMBRE

Beginning during Mexico's War of Independence, the precarious relationship between Catholic and indigenous ceremonialism in the Sierra del Nayar again began to shift. Missionaries could not maintain a consistent presence in the region, and so the ceremonies of the Náyarite of Santa Teresa and the other towns of the Sierra del Nayar were no longer constrained by outsiders. But rather than abandoning Catholic ceremonies, the ancestors of contemporary Náyarite continued the church-and-courthouse-oriented ceremonies that many had learned while the missionaries were influential in their towns. Like the centralized human sacrifice–oriented ceremonial tradition previously practiced at the Mesa del Tonatí, this Catholic-derived ceremonialism provided a focus for dispersed descent-group ceremonialism, a "higher" set of ceremonies linked to more inclusive political and religious authorities.

Documents concerning the Independence period in the Sierra del Nayar are rare, but readily available sources provide two pieces of evidence that clearly indicate that Náyari people integrated mitotes with Catholic-derived ceremonialism as their own comprehensive public political and religious tradition during the nineteenth century, and not during the eighteenth century as Grimes and Hinton earlier argued. First, during the middle part of the nineteenth century, the Náyarite of the Sierra del Nayar allied themselves with the rebellion of Manuel Lozada as autonomous towns, each with its own local political authorities and religious ceremonialism. Second, reports by explorers and anthropologists show that by the end of the nineteenth century, mitote ceremonialism and Catholic-derived ceremonialism were practiced together in Náyari towns, and that local officials derived their legitimacy from this combined costumbre.

The seeds of Cora alliance with the Independence-period rebel Manuel Lozada were sewn during the final years of Spanish colonialism in Mexico. During these years population increased dramatically throughout the lowland areas surrounding the Sierra del Nayar, and this demographic surge pushed members of the expanding regional population into Cora territory in order to exploit mines, trade, and ranch land (Meyer 1984: 29). By 1800, for example, there were 349 "Spaniards and people of other classes" resident in the Sierra del Nayar, or about 10 percent of the population (Meyer 1988: 272). At the same time, various liberal "reforms" whose aim was to secularize missions and finish off communal landholdings in indigenous areas of New Spain were also proposed. These pressures for the reorganization of mission communities (and so Indian lands) in the Sierra del Nayar continued to build until 1810, when the Mexican War of Independence disrupted the entire area.

During that eleven-year war, the Sierra del Nayar served as a staging ground for Insurgent attacks against the Royalists, who held the more heavily populated areas between the port of San Blas and the cities of Tepic and Guadalajara. Royalists, however, also fought for control of the mountainous region in and around the Sierra del Nayar. The Franciscan Rudesindo Angles, for example, served as commissioner of the mostly abandoned missions of the Sierra del Nayar and organized the Royalist defense of the region (Rojas 1993: 117). These Franciscan-sponsored Royalist forces eventually burned Santa Teresa and other Cora towns in 1812. Insurgents then responded by attacking the town of Atonalisco in 1815. As a result, Royalists thereafter concentrated on holding the main lowland population centers and ignored the Sierra del Nayar (Meyer 1989: 95). In other words, during the long War of Independence the Sierra del Nayar was an uncontrolled outlaw region in a crumbling Spanish colony at war. No priests or government officials maintained a continuous presence in the area, and anti-Spanish Insurgent militias comprised the only non-indigenous people living in the area.

Following the proclamation of Mexican independence, Franciscan missionaries from the College of Guadalupe (as well as some secular missionaries) are again recorded as working in the missions of Nayarit. Their influence, however, seems to have been slight (Rojas 1993: 135). Despite Franciscan opposition to the "bandits" allied with the emerging leader Manuel Lozada, by 1853 the Cora town of Jesús María had joined his incipient rebellion (Meyer 1984: 74). Shortly thereafter all of the Cora communities of the Sierra del Nayar, including Santa Teresa, joined Lozada under a Cora named Dionisio Gerónimo. In addition to mobilizing these Cora towns, Manuel Lozada, a former hacienda peon, eventually also managed to marshal thousands of other indigenous people (and some Spanish descendants), capture the city of Tepic, and then hold the entire region for seventeen years (1856–1873) "as a separate nation" (Meyer 1984: 247).

Lozada's "nation," however, was uneven, and the Cora, Huichol, and Tepehuan communities that recognized his leadership did so each for their own reasons. For Coras, these reasons seemed to center on the promise of local religious and political autonomy within a larger military confederacy. This promise was spelled out in the Plan Libertador, which was signed by 237 representatives from throughout the territory claimed by Lozada, a territory that included all of the Cora communities of the Sierra del Nayar. At the heart of this document was the "great principle that the pueblo should be governed by the pueblo" (Meyer 1984: 241). It included the provision that any nation that hoped to include the communities who supported Lozada, "whether in the character of Republic, Empire, or Kingdom," needed to recognize that these communities would be governed "by municipios that the people freely name by direct election, and that these towns or municipal bodies have the rights of absolute independence and sovereignty in the areas of government and treasury" (Meyer 1984: 242). This plan, however, was received as a "monstrosity" by lowland political leaders, who saw it as a threat to the consolidation of liberal Mexico (Meyer 1984: 242).

These politicians initially characterized the followers of Lozada as simply "bandits" or "thieves" (Meyer 1984: 76). However, by the time the Plan Libertador was put forth in 1873, the Náyari and other indigenous groups that had joined this rebellion were portrayed as a fanatical caste of *indios bárbaros* (Spanish: barbaric Indians) bent on destroying civilization itself (Meyer 1984: 115). Lozada was described not only as a bandit, but as a traitor, "guilty of selling himself to the imposed [French] empire when confronted by fine bayonets after loaning his mercenary services to contraband-running businessmen and always being addicted to the cleri-cal cause of reaction" (Meyer 1984: 227).

Indeed, Manuel Lozada's growth in power does seem to have been aided by "businessmen," particularly the English company of Barron-Forbes. By supplying Lozada with weapons and money, they hoped to iso-late Nayarit, then the seventh district of Jalisco, in order to expand their textile operations in Tepic and their lucrative export of untaxed precious metals (Meyer 1984: 110). Lozada also allied himself with the Austrian "emperor" of Mexico, Maximillian (put in place by France), a move taken as a direct slap by liberals who supported the reformist and nation-alist constitution of 1857.

But although Lozada may have been a traitor to the liberal cause of the lowland elites, he seems to have effectively represented the interests of the Náyari communities whose support he enjoyed. A wide variety of communities in and around the Sierra del Nayar joined Lozada under the call for "religión y tierras," which was described in the newspaper El País as a "laughable parody of the cry religión y fueros," the call that conservative Catholic cofradías (Spanish: brotherhoods of communal landowners) had used as a protest against the secularization of church privileges (fueros) during the same period (Meyer 1984: 96). This call for "religion and land," however, would have accurately reflected the goals of local cultural and territorial autonomy sought by the Náyari communities of the Sierra del Nayar at that time. Indeed, it was precisely religion and land that were threatened by the liberals whom Lozada opposed.

Liberals argued, for example, that lands were wasted in the hands of Indians, described as "savages who cut the tree at its base in order to col-lect its fruits with greater ease" (Meyer 1984: 115). The Indians them-selves were viewed as "the eternal enemies of progress" (Meyer 1984: 40), and their communities were described as "strange meeting places which with the name 'community' does nothing more than maintain the individuals that compose them in ignorance, misery, fanaticism and deg-radation" (Meyer 1984: 40). Legal rulings at the national level backed up these views, so that the Supreme Court of Mexico could interpret the Reform Laws in the liberal Mexican constitution of 1857 as meaning that "indigenous communities today do not have any existence recognized by law, and because of that they are neither moral persons nor may they seek redress from federal justice" (Meyer 1973: 155). Members of these communities were instead "free" Mexicans.

The Náyarite of the more remote Sierra del Nayar were not initially affected by the "cursed desamortization laws" (Meyer 1984: 39) that were passed and exploited by these liberal politicians to privatize communal lands, but the political organization of Manuel Lozada's "nation" that emerged in response to these laws seems to have meshed with the Náyarite's own desire for religious, political, and territorial sovereignty. This political organization was summarized by an observer in the aftermath of Lozada's execution in 1873: "The towns met in assemblies and there they worked out the principal points of their political agenda, having at the same time a military organization that recognized as its center the so-called General Headquarters of San Luis" (Meyer 1984: 247). This incorporation of politically sovereign communities within Lozada's overarching military confederation allowed him to mobilize large numbers of indigenous soldiers in pillaging lowland settlements—six thousand were mobilized for his final assault on Guadalajara (Reina 1980: 197). Moreover, it also gave local communities like those in the Sierra del Nayar the chance to develop their own ceremonially based forms of political authority and territorial defense.

Lozada's final words prior to his execution attest to this community-based political organization: "I do not renounce what I have done; my intention was to procure the good of the pueblo. If in the future disgrace should seize these towns, then many share the blame, not just me" (Meyer 1984: 229). With these words, Manuel Lozada, the "bandit" and "traitor" against the independent liberal nation of Mexico, revealed the nature of his power in the Sierra del Nayar: he had mobilized a diffuse confederacy of communities each bound by their own religious and political customs. Indeed, in the wake of Lozada's death, and the gradual dissolution of his confederacy, the Náyarite of the Sierra del Nayar refused to abandon their community-level sovereignty. Dionisio Gerónimo, who had previously served under Lozada and later was encharged by the federal government with pacifying the area after Lozada's execution, wrote that the town of Huaynamota was "in a state of rebellion, and does not want to put itself at the disposition of the higher government" (Reina 1980: 198). Later he sent another dispatch to the commander of the federal troops in Tepic complaining of his inability to establish a governmental presence among the different towns in the region: "They do not want to submit to this seat of government as they have in the past, but rather wish to live free of all types of authorities. They even refuse to obey ecclesiastical authorities" (Reina 1980: 199).

Despite the suggestiveness of these accounts concerning the community-level political foundation of Lozada's military confederacy, they do not provide a clear explanation of the place of public ceremonialism in the politically autonomous Náyari communities that emerged during the Lozada period. By the end of the nineteenth century, however, descriptions of the public ceremonies practiced in these local communities began to appear, and these descriptions provide explicit evidence that the integrated costumbre of Náyari towns like Santa Teresa was in place by this time.

The best of these descriptions is provided by the German ethnologist Konrad Teodor Preuss. Preuss worked in the Náyari towns of Jesús María and San Francisco for most of 1906 (Preuss 1998a). During that time he observed the ceremonial cycles of the Coras of those towns and recorded songs and stories relating to their public ceremonialism. His work shows that by the beginning of the twentieth century, mitote ceremonialism and church-and-courthouse-based ceremonialism were being practiced together. In an article for the German magazine *Globus* (Preuss 1998b), for example, he details the Catholic-derived church-and-courthouse-based ceremonial festivals of Jesús María. His descriptions of these ceremonies show that they were nearly identical to those that are practiced today in Santa Teresa. They describe the Moorish horsemen, the Urraca dancers, the Pachitas Festival, the Festival of the Deceased, the New Year's Festival, the Festival of Santiago, and the long and complicated Holy Week Festival with its black-painted "devils."

In addition to describing these church-and-courthouse-oriented ceremonies, in his book *Die Nayarit Expedition*, Preuss (1912) also provides detailed accounts of community-level mitote ceremonies such as are held today in Santa Teresa, and which were also held in Jesús María and San Francisco during his stay in those towns. Preuss, however, is less clear about whether descent-group mitote ceremonies (as discussed in the previous chapter) were celebrated in Jesús María or San Francisco during his stay in the Sierra del Nayar. In *Die Nayarit Expedition*, for example, he writes: "I never was sure of the number of [mitote] singers the Cora actually had. When I inquired, it seemed that they were almost on the verge of dying out. But originally it seems that each head of the house, i.e. the oldest one of a number of relatives who lived together on a rancherio [*sic*], had his own fiesta and was his own singer" (1912: 15). He also mentioned a particular singer, Leocadio Enríquez, who organized a mitote ceremony at his ranch and invited the German foreigner to attend for a price. Because Preuss did not want to set a precedent of being charged to attend these ceremonies, he declined. Nonetheless, he does suggest that mitotes were celebrated at particular ranches, and that one of the wealthier Náyari men of the town enjoyed the reputation of being an excellent singer in the private mitotes he arranged (Preuss 1912: 14). In the end, however, it seems that Preuss, like Hinton sixty years later, never attended these ceremonies, and so he did not discuss their possible importance for the constitution of descent groups. Despite this understandable omission, however, Preuss's writings clearly indicate that an integrated costumbre including both Catholic-derived ceremonialism and mitote ceremonialism had developed in the Cora communities of the Sierra del Nayar by the beginning of the twentieth century. This view is supported by the more limited observations of Náyari ceremonialism provided by the Norwegian explorer Carl Lumholtz.

Lumholtz traveled through the Sierra del Nayar in 1895, eleven years before Preuss began his studies in the area. He spent only a few months in the region, but his writings on the public ceremonialism of the Náyarite—although far from complete—closely match those of Preuss. Together they establish the practice of an integrated Náyari costumbre by the end of the nineteenth century.

Lumholtz arrived in the town of Santa Teresa in April, during its Holy Week Festival. At that festival, he was invited to eat at the home of the man portraying the Roman Centurion. Lumholtz then passed through the town of the Mesa del Nayar before descending to Jesús María and San Francisco, where he attended a cicada mitote in which a liquor-drinking ritual was performed. During that visit a Náyari curer objected to Lumholtz's practice of taking skulls from burial caves to form his ethnological collection, saying that "the dead helped to make the rain" (Lumholtz 1987: 509). By June he was on his way out of the Sierra del Nayar and into the Huichol (Wixárika) country to the east. His observations, though limited, are nonetheless quite telling. Not only do they support those of Preuss in establishing the importance of an integrated costumbre that included both mitote ceremonies and Catholic-derived festivals, but they also show that this public ceremonialism was being practiced in the area only two decades after the execution of Manuel Lozada.

Taken together, this historical and ethnographic information shows that the costumbre of Náyari communities like Santa Teresa was developed in an attempt to create autonomous and legitimate traditional governments during the period of Lozada's rebellion. At this time, Náyari people brought previously clandestine mitote ceremonies into the open and began to practice them in relation to the Catholic-derived ceremonies that had themselves replaced centralized preconquest ceremonial traditions.

After the execution of Manuel Lozada in 1873 at the hands of federal troops, the military confederacy headed by Lozada fell apart. In the wake of this loss, regional Spanish descendants (Vecinos), whose family ties extended out of the Sierra and into surrounding cities, exerted a steady pressure on the land and labor of the Sierra del Nayar. These Vecinos—with family ties to former colonial frontier towns like Acaponeta (Nayarit), Mezquitál (Durango), Valparaiso (Zacatecas), and Colotlán (Jalisco)—gathered in San Juan Peyotán and Jesús María, near the few government outposts and churches in the area. From these towns they used both governmental agrarian reform legislation and counterclaims against that legislation by the church as pretexts to invade neighboring indigenous lands. In times of relative peace they worked to extend their cattle ranches and to consolidate commercial routes. During times of war they organized armed groups of bandit-soldiers who terrorized neighboring Náyari communities until the indigenous people of these towns were forced to flee, leaving their land vulnerable to colonization. Indeed, as Beatriz Rojas (1993: 190) points out in her discussion of Huichol history, the building pressure by Vecinos to control the region through the end of the nineteenth and the beginning of the twentieth centuries, and "the impossibility of the Vecinos to accept that the lands of the Huichols [or Coras] are truly theirs," continue as enduring themes in the region to the present day. Before discussing this more recent history, however, I first discuss the political importance of the symbolism that developed through the performance of descent-group and community ceremonies as part of an integrated costumbre beginning in the nineteenth century.

5

The Symbolism of Community-Level
Ceremonies and Festivals

Those festivals are for everyone, for all of the people from here.

PEDRO FLORES

SINCE THE POST-COLONIAL PERIOD of the nineteenth century, the religious costumbre of Santa Teresa has been composed of both community-level and descent-group ceremonies. In recent decades the relation between the community and descent-group levels of this integrated costumbre has changed dramatically, but its importance in the failing struggle to legitimate community authorities (Spanish: *autoridades*) in terms of outlying descent groups was still plain to see during the period of my fieldwork. Indeed, historical documents show that this relation between community-level and descent-group ceremonies shaped factional struggles over traditional authority that emerged following the Lozada period, and then fanned the flames of violence after that factionalism shattered into back-and-forth blood-feuding among the people I eventually came to know. But even amidst this factional violence, Tereseños repeatedly commented to me on the importance of community-level ceremonies and festivals for holding the town together, and also for allowing it to fall apart.

Community-level ceremonies and festivals are fundamental for sustaining legitimacy because their symbolism represents the town's authorities as both "higher" and more inclusive than maize-bundle groups, which are correspondingly represented as being "lower" and as only one part of the whole community. In other words, the symbolism of these community-level ceremonies and festivals positions community authorities both hierarchically (higher to lower) and synecdochically (whole to part) in relation to descent groups. The construction of these symbolic tropes, however, depends on three more specific hierarchical and synecdochical relations: 1) the relation between the offices held by community authorities and the age-and-gender-stratified world of the maize-bundle groups; 2) the relation between the maize-oriented ceremonial "custom" (*yi'irá*) of maize-bundle-group and community mitote ceremonies; and 3) the relation between the rainy season and the dry season—between flowers and ash—as depicted in the Catholic-derived year-long ceremonial cycle. Perhaps the most important of the first of these hierarchical whole-to-part relationships is between community-level ceremonial elders and descent-group ceremonial elders.

Community-level ceremonial elders (sing. *-vásta*, pl. *-wáusimwa*) are considered to hold the highest offices among Santa Teresa's autoridades. Like maize-bundle-group elders, the three (some say five) community-level ceremonial elders inherit their offices based on seniority in male lines and fulfill their roles by supervising and overseeing ceremonies. However, their ceremonial responsibilities for sustaining health and well-being are much more inclusive than those of maize-bundle group elders, and their ceremonies are correspondingly more elaborate. The senior (and so "highest") of these community elders oversees a complicated set of community-level mitote ceremonies (referred to below as the community mitote cycle) oriented to the principal mountain peaks that surround the town. The "lower" two oversee a cycle of Catholic-derived ceremonies oriented to the courthouse and church, referred to below as the Day-of-the-Dead/Holy-Week cycle. In both cases, the self-sacrifice required of their offices is much greater than that of maize-bundle-group ceremonial elders. The fasts undertaken by these community-level ceremonial elders are more difficult than those undertaken by most maize-bundle-group elders, and their prayers—although uttered in the same format as those of descent-group elders—are longer and more complicated.

Tereseños told me stories of past community-level ceremonial elders who lived to be more than one hundred years old. They were spoken of with awe, as men whose calm strength and resolve to carry out physically taxing ceremonial fasts remained inspirational for Tereseños long after their deaths. During my own fieldwork in Santa Teresa, I was fortunate to meet one of these men. Gregorio Campos was the senior community-level ceremonial elder of Santa Teresa prior to his death in 1994. Like his ancestors, he was quiet and avoided argument or any type of harsh or hurtful behavior. At the same time, his stoicism and ability to "bear" (Spanish: *aguantar*) the privations and suffering that came with his position seemed almost superhuman to me. Long after others had dropped off to sleep, wrapping themselves in their wool blankets against the mountain cold, he sat awake. Some Tereseños claimed that such inwardly powerful community-level ceremonial elders have the power to convert themselves into rain clouds, to literally pass between the worlds of the living and the dead in order to help the community as a whole. Like the clouds, these community-level ceremonial elders are called tawáusimwa, and so are depicted as living representatives of the deceased descent-group elders (Coyle 1998). Others whispered to me that "Don Goyo" himself brought the winter's first frost by unburying a pure, white crystal hidden on the top of the center mountain called Tayaxuri (a.k.a. Kwei-marutse). Like maize-bundle-group elders, then, community elders like Don Goyo were seen to occupy a mediate position between the living and the dead. In this case, however, their position was more inclusive; Don Goyo stood between the people of the entire community and all of the deceased (male) ancestors who produced the current population of Santa Teresa.

Ranked just below the offices of the community-level ceremonial elders, the counselors (Spanish: *consejeros*) are also appointed for life as part of a council of elders (Spanish: *consejo de ancianos*). These leading officers differ from the *principales* of other "cargo systems" in Mesoamerica (Chance 1990: 27) in that they do not automatically receive their post as a result of passing through the entire series of lower offices. Instead, in Santa Teresa, long service in lower-level offices is necessary but not sufficient to be a counselor. More important is the position that a counselor holds in relation to his own patrilateral descent group. Although I was not able to quantify the observation, it is nonetheless quite obvious that in Santa Teresa the council of elders was almost without exception composed of ceremonial elders of maize-bundle groups. Because the council of elders in turn appoints the lower authorities who actually do the work of the two ceremonial cycles mentioned above, the participation of descent-group ceremonial elders again helps to create a sense that the ceremonies supervised by these authorities are oriented towards all of the members of all of the maize-bundle groups in Santa Teresa. Like the three community-level ceremonial elders, this council of elders and the lower authorities they appoint are all positioned above particular maize-bundle-group elders in an overarching hierarchy of traditional authorities.

At the level of the council of elders, this hierarchy is formed not only through the presence of particular men as both descent-group ceremonial elders and counselors, but also through the special role that these men play as the voice of the community authorities as a whole. Indeed, the use of the term "consejeros" is based on the sessions of ritualized oratorical "counsel" (Spanish: *consejo*) that they perform as part of community ceremonies. The discursive structure of this ritual oratory parallels that of the ritual speeches that maize-bundle-group ceremonial elders address to their ancestral maize during their three annual mitote ceremonies. For this reason it serves as a powerful symbolic vehicle that links inclusive community authorities to the legitimate traditional authority of descent-group ceremonial elders, while also distinguishing their own oratory as the single "higher" ancestral voice of the community as a whole.

All of the annually rotated offices of the community authorities are be-

99

low these two highest lifelong offices, but the lower offices are also stratified hierarchically. This stratification, however, is reproduced in ceremonial performance and so does not form a carefully differentiated "ladder"
in which each specific office occupies one rung, as in some other Mesoamerican cargo systems (e.g., Cancian 1965). Rather, annually appointed
cargo-system offices in Santa Teresa are in practice grouped into two
broad steps that are each occupied by several different equivalently positioned offices. There is no waiting list for specific offices in Santa Teresa,
and most people in the town are even unclear on the precise number of
offices that make up the cargo system. Rank order in seating or in processions tends to fluctuate, and people also differ greatly in their responses
when informally asked to rank each of the annually appointed offices. Instead, the relative positions of cargo offices in Santa Teresa are based on
the position of a particular office within the sets of ceremonies through
which offices are transferred from outgoing to incoming officeholder.

These sets of ceremonies for transferring offices constitute two
shorter cycles within the larger, year-long Day-of-the-Dead/Holy-Week
ceremonial cycle, which I discuss below. They are like small and medium-
sized gears meshing within the larger wheel of that whole cycle (see Figure 9). Only "lower" church-based officeholders enter their posts during
the first, shorter cycle of this inner gear. This smaller cycle begins its "ro-
tation" during the Festival of the Birth of Our Mother (September 8),
when prospective officeholders of these lower posts are first nominated.
These nominees are then presented publicly during the subsequent Festival of San Miguel (September 29). Then, during the Festival of Santa
Teresa (October 15), this cycle completes its course as incoming
officeholders formally accept their offices during the "handing-over-of-
the-stools" ceremony (Spanish: *entrega de los bancos*). This cycle of nomination, public presentation, and formal transfer is then repeated for
higher cargo-system offices following the completion of this shorter
cycle.

In the longer cycle the higher church-based offices, as well as all of the
courthouse-based offices, are transferred. Nominations for offices to be
filled during this cycle begin immediately following the Festival of Santa

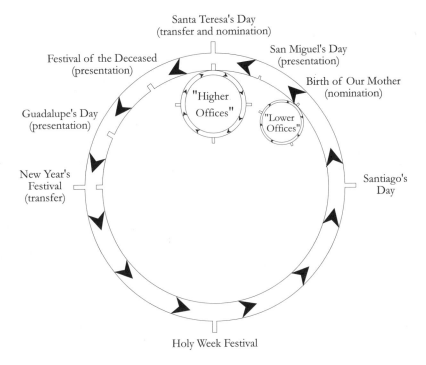

Santa Teresa's Day
(transfer and nomination)

San Miguel's Day
(presentation)

Festival of the Deceased
(presentation)

Birth of Our Mother
(nomination)

"Higher Offices"

Guadalupe's Day
(presentation)

"Lower Offices"

New Year's
Festival
(transfer)

Santiago's
Day

Holy Week Festival

FIGURE 9   Ideal Conception of Gear-Like Ceremonial Cycles

Teresa, after the set of ceremonies through which the lower church-based offices are filled has been completed. Then, during the Day-of-the-Dead (November 2) and the Festival of Guadalupe (December 12), the courthouse- and higher church-based officers respectively are publicly presented. Finally, following Epiphany (January 6), all of these incoming officeholders accept their offices during another handing-over-of-the-stools ceremony. In the "lower" and shorter cycle all of these ceremonies and festivals are completed in a few weeks; in the "higher" and longer cycle they take more than two months to complete.

During the first series of ceremonies that culminates on Santa Teresa's day, two pairs of outgoing male *mayordomos* and two pairs of outgoing female *tenanchis*, along with three individual *fiscales*, "hand over" (Spanish: *entregar*) their offices to the corresponding incoming officeholders (Spanish: *sayo*). As in all the annually appointed cargo offices in Santa Teresa (except the office of fiscal, which has three officeholders), the pairs of officeholders are composed of a senior (Spanish: *primero*) and junior (Spanish: *segundo*) member of the same office. During their year in office these senior and junior mayordomos and tenanchis are responsible for a number of ceremonial tasks. They care for the figure of Santa Teresa (as well as other saints located in the church); they help to clean the church each Saturday (except during Lent); they renew its two flowered arches (one inside the church and the other over its door); and they are central participants in any ceremony that involves Santa Teresa, particularly the one held on October 15 when their offices are "handed over."

The fiscals have fewer responsibilities. During ceremonial festivities they ring the two bells (one larger, one smaller) located in the ruined colonial-era church on the north side of the ceremonial plaza, and they renew the flowers that are tied to the three crosses in town (one on the south wall of the inside of the church, one outside the entrance of the church, and one on the outer east-facing wall of the courthouse above the table used by senior courthouse officials). Additionally, a pair of young girls, each called a *tenanchi tik+lan* (little tenanchi), also enter their cargo with these lower-level mayordomos, tenanchis, and fiscales. The little tenanchis ring a small bell during the festivals for San Miguel's Day and Santa Teresa.

Many more church-based offices are transferred following the series of ceremonies around the time of Epiphany, and because all of the court-house offices are transferred during this later festival, their association with Epiphany also places them one step above the lower church offices enumerated above. These higher church-based offices are composed of two pairs of mayordomos and tenanchis for Guadalupe and one pair for Jesus Christ. Like those for Santa Teresa, these "higher" mayordomos and tenanchis clean the church and help to renew the flowered arches each week. The mayordomos and tenanchis for Guadalupe also take care of the painting of that female saint in the church and participate in the fes-tival for Guadalupe celebrated on December 12. The mayordomos and tenanchis for Jesus Christ care for the figure of an infant that is usually kept in a small box in the sacristy to the south of the church's main altar. They participate in the festivals for that "saint," which are celebrated on Christmas Eve and during Holy Week.

The courthouse-based offices transferred later during this same series of ceremonies are composed of the offices of *alká* (one pair), *alasimayú* (one pair), *teniente* (one pair), *alguacil* (two pair), and *topil* (one pair). All of these offices are directly subservient to the pair of governors (*tatúani*; Spanish: *gobernadores*), who also transfer their offices in the festival following Epiphany, but it is difficult to rank them specifically. The alkás and alasimayús gather ceremonial paraphernalia needed by the governors. The tenientes and alguaciles call people to the courthouse, carry messages to outlying ranches or the municipal capital, and keep order during courthouse meetings or ceremonies. The topiles are the right-hand men of the governors, lighting their cigarettes, sweeping out the courthouse, and running various errands. All have the responsibility to be present with the governors during all of the ceremonies during the year, and all are also expected to carry out a variety of secular tasks. In practice, many avoid these obligations and do little more than participate in the ceremony through which their office is passed on to the incoming officeholder.

A variety of other officers also serve with the governors at the courthouse, but these are unpaid local officers of municipal and national bureaucracies, and not holders of traditional offices. Still, these officers, particularly the *comisario municipal* (municipal commissioner, or judge) or his *suplente* (substitute), as well as the *presidente del comité de bienes comunales* (president of the communal properties committee) and the *presidente del comité de vigilancia* (president of the oversight committee), occasionally participate with the courthouse-based officers in the ceremonies through which their offices are transferred from outgoing to incoming officeholder. I will have much more to say about the relationship between these offices and those of the traditional authorities when discussing the growing factionalism that I witnessed during the time of my fieldwork, but for now I will simply list them and outline their principal responsibilities.

Governmental positions include *comandante* (one pair); *policías* (five for each comandante); the above-mentioned comisario municipal (one pair); a pair of *jueces* for each of the larger outlying settlements and *anexos* (annexed lands) that pertain to Santa Teresa; *presidente, secretario, tesorero,* and various *miembros* of the comité de bienes comunales; and finally, presidente, secretario, tesorero, and various miembros of the consejo de vigilancia. The comandante and his policía carry guns and are supposed to keep order and apprehend criminals. The comisario municipal serves as a local-level judge of the municipal court. The jueces are also lower-level judges whose main responsibilities are as truant officers for the wildly unpopular schools that have recently been constructed in town and in many outlying settlements. The staff of the comité de bienes comunales is supposed to see that Mexican land laws are adhered to locally, and the staff of the consejo de vigilancia is supposed to enforce other governmental mandates. In practice, except for the comisario municipal and presidente de bienes comunales, most of these offices go unfilled or are filled in name only.

With the exception of these anomalous governmental offices, then, all of the offices of the cargo system constitute a stepped hierarchy above the level of particular descent groups (see Figure 10). At the highest level are the community-level ceremonial elders (tawáusimwa). Beneath these elders are the counselors (consejeros). Then beneath these lifelong officeholders are the annually appointed governors, who are sometimes linked with the comisario municipal and presidente de bienes comunales as "big authorities" (Spanish: *autoridades grandes*). Beneath these relatively powerful officials are all of the lesser courthouse-based officers, along with the church-based officers devoted to Guadalupe and Jesus Christ. Finally, the church-based officers devoted to Santa Teresa (along with the fiscals and the pair of tenanchi tik+lan) are somewhat lower than these other church-based officials.

The relative positioning of these community authorities, however, goes well beyond the hierarchy of offices. Instead, hierarchy is tied to a sense of synecdochical inclusiveness through the practice of two community-level ceremonial cycles: the maize-oriented "custom" of the

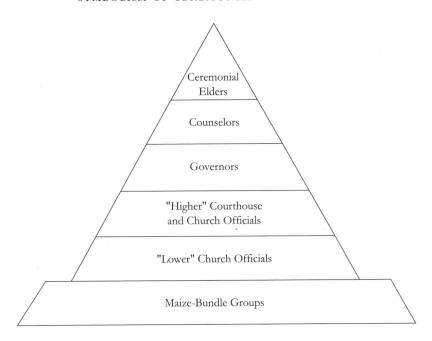

FIGURE 10 Ideal Conception of Different Levels
of Cargo-System Authorities Produced Through Performance
of Community Ceremonies and Festivals

community mitote cycle and the year-long, Catholic-derived Day-of-
the-Dead/Holy-Week ceremonial cycle. In the first of these cycles, symbols mobilized within the yi'irá custom of descent-group mitote ceremonies are elaborated upon within the context of larger, more inclusive
community-level mitote ceremonies. In using these symbols, community
officials also tap into deeply embodied notions of ancestry, territoriality,
and gender. These elaborated connotations of inclusive ancestry, territoriality, and gender then form a figuratively "higher" level of traditional
authority that is represented as being closer to the "upper" realms of the
deceased ancestors and ancestral deities whose disembodied forces drive
the natural world. In the second of these cycles—which I refer to as the
Day-of-the-Dead/Holy-Week cycle—the temporal oscillation between
wet-season and dry-season ceremonies is represented as corresponding to

biannual shifts between the legitimate authority of descent-group ceremonial elders during the wet season and community officials during the
dry season. This oscillation of ceremonies and seasons also refers to a particularly important folk narrative, a story that accounts for the cosmological origin of all Náyari people in Santa Teresa and provides a series
of moral and political lessons supporting the legitimacy of community
officials. I turn to a discussion of this narrative and its corresponding ceremonial cycle following a discussion of the community mitote cycle.

THE COMMUNITY MITOTE CYCLE

Three community mitotes corresponding to the three maize-bundle-
group mitotes comprise the community mitote cycle in Santa Teresa.
However, during the time of my fieldwork, community authorities focused their waning efforts on only two of these mitotes—the cicada and
parched maize mitotes—and either ignored the roasted maize mitote or
celebrated it on a very small scale. In the midst of this loss, the two remaining community mitote cycles that I attended in 1994 and 1995 nonetheless brought moments of great hope "for everyone, for all of the people from here." In both cases, this hope was built upon the remaining
images of hierarchical inclusiveness that these community-based ceremonies continued to produce.

The Community Cicada Mitote

At a fundamental symbolic level, both community cicada mitotes and
community parched maize mitotes create their sense of hierarchical inclusiveness because they are carried out a few days or weeks later in the
year than maize-bundle-group cidada mitotes. Moreover, they take much
longer to prepare for and to complete. But community cicada mitotes
also represent community authorities as overarching intermediaries to
the annual rains in a way that maize-bundle-group elders could not manage on their own. "It's like this," the ceremonial elder of one yi'irá group
told me. "Here it rained well and the maize grew because I always fast at

each of my customs; over there they are lazy and so they received nothing." Although each maize-bundle-group elder attempts to attract his own ancestors as the rains through fasting and prayer during his particular ceremonies, the continuation of the whole seasonal movement from dry to wet seasons is the responsibility of "higher" community officials. This encompassing responsibility is reflected and renewed in the symbolism of a liquor-drinking ritual that community authorities carry out as part of their cidada mitotes.

Unlike sporadic maize-bundle-group liquor-drinking rituals aimed at linking growing children with representations of the deceased-ancestor rains (as liquor), community-level liquor-drinking rituals take place every year in May. In this way these annual community rituals have a direct symbolic connection with the yearly change of seasons; they are linked to the rains that immediately follow them. This symbolic connection of liquor-drinking rituals with the rains in community cicada mitotes also provides an important context that shapes the meaning of two important symbols: sacred water (*wáw+*) and crosses (*watsiku*).

Preparations for annual community liquor-drinking rituals, like those for maize-bundle-group liquor-drinking rituals, begin with a pilgrimage "to join the waters." But pilgrimages taken by cargo-system officials to collect sacred water are to the most distant springs at the farthest edges of the Tereseño territory: the lake of Santa Teresa (*Nákuta*), whose patron is Tahátsi Xúrave in the east; the springs at Tenemasta (*Tyánutsa'are*), whose patron is Tayákwari (Our Grandmother) to the west; the mountain peak called *Kweinyarana'apwa* to the north; the cave called *Twákamuna* to the south; and, most importantly, the mountain peak called Kweimarutse (a.k.a. *Tayaxuri* or "Our Grandfather") at the center point. The use of waters drawn from these sites in the mitote ceremonies of the community authorities makes reference not to the ancestral territories of particular maize-bundle-group ranches, but to the most extensive boundaries of the geographical territory of Santa Teresa as a whole. At the same time, the ceremonial grounds at which the community mitotes are celebrated are not located at the home of any particular maize-bundle-group ceremonial elder, but are instead located near the summit of Kweimarutse itself, the center mountain of the most expansive boundaries of the Tereseño world. In the same way, the distillery and ceremonial plaza at which community cicada mitotes are celebrated (Spanish: *la taberna*) is not located at the household of any particular maize-bundle-group ceremonial elder, but rather on the very slopes of Kweimarutse, just a few hundred feet from Santa Teresa's principal spring. Because of this location on the slopes of Santa Teresa's center mountain, the water that is brought to this ceremonial plaza—and the liquor that is distilled there—is both literally and figuratively higher than the water (and liquor) of peripheral descent-group elders at their lower ranches.

The use of ceremonial crosses (watsiku) also creates a number of elaborations on the symbols and connotations produced within maize-bundle-group cicada mitotes, while also focusing this signification on representations of the seasonal rains. These yarn-woven crosses are commonly known as "God's eyes" by non-Indians in the region (and beyond). In Santa Teresa, however, their most direct connotation is to the cross-shaped world, chánaka, covered with clouds. Three watsiku crosses are made prior to the beginning of the five days of fasting and prayers that precede the final rituals of the community cicada mitote. The wooden crosses that serve as the framework for the watsiku are strung with five alternating bands of black and white hand-spun wool yarn. People say that these colors represent dark clouds. Balls of cotton, another representation of clouds, are placed on the corners of each cross. With this cloud symbolism, and their four-cornered shape, the watsiku are clear representations of the rainy season world. Moreover, their use in this mitote ceremony also suggests that they refer to the three community ceremonial elders—the Tawáusimwa—who supervise the ceremonies of the mountain peaks, the church, and the courthouse.

When I attended this ceremony in 1994, the community cicada mitote began with three watsiku crosses standing next to each other within an altar that was made on the ground adjacent to the distillery. As the liquor was distilled, it was also placed within the altar. Within this altar the crosses stood in a line facing outward, with the center one both taller and larger in diameter than the other two. In the evening prior to the beginning of the liquor-drinking ritual that concluded the community cicada mitote, cargo-system officials took each of these crosses out of the altar and carried them to the three places where they remained "to call the rains" throughout the wet season. The two smaller crosses were placed in the church and courthouse, and the largest watsiku was carried up to the highest point on Kweimarutse. Each of these locations pertains to a particular community ceremonial elder, who prayed through these crosses during the rainy season in the same way that maize-bundle-group ceremonial elders pray through descent-group maize. The three crosses, and the ritual spaces and ceremonial elders to which they pertain, were also referenced during the liquor-drinking ritual.

Whereas children entering a particular maize-bundle group are the focus of descent-group liquor-drinking rituals, cargo-system officials are the focus of the liquor-drinking ritual that is part of the annual community cicada mitote. During the ritual of 1994, for example, each of the male officials sat in turn on an '+pwári stool next to a female tenanchi of the church. With the sun rising behind them, and with crowns of flowers and an '+r+ prayer arrow tied to their heads (which I was told also occurs in descent-group liquor-drinking rituals), these conjugal pairs appeared to be a kind of royalty. Beneath them, resting on woven mats, were gourd bowls of shimmering liquor. As in descent-group liquor-drinking rituals, the communal drunkenness that is an outcome of this ritual is aimed at creating a common feeling among all the participants. In the community cicada mitote, however, this collective intoxication is focused on the conjugal pairs that are at the center of the liquor-drinking ritual. Drunkenness between male and female community authorities, then, serves as a metaphor for the cosmic sex between heaven and earth (the return of the rains) that is the basis of the annual renewal of life. In embodying this metaphor in ritual, cargo-system officials take ceremonial responsibility for the change of seasons throughout the Tereseño world.

This sexual metaphor was also extended in a final collective dance after everyone present had finished their gourd bowls of liquor. To begin this dance, all gathered in front of the ramada and the ceremonial elder painted the face of each participant with century-plant syrup applied from bamboo vials. Men received lines of paint from a needle-sized pick and women received circular designs applied with the mouth of the vial. The century-plant syrup and the painted designs made obvious reference to the sexuality of the cargo officials, elaborating on the metaphor of century-plant liquor and the rains as a kind of heavenly semen that impregnates women and earth. The dance that year was also memorable to me for its bawdiness. Male officials hung on to the intoxicated female tenanchis and made suggestive jokes as we staggered five counterclockwise circles as a group around the dance plaza to end the ceremony.

In summary, as community officials carry out their annual community cicada mitote, they also reproduce the position of their offices in relation to the various maize-bundle groups of Santa Teresa. By elaborating on and reorienting particular symbolic connotations that are most profoundly produced within maize-bundle-group mitotes, the mitotes carried out by community officials also construct a symbolic inclusion of one mitote ceremonial cycle in the next. Furthermore, by continuing to supervise this ancestral ceremony, community officials renew the complexly ramifying symbolic associations that link their offices with the change of seasons. In the context of these ceremonial performances, "nature" does not exist as a category independent of human action (or inaction). Instead, the change of seasons is represented as an entirely cultural outcome of the willingness of community officials to embody, and so renew, ancestral traditions that sustain the whole community of Santa Teresa.

The cicada mitote, however, is only one of the mitote ceremonies sponsored by community officials. In the following section I elaborate on this discussion of the hierarchical and synecdochical relationship between ranch and community-level mitotes.

The Community Parched Maize Mitote

The community parched maize mitote is the first ceremony celebrated after the second and "higher" series of annually appointed community authorities receive their offices following the new year, and it is the most important ceremonial responsibility of their term. The ceremony serves as a crucial display of the dedication and leadership abilities of incoming officials, particularly the two governors who serve in the highest offices of all annually appointed local authorities. Moreover, during the community parched maize mitote the hierarchical inclusiveness of these authorities is signified in two distinct ways.

The inclusiveness of the community parched maize mitote ceremony—like that of the community cicada mitote—is first signified by its geographic position in relation to all of the ranches of Santa Teresa. The ceremonial plaza at which the community parched maize mitote is celebrated is also located on the slopes of the center mountain, Kweimarutse. Indeed, the ceremonial plaza (in Spanish referred to as the *patio mayor*, the "highest court" or "upper plaza") is near the summit of the center mountain, even higher up than the other ceremonial plaza where the community cicada mitote is celebrated. A number of specific ritual symbols used only in the community parched maize mitote also signify the overarching inclusiveness of this ceremony—maize, prayer arrows, and the chánaka pole are the most important.

In the community parched maize mitote, a single bundle of maize is used instead of the many maize bundles representing group members that are found at all descent-group mitotes. This maize is grown in the "commons" (Spanish: *común*), a collective garden that (during my fieldwork) was located across Santa Teresa's main stream from the central plaza of the town. Like the gardens of ancestral maize grown by maize-bundle-group ceremonial elders, this much larger community garden is devoted to cultivating a special variety of white maize. The dried ears of this maize are kept not in any private house but rather in the governor's house, the stone building located on the community's central plaza, used specifically for holding the ceremonial paraphernalia of community authorities.

In addition to the white maize cultivated by the community authorities, four different varieties of colored maize are solicited from descent-group ceremonial elders who live at ranches dispersed over the geographic territory of Santa Teresa. During the community parched maize mitote that I attended in 1994, this maize was ground and poured into gourd bowls filled with sacred water during each of the five mornings leading up to the prototypical rituals of the mitote, just as in maize-bundle-group mitote ceremonies. In this mitote, however, instead of praying to the maize at the tapanco marking the eastern "door" to the mitote ceremonial grounds, the leading ceremonial elder of the community prayed to the different colored varieties of maize at each of the five cardinal directions: yellow maize in the east, red maize in the west, white maize in the north, blue-black maize in the south, and spotted maize in the center.

The maize used in the community parched maize mitote, then, is like the liquor distilled by community officials during the earlier cicada mitote; it has a hierarchical and synecdochical relationship to all the distinct varieties of maize cultivated by particular maize-bundle-group ceremonial elders. As at descent-group mitote ceremonies, this maize also serves as a metaphor for the ancestry shared by ritual participants. However, in the context of the community parched maize mitote, the unique characteristics of this maize represent the more inclusive ancestry that these overarching community mitotes reproduce. The community maize garden is bigger and more centrally located than peripheral descent-group gardens, and the different colored varieties of maize used within the ceremony refer to the most distant lands of the bounded Tereseño world, and thus to all the distinct maize-bundle groups that are sustained through the maize.

Similarly, prayer arrows used during the community parched maize mitote are made from feathers brought from maize-bundle-group ceremonial elders as representatives of the population of Santa Teresa as a whole, rather than from members of particular maize-bundle groups as part of their pilgrimages to "join the waters." The association of these prayer arrows with the five principal mountain peaks of Santa Teresa is particularly strong in this ceremony. In addition to arrows being placed under the ceremonial plaza's tapanco, as in descent-group mitotes, rows of three prayer arrows are also placed at each of the five cardinal points of the plaza. Tripods of arrows are also placed on the trails that lead out from the plaza towards the mountain peaks at the boundaries of the community's geographical territory, almost literally pointing to those peaks. After the ceremony is completed, these prayer arrows are then carried to these distant peaks by the community's leading ceremonial elder and four other senior consejeros.

This association of the community parched maize mitote with the most extensive boundaries of the Tereseño territory as a whole is also strongly evoked by a specially decorated pole that is assembled for this ceremony alone. The twelve-foot high chánaka pole is made of thick bamboo. Four struts radiate from the pole, securing a wheel-shaped hoop towards the top. This hoop is decorated with flowers, and with the same type of feathers used to make prayer arrows. A pair of blue feathers from the urraca (Spanish for the long-tailed jay that lives in nearby moist canyons) extends from the top of the pole. Above and below the principal wheel are a few other smaller wheels—like unformed worlds—each wrapped in white cloth tied tightly to the pole.

Recall that Tereseños consider this pole a map of the world. Indeed, it is probably the only explicitly named representation of the world in Tereseño ceremonialism. For this reason, the pole plays a particularly powerful role in linking hierarchical and synecdochical representations of territoriality with the community officials. As an explicit image of the world, this pole has a concrete meaning that most ritual symbolism in Santa Teresa lacks. Moreover, a number of ritual actions (like pilgrimages to gather sacred water at the five cardinal directions, prayers to maize and water in a gourd bowl, and dancing in a counterclockwise direction around a central fire), as well as more esoteric symbols (like the shapes of century plants, spindle whorls, and watsiku crosses), also find strong meaning as images of the world in their resemblance to the chánaka pole. In this way, the centrality of this ritual symbol within diverse chains of ceremonially produced signification mirrors the position of this "highest," most inclusive mitote ceremony in relation to particular descent-group mitotes. Maize-bundle groups depend on this distinctive pole—as they also depend on the liquor made each year at the community cicada mitote—to give concrete meaning to the symbols present in their own smaller mitote ceremonies.

The chánaka pole is placed at the center of a final dance-procession that completes each night-long community parched maize ceremony. As at maize-bundle-group parched maize mitotes, all of the participants in the evening's dancing join together at sunrise to dance five final circuits around the ceremonial patio. At this mitote, however, participants include the entire group of community officials, as well as representatives from the Day-of-the-Dead/Holy-Week cycle (discussed below). In the two years that I participated in the ceremony, mayordomos and tenanchis carried flowered arches on each side of an image of Guadalupe brought from the church, forming a small procession within the larger group. Courthouse authorities held the chánaka pole and ceremonial items associated with the courthouse offices (a lance, a flag, and ribboned staffs representing each of the courthouse offices). Others carried prayer arrows or smoked ceremonial pipes. Finally, a young girl called the *malinche*—a key participant in the Day-of-the-Dead/Holy-Week cycle—carried her own distinct flagpole while surrounded by the rest of her ceremonial group. The community ceremonial elder Don Goyo led this whole dance-procession, holding a large prayer arrow called the "turkey" (*s+pí*, Spanish: *gualojote*) before eventually "flying" off to the top of Kweimarutse to pray for the well-being of the entire community. Every year this pattern was repeated for five full nights, after which time the senior consejeros of the community gathered up the prayer arrows that marked the four corners of the "upper plaza" and began their treks to the mountains at the border of the Tereseño world.

Such hierarchical and synecdochical connotations in maize-bundle-group and community-level mitotes clearly position cargo-system officials above maize-bundle-group elders and other members of the community. Specific symbols at community mitote ceremonies resonate with those drawn from maize-bundle-group mitotes. At the level of ranch-based mitotes, such symbols are associated with fundamental concepts of selfhood and local identity. But the more elaborate community mitote ceremonies juxtapose those symbols with other unique and mysterious symbols (like the chánaka pole) and ritual practices (like the making and drinking of century-plant liquor) that draw the memberships of all of the maize-bundle groups into a common affinity beneath the community officials. These community officials are thus represented as "higher" than particular maize-bundle-group elders, and therefore responsible for continuing the maize-oriented yi'irá custom through which the general health and well-being of the community as a whole is secured and through which their own overarching legitimacy as traditional authorities is reproduced.

THE DAY-OF-THE-DEAD/HOLY-WEEK CYCLE

In addition to overseeing their maize-based dance yi'irá custom, community officials also supervise a series of festivals (*ye'estya*) comprising an annual cycle that I call the Day-of-the-Dead/Holy-Week cycle. This cycle is composed of ten major festivals that refer at several crucial points to a story that has been told in one version or another in the Sierra del Nayar for more than two hundred years (Neurath 1998: 91). This story describes the lives of two ancestral deities, the brothers San Miguel Xúrave and San Miguel Sáutari. During the time of my fieldwork, the symbolic connections between the festival cycle and this story helped interested participants and observers to isolate significant details and in this way discover implicit messages relevant to their own lives. Like me, the Náyari people with whom I celebrated Santa Teresa's Holy Week Festival over the years became part of the story of Xúrave and Sáutari through their participation in the festival, and linked their personal fates with these mythological characters. In doing so we learned a powerful lesson from the ancestral past about the proper place of traditional authorities in relation to the larger community and to the cosmos beyond. In the words of the late Don Goyo, this story and the festival with which it is associated have a single comprehensive moral and political purpose: They show us how to die.

Don Goyo's Text

I begin this discussion of the Day-of-the Dead/Holy-Week cycle with the text of the folk tale that is repeatedly referenced throughout this festival cycle. I have heard versions of this story several times both in Spanish and in the Náyari language. The text printed here was produced from a tape recording made during an interview with Gregorio Campos (Don Goyo), the late ceremonial elder of Santa Teresa. The interview, transcription, and translation would not have been possible without the help of a local Náyari friend and collaborator, who translated my questions to Don Goyo, and who agonized with me over the barely audible tape that resulted. Unfortunately, neither of us are linguists, and so our Náyari language transcription is most certainly flawed, but it is nonetheless included in an appendix for interested readers. The interview itself was carried out while we sat on the patio of Don Goyo's simple home on the afternoon of September 20, 1994. I remember it as a beautiful, clear day with clouds in the blue sky and carpets of purple wildflowers surrounding the patches of green maize plants whose ears were then ripening in the sun. He told this story without break in response to a question about the significance of blood as a ceremonial offering. I summarize its somewhat complicated plotline following this text.

1. Those Our Deceased Ancestors receive that which they all bring to them, blood of the deer.
2. Those Our Deceased Ancestors will receive it, that meat—a little of everything that is eaten.
3. And cotton that they will also hand over, so that they come back as we are hoping.
4. So that in this way the one who is Our Mother comes, that too I am saying.
5. So that no one ever bothers us. With that which we are accustomed to do.
6. We are not playing around in doing these things. We are accustomed to do it this way.
7. Always we are asking with Our Mother. Or Our Deceased Ancestors.
8. They exist to rear everything. In just that way [they raise] each of the things that are grown, and also forage with which the animals feed themselves, and maize—Our Mother—with which we live, and the sacred water that was left here.

9. So that with Our Deceased Ancestors, with them Our Mother [maize] who appeared is raised.

10. God left her here. In that way in which they made things in very ancient times.

11. From very far back come these things, he himself left them.

12. That same one, Santiago. With him we ask, with Our Horseman. I myself hand things over to him.

13. So that I will be helped. I don't know . . . So things appeared. In this way things were turned over [to us] all around.

14. So the sacred water of Our Mother appeared just as things were left behind by Our Elder Brother.

15. In that way everything was left behind. Sin, that one [the younger brother of Our Elder Brother] knows everything about that.

16. In that way they went to where their mother appeared, they went around the edges one then the other [Our Elder Brother and his younger brother].

17. Everything one of them went around making, each of the things— trees, animals, fruit trees. He [Our Elder Brother's younger brother] did not complete his obligation.

18. Only later after passing through here did he arrive back. In the place where their mother appeared.

19. So she asked him. That is, whether he did as he should have.

20. Whether he completed it well, "as I told you all to do."

21. That one was first, the one who committed no dirtiness [Our Elder Brother], and later the other one arrived [Our Elder Brother's younger brother].

22. Afterward she asked if he had done well. Finally that one arrived.

23. Finally they were both inside of the house, and he said this: "It's not so important."

24. "And let's just see. I committed more dirtiness. I'm nothing. I didn't complete my obligation. I didn't do well, fine. And so let's just see which of us turns out better."

25. They started to make things: cattle, dogs (the dog was first), and also the cat.

26. Both of them were told by their mother to make pinole of amaranth.

27. He [the one who arrived later, Our Elder Brother's younger brother] told him [he who arrived first, Our Elder Brother], "I'm going to make them right now." And so he just grabbed a piece.

28. He asked her, "Mother, help me." Then they [he and his mother] made the cat.

29. He told her, "Mother, call to them." The dog they also made. And he told her to call them.

30. And it ran to its female relative. And the other one [Our Elder Brother], fine. He didn't make anything.

31. They also made livestock. They made them and placed them around. They finished them to last forever.

32. His female relative helped him. They also made the bull, so that they would hand over [calves for the benefit of people].

33. Those and the horse. In that way they made these things, and in that way that other one [Our Elder Brother who arrived first] also made things.

34. They weren't much just standing there. They were just all alone without little ones.

35. And the other one [Our Elder Brother's younger brother who arrived last], it didn't take long for him.

36. One little one. Two little ones. Five little ones, they were already there.

37. Cattle, pigs, goats, sheep, horses, they were already walking all over the place.

38. The other one [who arrived first] spoke in this way to his mother when those [of his younger brother each] had five little ones.

39. "There mine are alone without little ones. But they are still nice."

40. So he said these words to his female relative, "Make them like that [like the others]."

41. [She said] "You will collect water. You will also make a short stick of this height [a prayer arrow]. You will also put feathers on it. For five days you will make offerings of water."

42. Fine, and so he made a prayer arrow. And then it did give little ones to he that had not had them.

43. They say: "It is never good to ask anything of him, he that committed no dirtiness. That one is tough."

44. And that other one—San Miguel Sáutari is what he is named—that young boy ended up doing well with his work.

45. This comes from way back. That it is really tough with that other one [Our Elder Brother]. That nothing came out at all with him, not a thing.

46. So it seems to me, it may be that way. When I ask something of him, or if I should ask something of San Miguel Sáutari.

47. He knows if I do well. So that they [San Miguel Sáutari's animals, owned by people] will all be producing.

48. That one there stayed where he remained. That [other] one [San Miguel Sáutari] passed through here.

49. In that way he left behind all of his sins, and he put his hat over there in a pine tree, and he tossed some worms [that resulted from a gangrenous wound to his genitals] into a madrone tree, and his hat we commonly eat as the mushrooms that grow under pine trees.

50. And over there a piece of him [his penis] pulled off, where the rock and the *mwáxa* tree [a tree that grows out of solid rock] that he made is located.

51. And he left behind everything, that sweet potato. And the *yeri* sweet potato. That one left everything. Or so they say.

52. And that one Our Elder [Jesus Christ] who appeared on the day of his birth.

53. That is how they knew to celebrate, by the day of his birth. And the other one by the day of his death.

54. Those were the ones that killed him, those devils. From that time come these things.

55. In that way he made himself appear dead.

56. To show that perhaps we will be dying like that.

57. And then that one went with his Elder, that we might also do the same.

58. So that if one is lacking in some way he will die.

59. I will be killed by them, for whatever sin I might have with him [San Miguel Xúrave], because he is dangerous.

60. But he also might help those of us who may have an animal.

61. And maize, a little bit of everything was left by Our Elder.

62. It is just that in that way he helps, so that he might give me a few of the the things that he left here.

The story translated here tells of the travels of San Miguel Xúrave and his younger brother San Miguel Sáutari around the northern and southern edges of the world, respectively. Xúrave makes the trip quickly and without "sinning," but Sáutari dallies along the way. He has sex with plants, animals, and rocks, bringing the world to life (but losing his penis in the process). Later, after returning to the east where his mother and older brother are waiting for him, the two brothers have a competition to see who can make the most fertile animals. They form animal figures out of amaranth, but the only way that Xúrave can compel his animals to move is by making prayer arrows, offering water, and fasting for five days. On the other hand, with the help of his mother, Sáutari's animals jump all over the place and have plenty of offspring. The simple moral of the story is that sexual "sin" is necessary for life on earth, but that fasting and the making of offerings to the appropriate ancestral deity is another—more dangerous—way to harness fertility and wealth.

This folk tale of San Miguel Xúrave and San Miguel Sáutari is satisfying and complete in itself, but Don Goyo's story also points out that the events it recounts continue to be celebrated in the ceremonies that make up the Day-of-the-Dead/Holy-Week cycle. He says, "From that time come these things" (line 54). Indeed, particular symbols and rituals of the Day-of-the-Dead/Holy-Week cycle are clearly juxtaposed with characters and scenarios from this story to form connotations that elaborate on its simple moral. In Don Goyo's words, these symbols and rituals, in association with this folk tale, "show that perhaps we will be dying like that" (line 56). Specifically, the depicted death of an elaborated Sáutari character in the Day-of-the-Dead/Holy-Week cycle is linked not only with the deaths of all living Tereseño people ("we"), but also with the transformation of (some) living people into the rains. These animate rains are then associated with the traditional authority of the cargo-system elders, who take over for these ancestral rains during the dry season and then supervise the ceremonies that bring them back by means of a symbolic human sacrifice the following year.

From Narrative to Festival Performance

The Catholic-derived Day-of-the-Dead/Holy-Week cycle in Santa Teresa ends and begins again with a sacrifice at the culminating moment of Holy Week that is referred to by Cora people in the town of Santa Teresa in Spanish as *la gloria* (the Glory). However, perhaps the best place to begin a description of the cycle (in terms of the brothers San Miguel Xúrave and San Miguel Sáutari) is in November, after the rainy season has come to an end and the series of festivals that most clearly point to Holy Week begins. This series includes the Day-of-the-Dead, Christmas, New Year's, Pachitas, and Holy Week festivals.

THE FESTIVAL OF THE DECEASED The Day of the Dead—locally referred to in Spanish as *la fiesta de los difuntos* (the Festival of the Deceased)—links the whole Day-of-the-Dead/Holy-Week cycle, and thus the story of San Miguel Xúrave and San Miguel Sáutari, to the ongoing agency of "the deceased" in the contemporary world of Santa Teresa. These links are formed by a series of connotations produced through the use of particular symbols that include "owls" and a life-sized figure of a deceased man, made of flowers, that is referred to as *Tayaxuk+* (Our Deceased Grandfather).

The festival begins on the morning of the eve of All Souls Day, when mayordomos and tenanchis mound marigold flowers into the shape of a corpse (tayaxuk+) inside the church. A table for this figure is prepared with white sheets, and once the tayaxuk+ is finished it is covered with a special black and purple burial shroud that will later be used to cover a crucifix during Holy Week. Next to this table are more items associated with Holy Week: two candle-staffs and the small crucifix that will be carried by red-robed boys, and a pair of woven mats on which the apostles (*apostulus*) of Holy Week eventually kneel before offering smoke to the figure of the crucified Christ. In the Festival of the Deceased, these mats eventually hold a pile of steamed squash and other foods of the season that are brought to the church by all of the households in Santa Teresa. Once all of these items are put in place, and the flowery figure of Our Deceased Grandfather is completed, the church is closed until nightfall.

· The main ceremony of the Festival of the Deceased occurs well after nightfall. It centers on a pair of young boys wearing red robes who are identified as "owls" (*mwak+ritsi*). Indeed, this festival as a whole is sometimes referred to by Tereseños simply as "the owls." These boys are dressed in their robes in the sacristy where the figure of an infant Jesus

Christ is kept during most of the year. In this room a crucifix that will eventually serve as a counterpoint to this figure of the infant Jesus Christ during Holy Week is tied to one of the three boys' waists with a black horse-hair rope.

Like the crucifix, burial shroud, woven mats, and owls, this rope has a connection with Holy Week. It is used by one of the apostles in that later festival to tie a large and heavy crucifixion cross to his waist in the same way that the young owl wears the much smaller image of the crucified Christ tied to his waist during this festival. One of the other two boys who flank this owl carries a pitcher of sacred water with white tsuwá flowers, and the other carries a small bell. A ceremonial specialist who knows the Catholic prayers that pertain to this festival supervises these boys.

After night has completely fallen, all of these owls leave the church and follow a counterclockwise path to the dry-season homes of Tereseños that are scattered on the prairie surrounding Santa Teresa's church. As they walk through the night, the red-robed boys and all of the other children that accompany them begin to hoot like owls. As they arrive at each of the houses in turn, the man who leads these boys recites the same type of mysterious Latin prayer that will later be repeated during Holy Week. He then "bathes" the house with sacred water carried by one of the owls, flinging it with grand crossing motions from the tsuwá flowers. After these blessings have been completed, the assembled crowd—which is composed mostly of children—immediately clamors for offerings by hooting out, "*Heloti* [green maize ears] k+, k+, k+; *xutsí* [squash] k+, k+, k+; *yaná* [tobacco] k+, k+, k+ . . ." They mimic the sound of owls while playing on the suffix that means "deceased" (Casad 1984: 208). These owls continue their counterclockwise circuit through the night, eventually returning just before sunrise to the plaza. There they stop first at the courthouse and then return to their patron, Tayaxuk+. At the church, the offerings that have not been eaten by the children are added to the pile of food that lies in front of the shroud-covered flower-corpse, and the owls return their vestments to the sacristy, where they are stored in anticipation of Holy Week.

At sunrise the authorities assemble around the table on the veranda of the courthouse and then cross the plaza to the church, where they begin to disassemble the figure of Our Deceased Grandfather by taking away the flowers that formed it. The mayordomos and tenanchis follow, and then the rest of the people who are gathered in the church continue to remove the flowers. These flowers are taken back to each household, where they are hung to dry and, eventually, disintegrate. In this way, the Festival of the Deceased not only focuses attention on the deceased ancestors of Náyari people (as Our Deceased Grandfather), but also identifies the exact point in the year when this unitary representation of the deceased leaves Santa Teresa. Indeed, Tereseños report not only that the owls represent the souls of the dead, but also that in going from house to house these owls stock up on provisions for the return trip to their dry-season home. Moreover, the deceased ancestors who are represented by Tayaxuk+ and the owls are also strongly associated with the seasonal rains, which come to an end during October.

As the Festival of the Deceased comes to a close the leaders of the Holy Week Festival—the two horsemen referred to in Spanish as *centuriones* ([Roman] centurions)—begin their religious fasts from liquor, salt, and sex. These fasts, along with the other symbols linking the Festival of the Deceased with Holy Week, make it clear that each particular festival cannot be understood outside of the context of the festival cycle of which it is a part. Indeed, Tereseños state that Tayaxuk+ is simply a different representation of the same deity that is the focus of Holy Week. This latter deity is commonly referred to as *Hesu Kristu Tavástara* (Jesus Christ, Our Elder). In a recorded interview from 1994, ceremonial elder Amadeo Flores was quite explicit in regard to this view. "That [flowered figure] is Tayaxuk+. That is the Jesus Christ that they will make. The [same] Jesus Christ that is lying over there that they never take out of the box [the figure of the infant Jesus in the sacristy]. This same one they are going to make there so that everyone sees it. That is the one they are going to worship. . . ." When I asked Flores if this was the same figure that they would kill during Holy Week, he responded, "There you go! That is the same one. It is just that they make him at this time of year."

But if the correspondence between the ritual symbols of the Festival of the Deceased and those of Holy Week is clear, the specific relationship of "Jesus Christ" not only to "the deceased" but also to the characters San Miguel Xúrave and San Miguel Sáutari is much more difficult to pinpoint. Help in this interpretive effort arrives during the subsequent festivals, when the multifaceted identity of Jesus Christ (Hesu Kristu Tavástara) begins to be revealed.

THE CHRISTMAS FESTIVAL Preparations for the Christmas Festival (Spanish: *la fiesta de la Navidad*) begin on the morning of Christmas Eve. In the church, the mayordomos and tenanchis lower the box containing Joseph and Mary (as Dolores) from its normal position in the pantheon on the wall behind the altar and place them in a manger scene on the floor of the church in front of the altar and opposite the sacristy. The festival begins a few hours before midnight, when the dancers gather in the courthouse to receive tamales that are brought by the cargo-system officers, who will transfer their posts in the upcoming New Year's Festival. The town's ceremonial dancers—a kind of matachines dance company (Rodríguez 1996) referred to locally in Spanish as the *Urracas* (Blue Jays)—begin to perform inside the courthouse. At midnight, two tenanchis light incense holders and place them in front of the Urraca violinist. Church-based officeholders then each take a single candle from their shoulder bag and light it. Holding these lighted candles, the mayordomos and tenanchis all surround the Urraca dancers who again begin to perform their shining, twirling dance. Holding their candles in front of them, the mayordomos and tenanchis circle the dancers five times in a counterclockwise direction before moving as a group across the dark plaza to the church. This group heads straight for the sacristy where the boys who appeared as the "owls" of the Festival of the Deceased again put on their red robes. The lead Urraca dancer then carefully takes a small figure of Jesus Christ (Hesu Kristu Tavástara) out of a box in the sacristy where it is hidden. People say that this figure is born during the festival to grow up very rapidly and then be killed by the "devils" (*tyárutse*) or "Jews" (Spanish: *judíos*) who appear during Holy Week.

The group exits the sacristy with this figure, and the red-robed boys move to the back of the manger scene at the altar of the church and crouch down. The ribbons and mirrors of the twirling Urraca dancers flash in the candlelight through copal smoke as the leader of the dancers places the figure of the infant on a cloud-like bed of cotton between Joseph and Dolores. The boys behind the manger immediately begin to blow on whistles. Someone once whispered to me at this moment that these whistles were "the sound of Jesus crying," but it sounded to me like the hooting call of the owls that these boys earlier portrayed. In any case, everyone present in the church at this late hour then takes the opportunity to "visit" the newly born Hesu Kristu Tavastara by making ritualized offerings.

Once all have approached the figure of Jesus, the Urraca dancers again perform. This time, however, they add a theme to their dancing that is undertaken only during this festival. The eight dancers break into groups of two, and each of these pairs of dancers begins to circle opposite each other in a counterclockwise direction. Two of these pairs then extend their fans out horizontally at the level of their belly buttons so that they are joined. These pairs then cover the joined fans with black shawls (Spanish: *rebozos*) like the ones worn by all Náyari women in Santa Teresa. Once these two pairs of dancers are joined in this way, the other two pairs then join them in the same manner to make two groups of four dancers, all joined by rebozo-covered fans. As the festival comes to a close these dancers circle around the central axis formed by their joined fans, and so symbolically point to the image of the world formed through mitote ceremonialism. Their world model carries a number of important connotations that link it both to the preceding birth of Hesu Kristu Tavástara and to the story of San Miguel Xúrave and San Miguel Sáutari; it combines a whole series of meanings into a single powerful representation.

These dancers are strongly associated with the femaleness of the church. This connotation is emphasized in the Christmas Festival because these dancers serve as the maternal vehicle through which the infant is "born." The connotation is re-emphasized by the use of prototypically female rebozos on their fans, and by the fact that these shawls seem to extend out from the dancers' belly buttons as if they were umbilical cords. At the same time, in the context of this festival, these dancers are also associated with the deceased (paternal) ancestors. In the courthouse, for example, they are surrounded by candles such as would surround a corpse during a night-long vigil (Spanish: *velorio*) prior to its burial. Also, the "crying" or "hooting" whistles of the red-robed boys point to their role as owls in the earlier Festival of the Deceased.

This conflation of seemingly disparate female and male connotations within the singular image of the rotating dancers joined in a cross-shaped figure also helps to account for the identity of Hesu Kristu Tavástara in terms of the story of Xúrave and Sáutari. Specifically, the role of the red-robed boys as deceased-ancestor "owls" during the Festival of the Deceased plays on a double meaning of them as representative of a still-half-formed male child, the embodiment on earth of the departing heavenly deceased ancestors. When the deceased ancestors "fly off" during the Festival of the Deceased, they also leave a male child in their place to be born during the Christmas Festival.

The name of this child—Hesu Kristu Tavástara (Jesus Christ, Our El-der)—also indicates this paternity, as it continues an interesting series of dual images that Jesus Christ embodies in Santa Terasa. In this case, the second part of his name—Tavástara—refers to an old man, literally an "elder" like Tayaxuk+. But at the same time the first part of his name, Hesu Kristu, points to the young boy who is born on the earth during the Christmas Festival only to die during Holy Week. Crucially, this dual im-age of Hesu Kristu Tavástara as both old man and young boy, as a boy-deity walking the earth among people, also serves as a key link between the whole Day-of-the-Dead/Holy-Week ceremonial cycle and the story of San Miguel Xúrave and San Miguel Sáutari.

In the story told by Don Goyo, for example, Sáutari is depicted exactly as the kind of earth-bound deity that Hesu Kristu Tavástara also repre-sents. As Don Goyo said, Sáutari passed through having sex with all of the animals, plants, and even rocks that are today found in the world. He went along making everything and left behind everything. In contrast, San Miguel Xúrave returned directly to his mother, never mixing with humans and thus avoiding all sin. But even Don Goyo was not very clear on the identity of San Miguel Sáutari viz-à-viz "Tavástara." For example, he mentioned "San Miguel Sáutari . . . that young boy" (line 44), seeming to point to the representation of Hesu Kristu as a young boy, but then in the next breath he also mentioned Tavástara, saying that he, too, left everything here on earth. Thus, he seemed to differentiate Hesu Kristu Tavástara from Sáutari. When interpreted in relation to the festival cycle to which this story pertains, however, this seeming opposition between Hesu Kristu Tavástara and Sáutari evaporates.

Like the ceremonially produced dual image of Hesu Kristu Tavástara as both an old man (the flowery figure of Tayaxuk+) and a young boy (the figure of Hesu Kristu in the manger), the infant born during the Christmas Festival in Don Goyo's story is also portrayed as a conflated dual image: both Sáutari (Hesu Kristu) and Tavástara. However, the two sides do not remain stable throughout the ceremonial year. Instead, the Christmas Festival is the point at which the Christ figure begins to shift from being an old man—a descendent of the deceased ancestors—to being the young boy named Sáutari. It marks the moment at which this shift begins to take place because it is the moment that Hesu Kristu Tavástara is born on the earth, and so begins to participate in the sins of living humans.

But if in Don Goyo's text Hesu Kristu Tavástara as Sáutari is human-like because of his brief, transitory presence on earth and the proclivity for sexual sin that naturally accompanies his earthly sojourn, he also cleans himself to return to his pure mother. He does this by abandoning all of his earthly sins at specific places across the landscape, and in this way shows that "perhaps we will be dying like that" (line 56). In providing such an example, this story, and the ceremonial cycle with which it is linked, serves as a point of reflection, an encompassing morality play that is intertwined with the daily lives of people who are born and die within the repetitions of this festival cycle. For the authorities who enter their offices as part of the cycle, this morality play tells a story about the superficiality of human political authority when compared to the overarching authority of the deceased ancestors. However, it also suggests the possibility of redemption as some living people—like San Miguel Sáutari before them—manage to leave their earthly sins behind and continue on as deceased ancestors in the flowery world of the rains. This contradictory moral and political lesson sharpens beginning during the festival that follows, just as Hesu Kristu Tavástara also slowly develops the traits that even more clearly link him with San Miguel Sáutari.

THE NEW YEAR'S FESTIVAL   The Christmas Festival in Santa Teresa is quickly followed by the three distinct ceremonies that comprise the New Year's Festival (Spanish: *la fiesta del año nuevo*). The three ceremonies that make up the New Year's Festival are divided from one another by five-day intervals. They are referred to as the "handing-over-of-the-staffs" (Spanish: *la entrega de las varas*), the "Little Bulls" (Spanish: *los toritos*), and the "handing-over-of-the-stools" (Spanish: *la entrega de los bancos*) ceremonies. Of these, the handing-over-of-the-staffs ceremony focuses on the transfer of cargo-system offices (discussed in the first section of this chapter), while the Little Bulls and handing-over-of-the-stools ceremonies provide a series of symbolic links with the story of Xúrave and Sáutari. Thus, I will focus only on the latter two ceremonies here.

The Little Bulls Ceremony   The Little Bulls ceremony takes place soon after the conclusion of the New Year's Day handing-over-of-the-staffs ceremony, when the ribboned wooden staffs that represent the different offices of the cargo system are passed from outgoing to incoming office-holders. During the two years that I witnessed the Little Bulls ceremony in Santa Teresa, it was held on Epiphany (January 6), locally called the Festival of the Kings (Spanish: *la fiesta de los reyes*). In some other Cora towns (e.g., Mesa del Nayar and the municipal capital of Jesús María), the ceremonies of this day include both a Little Bulls ceremony and a handing-over-of-the-stools ceremony, but in Santa Teresa during the period of my fieldwork the latter ceremony had been put off until after the Little Bulls ceremony. Similarly, the handing-over-of-the-staffs ceremony was once also probably included as part of the Festival of the Kings, but because Mexican law requires local authorities to enter their offices on the first day of the year, this ceremony has been moved forward. In any case, the disruptive "devils" (tyáru, sing.; tyárutse, pl.) who are linked to Holy Week begin to emerge during the New Year's Festival. These characters are clearly associated both with the entrance of the main political authorities of Santa Teresa and with the political and moral lessons implicit in the story of San Miguel Xúrave and Sáutari.

The Little Bulls ceremony begins exactly at noon, when the young boys who play the toritos start to run. These young boys are also sometimes referred to as "Jews" (Spanish: *judíos*) or really "Judases," based on their similar appearance to the "Jews" who later appear during Santa Teresa's Holy Week Festival. Don Goyo and others refer to these characters as "devils" (tyárutse), those who kill Hesu Kristu Tavástara (in his aspect as Sáutari) during Holy Week. Both the toritos and the judíos appear without shirts and with their pants rolled up. Their faces and bodies are painted black, or white with black stripes and spots. Both the toritos and the judíos also run from place to place in two single-file lines during their respective festivals. However, the toritos are younger—between about six and twelve years of age—than the judíos, and they carry carved wooden "horns" (Spanish: *cuernos*) rather than the wooden "sabers" (Spanish: *sables*) that will be carried by the judíos. Also, the toritos make a cattle-like mooing sound whose high pitch evokes the hooting call of the "owls" that some of these boys earlier portrayed.

The toritos prepare for their run beneath a large pine tree that grows out of the banks of a creek that passes a few hundred meters to the west of the plaza of Santa Teresa (the same creek in which the tyárutse will bathe following Holy Week). They paint themselves there under the supervision of an adult "captain" and a single old man on horseback called the *wacharu* (from the Spanish *vaquero*, "cowboy"). The toritos run from the pine tree in two single-file lines to the top of a small peak that lies directly to the north of the plaza of Santa Teresa. This peak is topped with a wooden cross, and the toritos gather leaves from oak trees that grow all over the peak and toss them around the base of this cross. They then circle the cross in a counterclockwise direction five times and charge down the hill towards the plaza. However, a gate in a fence on the west side of the plaza temporarily blocks their entrance. This fence is also used by the

FIGURE 11 Toritos

courthouse authorities to keep the tyárutse, who run in a similar pair of single-file lines, out of the plaza during Holy Week. The toritos' response to this gate is the same as the response of the tyárutse later on: they run back and forth in lines between their captain and the wacharu, both of whom are stranded with them outside of the gate. Eventually, however, the gate is opened and the toritos stream into the plaza carrying more of their oak leaves from the nearby peak.

The group of toritos—about thirty young boys during the two years that I witnessed this ceremony—respond to this opening by stampeding directly to a stone cross in front of the church, dropping their oak leaves at its base, and running around the cross five times in a counterclockwise direction. The group then separates back into two single-file lines, one line running around the north side of the plaza and the other running around the south side; their paths seem to evoke the separate directions taken by Xúrave and Sáutari in their travels around the world. This reference is confirmed by the way that the lines of boys return to their "mother," the church. Rather than completing an entire circuit of the plaza in order to return to the church—as would be common during a church procession—both lines travel straight back from the west through the center of the plaza towards the church door. Similarly, people commonly say that Xúrave and Sáutari both proceeded halfway around their respective edges of the world and then cut straight back from the west towards their mother in the east.

Arriving back at the church, five of these boys are led inside (just as five tyárutse will later be brought inside at the end of the Holy Week Festival). Then, at the altar of the church, their "captain" recites a Catholic prayer to the pantheon of saints, which, as during Holy Week, is covered with a white cloth. Outside, the mooing "little bulls" wander around locking "horns" with one another. Others fight a bit more aggressively, fencing and slashing with their horns in the same way that the tyárutse use their wooden "sabers" during Holy Week. A number of people have commented to me that both the toritos and the tyárutse (who also frequently fashion horns in their hats) are like real bulls: when crowded together, they tend to fight.

The references to Holy Week continue. As in that later festival, the toritos proceed from the church in a counterclockwise direction around the plaza. They disrupt observers as they pass by and clack their horns against the walls of all the buildings that surround the plaza. At the courthouse, they wander around rubbing up against the authorities' table and bumping into officials as if foraging. The toritos are very young boys and so people find this disruption humorous, even saying that the toritos bless the courthouse by entering it. But at the same time, the sense that these boys are taking over the spaces of the cargo-system officials is also strong, particularly because they are clearly precursors to the much more aggressive, and even dangerous, devils.

As the toritos trample their way through the courthouse, the elderly wacharu sits on his horse across the plaza and begins to drink liquor with ritual solemnity. This elderly man also symbolically points to the centurions of Holy Week, not only because of his horse and his association with the devil-like toritos, but also because of the circular hat that he wears. This hat is of the same type that is later worn by characters in the Pachitas Festival, and then again by the senior centurion during Holy Week. In the Little Bulls ceremony, the hat is decorated with two ribbons that cross in the center. It thus serves to continue the world image found so prominently in mitote ceremonialism. Furthermore, it sets the stage for a series of elaborations on this symbolic theme as characters in later festivals add elements to this circular hat.

The wacharu's drinking of liquor is another reference to Holy Week. In that festival, the liquor-drinking of the devils and the centurions is set in contrast to the liquor that pertains to the cargo officials. The toritos first drink this liquor linking them to Holy Week after their brief disruption of the courthouse. Before drinking, however, they begin to mill about in the plaza, locking their wooden horns and charging after each other. Eventually, the wacharu orders some of the men who are standing around the plaza to round up the toritos, and they head out alone or in pairs to cut particular young boys out of the "herd" that is gathered in the center of the plaza. Most of these "herdsmen" are married adults with families who have long since completed their roles as toritos and then devils. For these reasons they are all potential cargo officers, and their service here seems to lend support to the new courthouse authorities; they work together to re-establish order after the small and rather silly disruption caused by the young boys masquerading as little bulls.

These men drag the young boys by their horns to a point near the church where they apply a "brand" to the side of each boy's white-painted torso and then give the boys liquor. This brand is applied with more of the black paint with which some of these toritos have already decorated themselves. The paint is applied in the shape of a black cross, and once they are branded the boys immediately stop acting like bulls and sit calmly to one side of the plaza. People say that the painted brand is like salt: it domesticates the wild animals, making them docile and manageable. In the end, all of the toritos are branded in this way before receiving a collective meal of beef broth. The ceremony ends after this meal, when the horseman and the captain lead the boys in a group back to the creek where they wash off their paint.

Each young boy in Santa Teresa should participate in the Little Bulls ceremony for five years. They then begin the first of fourteen years as devils in the Holy Week Festival. After this long period of participation in these Holy-Week-oriented festivals, most men abandon these ceremonies to focus on completing the responsibilities associated with church or courthouse cargo offices. Quite a few others, however, particularly those with a reputation for reckless fighting and drinking, may continue as captains and eventually even centurions during Holy Week. These men may avoid—or be isolated from—church or courthouse offices for their entire lives. Instead, they participate in the community-oriented costumbre only through their continued affiliation with the Holy Week ceremonial tradition. In the Little Bulls ceremony, this sense of an antagonistic authority structure (with its own liquor) is initiated. The subsequent Pachitas Festival builds upon this idea, which then comes to a head during Holy Week, when belligerent and drunken devils threaten the basis of cargo-system authority in the town.

Moreover, this opposition between the sagacious restraint that is supposed to typify cargo-system officials and the disruptive youthfulness of the toritos/devils also refers to the evolving relationship between the two sides of the Hesu Kristu Tavástara character. Since Hesu Kristu Tavástara is born during the Christmas Festival, it seems as if he should embody the austere characteristic of the deceased elders for whom he is named. His birth takes place with great solemnity and seriousness following the Festival of the Deceased, and this birth is closely related to the subsequent festival when the adult and elderly men who serve as the senior cargo officers in Santa Teresa enter their posts. At that point in the

Day-of-the-Dead/Holy-Week ceremonial cycle, Hesu Kristu Tavástara seems to serve as a token from the deceased ancestors to living authorities; he is left by the deceased-ancestor rains in order to lend their divine legitimacy to the living authorities who are encharged with controlling the town of Santa Teresa during the dry season. But beginning with the Little Bulls ceremony and continuing through Holy Week, the other side of this two-sided Hesu Kristu Tavástara character becomes increasingly prominent. The emergence of Sáutari from behind the shadow of his double provides both political and moral lessons for participants in these festivals.

Politically, the youthfulness of the disruptive toritos and devils is related to the passionate energies of young men who involve themselves and others in foolish conflicts and short-sighted schemes. Such young men are unwilling to defer their own desires, and instead let themselves be swayed from careful completion of ceremonial obligations by their drunkenness and their sexual attraction to women. But as boys and young men mature, the stories and festivals that they have received from their ancestors tell them that they should abandon this part of themselves. They should leave behind the disruptive sexuality that is associated with their roles as toritos and then as devils in order to discipline themselves for the ceremonial responsibilities that they face as cargo officials. Should they choose to ignore these lessons, they remain forever isolated from the courthouse and thus from traditional authority.

Morally, this restraint places men on the second step of a stairway that leads upward to the heavens. As cargo officers, older men should begin to abandon their sins here on earth like Sáutari abandoned his sins around the landscape. By cleaning themselves in this manner, they also prepare themselves for their own deaths, when they will ascend another step to join their even-more-purified ancestors. In this way, participation in the most "sinful" and disorderly festivals associated with Holy Week shows Tereseños that perhaps they themselves "will be dying like that." It forms a step-wise path through which the lustful part of a man should eventually die off in the same way that the lustful part of Hesu Kristu Tavástara is eventually killed during Holy Week, so that his more austere double may be reborn in heaven. This lesson becomes more and more clear as the ceremonial cycle moves on to the Pachitas Festival, when the correspondence between the life-courses of the men of Santa Teresa and the earthly experiences of San Miguel Sáutari become plain. Before this festival begins, however, the decorated '+pwari stools of the senior cargo-system officials are "handed over" in the last of the three New Year's festivals.

The New Year's Handing-Over-of-the-Stools Ceremony Like the ribboned staffs earlier transferred from outgoing to incoming officeholders on New Year's Day, a stool that represents each office is also "handed over." The stools ('+pwari) of the handing-over-of-the-stools ceremony are identical to the special stools used by bow-drum singers in mitote ceremonies, except that the back and arms are exaggerated to form a wooden framework that completely surrounds the seated person. Prior to the ceremonial "handing over" of these stools, this framework is decorated with hundreds of bananas. The banana-covered stools are then finished with a cover of cardboard, upon which pieces of bread shaped like crocodiles are fastened. The end result is a peculiar banana-throne that completely encompasses the incoming cargo officer seated on it.

Each outgoing officeholder also prepares, in addition to the stool itself, a bundle of fresh sugar cane and a crown of sweetened pinole tamales. The bundle of sugar cane, which serves as a scepter, is hung with baked donut-shaped pieces of bread and honey-sweetened pinole tamales that seem to sprinkle out of the sugar cane's green foliage. Prior to the beginning of the ceremony, this sugar-cane scepter is placed against an arm of the stool and the sweet pinole crown is placed on the seat. These decorated banana-thrones are then lined up next to each other in front of the courthouse facing the church to the east.

The actual handing-over-of-the-stools ceremony begins inside the church. All of the outgoing and incoming officeholders kneel at the altar facing the saints and pray under their breath. After finishing this prayer, they leave the church together. Outside, the incoming cargo officers stop and line up next to each other in front of the church across the plaza from the decorated '+pwari stools that they will soon occupy, while their *sayos*—the outgoing officeholders—continue across the plaza and line up in front of their respective stools. The outgoing officeholders then pick up their sugar-cane scepters and walk together back across the plaza towards the church. The sayos meet in pairs in front of the church, and each of the outgoing officeholders separates one sugar cane from the rest of the bundle and offers it to their respective sayos. This single cane is tied to the bundle with a colored ribbon, and the outgoing officeholders use this ribbon to pull the incoming officeholder towards the decorated stools that are being "handed over." After they have crossed the plaza in this way, each of the incoming officeholders is guided into a banana-draped '+pwari stool by his sayo. The sweetened pinole crown is placed on his head, and the sugar-cane scepter is again tilted against the banana-throne that represents the office that each person has now entered.

The bananas that are hung from the incoming officeholders' '+pwari stools share a fundamental sexual theme with mitote symbolism. Recall that in maize-bundle-group mitote ceremonies bananas are frequently served in maize-based pinole (Our Mother) as a representation of the sexualized cosmos. Phallic-shaped sweetened pinole tamales are also served in this pinole during mitote ceremonies, and so the sweetened pinole crowns worn by the entering officeholders share the connotation produced by the bananas. Furthermore, on the sugar-cane scepter these sweetened tamales hang next to more-or-less vaginally shaped pieces of bread (*xúmixk*). Both are depicted as raining out of the green foliage of the fresh sugar cane, which resembles a growing maize plant. Beneath these pieces of bread and sweetened pinole tamales are mythical animals, a microcosmic natural world that seems to be the result of that primordial, sexual rain. The symbolism mobilized through the association of cargo officers with these banana-decorated '+pwari stools, then, positions incoming officeholders as representatives of the male half of the sexualized cosmos.

This sexualized representation of cargo officeholders as the leading males of the community, however, is not without its contradiction, which is also linked to the symbolism of the decorated '+pwari stools. As was mentioned previously, in the Náyari language the name for banana (xána)

FIGURE 12 Cargo officer on '+pwari stool
during the New Year's Festival

is associated with the name for sin (xának+re), and this double meaning
indicates the contradictory position that cargo officers maintain in relation to their own sexuality. On the one hand, sex is a necessary func-
tion—a type of work—that men must perform with their "domesticated" wives. But on the other hand, sex is also a sinful temptation that
threatens the ability of cargo officers to fast, and thus successfully complete the ceremonies from which the force of natural reproductive abun-
dance is ultimately said to emerge. Similarly, the banana-decorated

137

'+pwari stools connote not only the legitimate authority of incoming officeholders to oversee all ceremonies related to the "female" church, but also their weakness and inability to fully complete the rigorous fasts required of them as officeholders. This message takes on increasing salience as the sinful and eventually disruptive aspect of Hesu Kristu Tavástara takes center stage in the subsequent festivals.

THE PACHITAS FESTIVAL Through its focus on a young boy and girl, the Pachitas Festival (a kind of carnival) dramatizes one aspect of the "sinfulness" of the younger side of Hesu Kristu Tavástara. This long festival begins shortly after the conclusion of the New Year's Festival and ends on Ash Wednesday, when the special round hat previously worn by the wacharu is "handed over" over to the centurion-horsemen of Holy Week. These horsemen then lead the devils in symbolically killing Hesu Kristu Tavástara during that festival, and in this way complete the fate of the character who was initially conceived during the Festival of the Deceased and then born during the Christmas Festival.

To carry out the festival, its participants—most of whom are newly appointed mayordomos—are encharged by the new courthouse authorities with the task of "finding Hesu Kristu Tavástara." However, despite the weeks that this group spends in supposed pursuit of this character, they fail to locate him. Indeed, people commonly report that the participants in the Pachitas Festival are unable to complete their task because they are "sinful" and weak. Thus, they share a characteristic with both the cargo officers and the earthly character of Hesu Kristu Tavástara, who in the figure of a red-robed young boy joins the other revelers of this festival.

During the Pachitas Festival, then, an important aspect of the younger side of the two-sided Hesu Kristu Tavástara character strongly emerges. Like Sáutari on his earthly journey, this young boy and his drunken and festive associates seem only interested in self-gratification. But as the story of Sáutari's travels makes clear, although Sáutari immerses himself in sexuality, this earthly sinfulness also brings life to the dry-season world. Furthermore, Don Goyo's story also points out that Sáutari eventually casts off his sins at specific places around the landscape in order to return to his mother. In just the same way, during Lent all of the people associated with the Pachitas Festival—in the end, all of the Náyari people of Santa Teresa—should also cast off the sins that they have acquired during this long, raucous festival. In these ways, the Pachitas Festival reveals one aspect of the human-like character of Hesu Kristu Tavástara (as San Miguel Sáutari), and so sets the stage for the culminating political and moral lessons of Holy Week.

The Pachitas Festival begins on January 13 and ends on Ash Wednesday, the beginning of Lent; it is the longest festival of the year in Santa Teresa. The festival starts in the church with the assembly and raising of a flag that is emblematic of the festival as a whole. For the five days after it is first "raised," this Pachitas flag is attached to the apex of a flowered arch that has been placed over the saints that line the eastern wall of the church. At this point in the festival the white flag is decorated only with crepe-paper flowers at its corners, and with fresh flowers and a urraca-feather wand extending upward from the top of the flag's pole. Multicolored ribbons and a pair of bells also hang down from the top of the pole. The flag itself is appliquéd with a single ribbon in the shape of a circle topped with a cross. For the five days that this flagpole is attached to the flowered arch in the church, it occupies the exact position on that arch that is usually reserved for a single white bell-shaped campanilla flower. Both the shape of this flower and the bells of the flagpole refer to the bells of the church, and thus to a sense of sacred, earthly femaleness.

On the fifth day after it has first been raised, this flag is taken out of the church by the singers, violinists, mayordomos, and tenanchis who comprise the pachitas group (Spanish: *pachiteros*). Most prominent among this group are the three young girls who trade off sounding the bells attached to the flagpole by stamping the pole on the ground in time to the music of the singers and violin players. This bell-ringer—called in Spanish *la malinche*—wears the same distinctive round hat as that of the wacharu-horseman that led the toritos. However, the hat is now covered with clean white cloth like the cloth used to make the flag that the young girl "plays" by ringing its bells. It is also decorated with colorful ribbons that form a cross with its junction at the highest center point of the hat. This hat is later worn by the senior centurion of Holy Week, when it is covered in black cloth marked with a red cross. At this point in the festival, a red-robed young boy—called in Spanish the *monarco*—has not yet joined the rest of the pachiteros, and so the girl at the time portraying la malinche with her circular hat is the center of the group. Indeed, the group of pachiteros as a whole is often referred to as simply "las malinches."

The pachiteros begin their collective search for Hesu Kristu Tavástara on the first day that the flag is taken out of the church. At that time they form a tight, protective group around the young girl chosen to carry the flagpole as they proceed on a counterclockwise path to the four small boundary stones at the edges of the prairie that surrounds the town of Santa Teresa. These stones mark the footpaths entering Santa Teresa from each of the four directions, and at each of these stones the pachiteros sing and make offerings like the ones they will later make at particular households. In subsequent days the pachiteros follow a shorter counterclockwise path that connects all of the Náyari dry-season homes in the vicinity of Santa Teresa, the same path that the owls of the Festival of the Deceased followed earlier. At each of these houses the pachiteros are ostensibly looking for Hesu Kristu Tavástara, but they do not look very hard. Instead they sing and dance with members of each household in exchange for food, liquor, and cigarettes.

The unusual songs of the Náyari pachiteros have been described in a number of publications (e.g., Téllez Girón 1987), all of which specially note that they are sung in a mix of Spanish, Latin, and Nahuatl that is largely incomprehensible to the performers themselves. Pachiteros in Santa Teresa also candidly admit that they do not know the meanings of most of the words that they sing and point to this incomprehensibility as proof that the ancestral songs are, in fact, "very old." They say that these songs, like the other "customs" that Coras continue to practice in Santa Teresa, were passed down from their ancestors, and for this reason the language of the songs is not entirely understandable to them. However, many of the Spanish lyrics are plainly understood and have clear meaning within the context of the performances. For example, the words "dance, flag, dance" (Spanish: *baila, baila, la bandera*) are part of one of the first songs that the pachiteros sing on arrival at a house. The words refer to the flagpole that the malinche stamps into the ground in time to the music. Other short phrases from the songs refer to the purity of the malinche, and to the food and liquor that are given to the pachiteros by members of the households at which they sing. The rare hand-copied song books from which some men sing contain many more relevant Spanish phrases, but these phrases are often lost in the exuberant collective singing of the mysterious "ancient" songs. During this singing, householders and pachiteros often pair off to dance. Facing the same direction with their arms around each other's shoulders, they skip in a counterclockwise circle around the malinche as she rings out the song's beat by thumping her flagpole on the ground.

After such preliminary songs (which may continue for hours if the householders provide adequate liquor and cigarettes), the eldest pachitero makes the distinctive offerings of the group. First, he takes the flagpole from the malinche and scratches a cross in the dirt. He then pours yellow pine-tree pollen (Spanish: *pinolito*) into the center of the cross and decorates it with flowers. Just then the pachiteros sing out, "A flower at every corner, pinolito right in the heart" (Spanish: *cada esquina una rosa, pinolito en el medio corazón*). As the pachiteros prepare to leave, members of the household often tuck peach blossoms and other cultivated flowers into the malinche's white hat so that it is eventually completely covered with multicolored flowers. Like the malinche's bells and clean white flag, these blossoms point to the identity of this girl as a representation of "Our Mother," a pure virgin whose "flower" would be irresistible to the sex-crazed San Miguel Sáutari.

After several days (and nights) of singing and dancing at each house in turn, the pachitero group expands to include the monarco character. In contrast to the malinche, the monarco has no bells on his flagpole, and his clothing, hat, and flag are red rather than white. This red color clearly refers to the red-robed boys who appeared first as the "owls" of the Festival of the Deceased and then again tooting whistles during the Christmas Festival. In the context of dancing and playing music with the malinche,

FIGURE 13   The Pachitero group

the red-robed monarco takes on the sexualized characteristics of Sáutari. Indeed, even the name "Sáutari," which is based on the verb stem -*sáuta*- ("cut flowers"), seems to point to the sexually charged relationship of this young boy with the flower-draped malinche. At the same time, however, because the monarco is actually a preadolescent boy, he seems to maintain the sinless purity and innocence that Hesu Kristu Tavástara will once again claim during Holy Week.

During the days leading up to Ash Wednesday, the flags and costumes of both the malinche and the monarco are slowly elaborated until they are both fairly dripping with ribbons, crepe paper, and flowers. The flagpole of the malinche receives two more flags that look like wings next to the body of her original flag. These two "wings" are attached to the central flag with a small arch decorated with multicolored crepe paper, a reference to both the flower arch of the church and the crepe paper that will soon decorate the devils of Holy Week. The flagpole of the monarco receives a hoop decorated with more multicolored crepe paper. This hoop refers not to the church, but to the world-shaped chánaka "wheel" of the community mitote festival and to the crepe paper of Holy Week. During both the Pachitas Festival and Holy Week, many people collect pieces of this colorful crepe paper to hang on their fruit trees and in their gardens. In doing so, they indicate that this crepe paper—like the sinful "flower cutting" of the monarco—serves to bring back the actual flowers of the rainy season.

The elaborations on the costumes and flagpoles of the malinche and monarco also help to continue a sense of movement. They create a symbolic trajectory from one ceremony to the next, a movement that seems to precede (or even direct) the seasonal movement from wet season to dry season and then from dry season to wet season. The slowly building elaborations of the malinche's and monarco's costumes, and the increasingly bawdy drunkenness of the pachiteros and householders who accompany them, reach a peak on the evening preceding Ash Wednesday, when the Pachitas Festival ends in a spectacle of flowery color.

On that evening the pachiteros assemble for their last day and night of singing, only to separate into two different and competing groups. The first of these groups now pertains specifically to the malinche. They signal this affinity by wearing in their hats white bell-shaped campanilla flowers like the flower the malinche wears in her hat during this final day of the festival. The costume of the monarco is also modified by the addition of a flower. In his case, however, the flower is not a campanilla but a huge white calla lily. This flower very closely resembles the new white campanilla worn by the malinche, except for the long yellow spadix that protrudes from the flower. This phallic-looking spike exudes a powdery

yellow pollen that is like the pinolito used by the pachiteros in this festival. These two flowers, then, again imply a sexualized relationship between the malinche and the monarco that is analogous to the relationship
of Sáutari to the flowers, plants, trees, and even rocks that he brings to
life during his travels on earth.

The pachiteros who pertain to the monarco during this last day of the
festival also wear green spiky shoots of calla-lily plant in their hats. These
spikes resemble century-plant leaves, and so point to Holy Week when
syrup made from century plants will be used as paint for the devils. At
this point, both the malinche and the monarco wear bandoleers filled
with live cartridges across their chests. They use the cartridges to fill re-
volvers that they fire into the air during the night. These guns give them a
serious look, as if they hope to suddenly forget all the previous nights of
debauchery for a last sincere pursuit of Hesu Kristu Tavástara. But despite
the newfound weaponry of the malinche and the monarco, the pachiteros
again look right past the character they seek, and continue to sing and
dance with the red-robed monarco in their midst.

The pachiteros begin their final day and night of singing and dancing at
the courthouse, where they sing several tunes for the assembled authorities. The group then splits in two and follows their respective flags in opposite directions to the houses around town. They separate in order to
pursue Hesu Kristu Tavástara, just as the devils later break into two "armies" to continue this pursuit during Holy Week. Then, after a few
hours, the two groups come together again in front of the courthouse.
The first group to arrive begins to sing but is then interrupted by the
other group, which slams into them, disrupting their performance. One
of the cargo system's governors urges a competition, and so the groups
alternate singing and pounding their flags while the other flag is forcefully
quieted by a member of the opposing group.

As this competition continues—seemingly a competition to prove
whether the malinche or the monarco has been working harder to find
Hesu Kristu Tavástara over the previous weeks—the groups also stand
back to back and rotate around each other in a small counterclockwise
circle in front of the courthouse. While doing this they each carve a pair

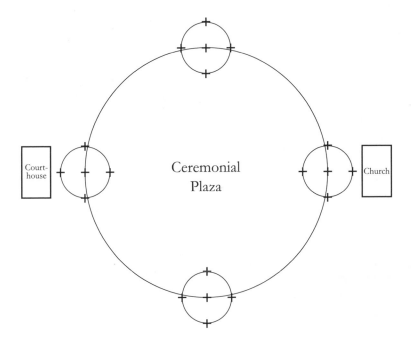

Court-house

Ceremonial
Plaza

Church

FIGURE 14 Pattern of Pachitero Crosses Around the Ceremonial Plaza

of pinolito-filled crosses in the dirt at opposing cardinal directions to make a circle that is itself marked at its four corners by smaller crosses. The two competing groups then continue to mark the southern, eastern, and northern edges of the plaza with these crossed circles before eventually returning back to the courthouse. In the end, they mark a circuit like those danced in mitote ceremonies. Here, however, this larger circle refers to a single centralized cross-shaped world that will eventually receive a series of wooden crosses prior to the final ceremonies of Holy Week (the "way of the crosses," although this term is rarely used in Santa Teresa). Once they have finished drawing out this pattern, the pachiteros are covered in a shower of yellow pinolito tossed by cargo officials from bamboo containers like those used at liquor-drinking rituals to apply sexualized designs to people's faces. Then, after exhausting their pinolito, these officials bring out containers of commercial dyes, which are also splashed over the pachiteros until they become entirely saturated in color. Finally, multicolored store-bought candies are brought out, and big handfuls of them are tossed in colorful arches over the assembled group. This candy attracts children, who root around beneath the pachiteros in search of the sweets.

People say that the pollen and dye are like rain and the hard candies are like hail. This colorful shower of pollen, dye, and candy, then, reflects the type of rainy-season fecundity that San Miguel Sáutari is said to have brought to the earth. But although the pachiteros, like Sáutari, seem to succeed in (re)creating the colors of life through their sexualized travels through the town of Santa Teresa, they nonetheless fail to find Hesu Kristu Tavástara, the young boy who, as the monarco, travels among them. As a result, the responsibility for completing this task is transferred to the centurions of Holy Week as the Pachitas Festival continues.

The pachiteros begin the ceremony that concludes their festival by hanging the flags of both the malinche and the monarco over the flowery cross behind the table of the courthouse officials. From this cross the pachiteros then proceed immediately across the plaza to the front of the church where the senior centurion of the Holy Week Festival is waiting for them. At the church the young malinche removes her hat and hands it to the centurion. People report that she speaks to the centurion, blaming her inability to find Hesu Kristu Tavástara on her "dirtiness." Unlike the centurion (who began his fast at the end of the Festival of the Deceased), she and the rest of the pachiteros have failed to fast from bodily sin, and so they were unable to hunt down the little boy among them.

Almost immediately after the centurion receives the malinche's round hat, the young men standing near the centurion are ordered by him into two single-file lines extending from the front of the closed church. An old man then begins to play a driving tune on a reed whistle like those later carried by the devils. The sound of this music seems to penetrate into the young men and they begin to bounce back and forth on the balls of their feet. The two lines of young men then start to run back and forth in front of the church as they shout and sing in the distinctive manner of the devils. At this point, just before the beginning of Lent, the army of devils who will persecute Hesu Kristu Tavástara begins to gradually emerge.

At midnight the pachiteros end their festival in the church. In front of the altar, the malinche and the monarco pound their flagpoles as they have throughout this festival, but now no music plays to accompany them. Instead, the steady thumping again foreshadows the devils, who will eventually pound their "sabers" in the same way to conclude the Holy Week Festival. In both cases (as with the toritos who used their "horns" in a similar manner), the thumping seems to be some kind of divine and pure language that is meant to transmit forceful intentions upwards to the pantheon of saints. It communicates prayers in a way that human speech cannot.

The festival comes to a definitive end as the mayordomos cover all of the pachiteros in a final drenching rain of yellow pinolito and multicolored dye. An impressive contrast to this final display of color, however, is immediately provided by the ceremonial elder of the church, who marks the forehead of each pachitero with a cross of black ash like that which will later be used as paint for the devils. After putting the costumes and flags back in the sacristy, the group assembles one final time at sunrise to mark the completion of their ceremonial festival.

On the first day of Lent, the people who participated as pachiteros gather at the courthouse, and the young girls and boy who portrayed the malinches and monarco are returned to their parents by the mayordomos and tenanchis who cared for them over the previous weeks. The rest of the pachiteros receive beverages brought by the courthouse officials. The most important of these beverages (which also include coffee and chocolate) is called in Spanish the *mistela*, an infusion made of *arrayanes*, the sweet berries of a thorny tree that flowers during the dry season. This beverage is free of alcohol and has a bright color that resembles dye, and so it is perfectly suited for the first day of Lent: its color points to the life-bringing floweriness of the Pachitas Festival that has now ended, while its lack of alcohol signifies the religious fasts that all of the Cora people of Santa Teresa should begin during the dry days of Lent.

LENT AND HOLY WEEK The Holy Week season in Santa Teresa begins slowly during Lent and reaches a crescendo on Holy Saturday, when it suddenly concludes. Throughout this period the people of Santa Teresa are supposed to cast off their sins, just as Sáutari is said to have abandoned his sins here on earth before returning to his mother in heaven. However, for both Sáutari and the Náyari people who accompanied him during the long course of the Pachitas Festival, habits are hard to break. So as the dry season turns drier and the indulgent character of Sáutari remains undiminished, his colorful and carefree sexuality takes an ugly turn, and an embedded double image within the two-sided character of Hesu Kristu Tavástara is revealed.

Although Sáutari represents only one half of the two-sided Hesu Kristu Tavástara character, the transition from the Pachitas Festival to Holy Week shows that Sáutari himself is composed of another, deeper duality. On one side is the now familiar aspect of Sáutari as the colorful "flower cutter" who sang and danced his way around the world in the same way that the pachiteros traveled from house to house during their festival. During Holy Week, however, the sexuality that characterizes Sáutari becomes increasingly dirty and disruptive, and the other half of this side of the Hesu Kristu Tavástara character emerges. During this period San Miguel Sáutari is transformed into the ash-covered "devils" (tyárutse) that kill Hesu Kristu. In other words, as a result of his own unrestrained sinfulness, San Miguel Sáutari essentially kills himself so that his other half (Távastara, "Our Elder," or San Miguel Xúrave) might rise to heaven.

This transition from the Pachitas Festival to Holy Week also brings about a political crisis in Santa Teresa—a type of collective suicide—that mirrors the internal purging of Hesu Kristu Tavástara. During the New Year's Festival, the cargo-system authorities of Santa Teresa still seem to embody the spirit of Tavástara; they are austere old men whose fasting points to their legitimacy as traditional authorities. But their banana-covered stools also point out their human weakness, which then unfolds into the Sáutari-like sexual indulgences of the pachiteros. When the pachiteros fail to complete their responsibilities, the cargo officials are then forced to seek out more drastic measures, and so during Holy Week they transfer all of their authority to the centurions. These centurions, however, are unable to control the violent and sexually aggressive devils who plunge the town into chaos. In other words, the young men who take over during Lent as devils are the "dirty" twins of the pachiteros just as the tyárutse characters they portray are the "dirty" flip side of the colorful "flower-cutting" Sáutari. Still, by murdering "Jesus Christ" in a chaotic frenzy at the end of Holy Week, the devils also are meant to perform a type of cleansing. They open the way for the cargo-system officials to reassert the political legitimacy of their authority structure prior to the approaching rainy season, when these rains—as the deceased ancestors— again claim the town.

In Santa Teresa, Lent is divided into six week-long periods beginning on Ash Wednesday followed by the four-day period of the Holy Week Festival, which begins on the Wednesday of Holy Week. These six weeks prior to Holy Week are marked by the slow emergence of the tyárutse and by the repeated patrolling of the town against the gradually increasing threat that they represent. On each Wednesday during Lent the captains (Spanish: *capitanes*) of the tyárutse, referred to in Náyari as the *matanyatyi* (those in front), mark the four trails that enter the town of Santa Teresa. They use sabers that will eventually be painted black and white to draw crosses in the dust on those trails. Each Wednesday they place those crosses closer and closer to the plaza, and thus closer and closer to the church and courthouse that they will eventually invade. This marking begins at the small stones that the pachiteros earlier decorated with their own flowery crosses to begin their festival and ends during Holy Week in the plaza where the malinche earlier turned her hat over to the senior centurion-horseman who leads the tyárutse. During the last week of Lent the centurions and devils join the captains to mark crosses on the path that circles the plaza to the north. In this way, by slowly moving their crosses inward on these four trails and by gradually increasing their numbers, the centurions, captains, and devils help to create a sense of dread. Throughout Lent, these young men seem to creep inward towards the heart of town, bringing disorder and chaos with them as they come from the outside.

In response to this external threat, representatives of the courthouse authorities patrol the borders of town. Every Wednesday of Lent these representatives proceed in a counterclockwise direction to each of the points along the path that encircles the town's ceremonial plaza. At these points they draw their own crosses in the dirt with a small lance as they slash a white flag (the *xandaru* or "soldier") through the air in a dramatic crossing motion. Then, on their return to the plaza, they lean their lance and flag across the flower-decorated courthouse cross affixed to the wall behind the authorities' wooden table before checking the gates that block entrance to the plaza against the gradually increasing threat of the tyárutse.

This threat takes its first serious form on the Wednesday night of Holy Week, after a full day of preparations for the Holy Week Festival at both the church and the house of the senior centurion. At the church, preparations focus on the construction of an elaborate Holy Week altar and on the painting and decoration of a special crucifixion cross. This impressive Holy Week altar is made of wooden scaffolding that supports a wide staircase edged with thick green foliage and "hats" (*múkutsi*). These "hats" are woven hoops of yucca leaves (*tak+*) that resemble the circular hat of the centurion earlier received from the malinche. Candles (*kanti*) are placed within each of the hoops that edge both sides of the wide staircase that climbs the middle of the Holy Week altar. These candles are made of special wax (*x+xka*) that is saved from year to year, and whose name seems to refer to the name of the harsh Tereseño dry season (*x+xkata*). Like candlewax, the desiccated grasses and shrubs of Santa Teresa burn during this time of year, leaving black ash like that used by the tyárutse to paint themselves for this festival. In the end, the large altar within the church resembles a green, flower-covered mountain (or a pyramid). Indeed, the following day it is used as a kind of "Garden of Gethsemane" on the "Mount of Olives," although I never heard anyone describe it in such orthodox terms.

Outside the church, apostles prepare the crucifixion cross to which an image of the dying adult Hesu Kristu Tavástara is tied on Thursday. These twelve apostles are normally the oldest men in Santa Teresa. Like the centurions and captains (and outsiders like myself who are occasionally "kidnapped" to serve with the devils), they serve five-year terms. The role of these apostles is to fast and stay awake through the Thursday night of Holy Week, accompanying Hesu Kristu Tavástara on a night-long crucifixion. The cross they prepare is painted a lifeless black and white, like the bodies and sabers of the devils and captains. Once painted, the cross is leaned against the north wall of the church near the door.

After the altar and apostles' cross have been assembled, the church is closed and attention shifts to the centurion's house where the devils come together to begin the Holy Week Festival. Against the east wall of this house, a small altar is built and stacked with food, cigarettes, and quarts of liquor. The senior centurion's hat—now covered with black cloth—and his old sword lean against the wall next to the cavalryman's cross that is carried by the junior of the two centurions. Tall reeds that will later be used as "lances" by the devils are leaned outside the house on either side of the door.

The devils begin to arrive at the centurion's house on Wednesday, at which point one of the captains for the devils addresses the centurions. He speaks to the senior centurion as his father, accusing him of leaving the devils to grow up alone in "Santa Rosalena," a place that is said to be somewhere to the west. They say, "Look, all we have are our pants and my jacket [the ashy, black paint], but my mother sent me out to find you, and now that I have found you I will do whatever you order." The senior centurion then addresses the devils as his children and promises to protect them as he rides his horse among them during the festival.

Many of the devils who arrive at the centurion's house on Wednesday afternoon are already painted. Their paint is black on white like that of the toritos, but their costumes are more elaborate. Rather than the small wooden "horns" of the toritos, each of the devils carries a long wooden "saber." Devils also wear hats decorated with long streams of multicolored crepe paper. Sometimes this crepe paper is also used to decorate little horns formed onto the top of their hats, playing on the dual identity of the devils as now nearly adult bulls. Most devils also carry a reed whistle on which they play a hypnotically repetitive four-note tune. Others carry

FIGURE 15 A devil of Holy Week

drums, and when the large group assembles, the din from these simple musical instruments is overwhelming.

Many devils also have dead forest animals slung over their shoulders. These rotting animals can include snakes, small jaguars, squirrels, or co-atis, but perhaps the most popular is the skunk. Skunks (black and white, like the devils) are captured live, and during the festival they spray quantities of scent on the assembled group. Inevitably the mob will kill such a terrified skunk with pummeling blows from their sabers, after which it is tied with string from snout to tail and hung across a shoulder like the other rotting animals that the devils have brought with them. The devils joke that these animals are their "horses" (as opposed to the real horses of the centurions), and so they often straddle them and comically buck and rear about as they hold the noxious little corpses between their legs. Like the slow movement of the crosses towards town during Lent, these animals signify that the disgusting (but also hilarious) devils come from "outside" (*tyát+ki*), the place to the west that is referred to by the devils as Santa Rosalena.

The devils are also well known for their obscene songs. These songs emphasize creativity over continuity, and the aggressive display of raw emotions over the collective pursuit of common ceremonial practices. As young men fight and stagger drunkenly together around town, they try out new verses and phrasings, but older songs are perennial favorites. Some songs, for example, ridicule the apostles and their elder-focused ceremonies:

> Tuxa, tuxa nákuxe
> Tuxa, tuxa nákuxe
> ("Gourd bowl, gourd bowl, is deaf")
> Siku, siku ú'urari
> Siku, siku ú'urari
> ("Bow drum resonator, bow drum resonator, lets out farts")
> Nyechika yet+ tyevicha'a hutza, yehwi
> Nyechika yet+ tyevicha'a hutza, yehwi
> ("My female dog is pregnant, but she isn't married, and how")
> x+pu, x+pu putyauku
> x+pu, x+pu putyauku
> ("Hole, hole, she sure has one")
> Mwaxá, mwaxá t+ke hé'eratza
> Mwaxá, mwaxá t+ke hé'eratza
> ("Female deer, female deer, she sure is meaty down there")
> x+pu, x+pu putyauku
> x+pu, x+pu putyauku
> ("Hole, hole, she sure has one")

Such a song might end with the popular chant "Apostulu '+ra'ara, hahá!" ("The apostle screws his wife, hahá!"). Many other songs are directed at teenage girls:

> Mukawayé mu liya
> Mukawayé mu liya
> ("There goes the girl")
> Nyekeyé mwixatye
> Nyekeyé mwixatye
> ("Didn't I tell you")
> S+ pu'uri, yéh s+ pu'uri
> S+ pu'uri, yéh s+ pu'uri
> ("But it's someone else, someone else spoke to me")
> Kapahé nyeheva
> Kapahé nyeheva
> ("So don't talk to me")

This type of song might end with a dismissive or obscene chant to the particular girl that has drawn the attention of the devils: "liya, liya chaparita!" or "liya, liya carnuda!" ("shorty" or "meaty"). Like the rest of the devils' behavior, these songs are both scandalous and funny; they threaten the patriarchal authority of the town's elders while also providing a type of vigorous new energy that is beyond the capacity of those old men.

This energy is also displayed in the movement of the devils. Throughout the Holy Week Festival these young men are in constant motion. They bounce from foot to foot and challenge each other to duels, swinging their sabers in great circles and clipping the dusty red soil before slamming their heavy wooden swords together. Bloody injuries are common and tend to heighten the excitement. The captains attempt to keep the frenzy down, but they often fail, or themselves enter the fray. On horseback, however, the centurions have a tactical advantage over the devils. By charging through the group and forcefully compelling them to move in one direction or another they attempt to channel the devils' unfocused energy towards the goal of the festival: taking control of the town in order to kill Hesu Kristu Tavástara.

The centurions begin this disciplinary effort on Wednesday afternoon when they form the devils into two groups so that their captains can lead them. The groups then begin the distinctive pattern of running back and forth (like the toritos), which they continue throughout the festival. The captains and centurions first lead the devils in running around the path that encircles the town towards the west side of the plaza, where the whole group is repelled by a closed gate. The group then reverses direction and follows the path back to the opposite gate of the plaza. This gate is also closed, so the group begins to run back and forth there. This site— immediately to the south of the church—then becomes a center of gravity for the devils, who return there later in the night. This is the former location of the graveyard of Santa Teresa, so it emphasizes the connection of the centurions and the devils with the Festival of the Deceased.

At this former graveyard, the centurions solicit descent-group maize from each of their "children" and this maize is joined together in the centurion's distinctive gourd bowl–shaped hat to be brought back to the centurion's house. There it is placed with sacred water in two actual gourd bowls, one for each centurion. The centurions pray through this joined maize just as descent-group elders pray through their own special maize. The centurions then leave this offering on an edge of their house pointing towards the center mountain, Kweimarutse, until morning.

In a number of ways, this simple act of joining maize brought by the different young men portraying devils re-emphasizes the epochal nature of the whole festival cycle. Because of its gourd-bowl shape, the centurion's hat (earlier worn by the wachero and then the malinche) is like a map of the seasonally changing world. By joining maize in this hat, this cosmological significance seems to reach out towards the young men who have deposited their maize—and so their souls—in that hat. The foolish vulgarity of these devils, then, although driven by their youthful aggression, also links them with the cosmological fate of Sáutari. Like Sáutari's sexuality, which becomes absurdly exaggerated as he travels across the land, their concupiscence has become so extreme that they have turned into "devils." But because they share Sáutari's fate, it should also becomes clear to these young men that only by slowly leaving this sin behind—like Sáutari abandoned his sin around the landscape—can they discipline themselves to be appropriately restrained adult men. As they move out of their dirty ceremonial role, they should purify themselves enough to claim traditional political authority and eventually perhaps even a place in heaven with their deceased ancestors, the rains. But for now, such self-denial seems impossible for these young men, and so as night falls they congregate at the former graveyard on the south side of the church, where they spend the first of three nights dancing and fighting in the cold.

On Thursday the courthouse officials of Santa Teresa explicitly hand their authority as the town's traditional leaders over to the centurions. The centurions use this authority to pursue and symbolically crucify Hesu Kristu Tavástara, which begins the ritual cleansing of sins that allows this character—and by extension all (male) Tereseños—to move upward to heaven. This transfer of authority begins in the morning. While the devils and captains paint themselves, the apostles, centurions, mayordomos, te-nanchis, and other ceremonial specialists gather in the church. Outside, the senior civil officials assemble in the courthouse to watch their representatives complete a final circuit around the plaza with flag, lance, and staff. Once these representatives have marked crosses in a counterclock-wise direction around the plaza, all of these civil officials then briefly join together on the veranda of the courthouse, where a white-wrapped bundle containing all of the staffs pertaining to each of the courthouse offices is laid open on the table. The senior governor carries this bundle across the plaza to the church accompanied by the other courthouse officers, some of whom also carry the flags and lances of these authorities.

This group enters the closed church, which at this point is guarded against the devils by a small contingent of cargo-system officials. With great solemnity the governor passes the bundle of staffs to the senior cen-turion, who places it to one side of the large, leafy altar. This transfer sig-nifies that at this point in the festival, on Thursday morning, all tradi-tional political authority over the town of Santa Teresa has passed from the courthouse officials to the centurions. For this reason, courthouse officials should not enter the courthouse or approach the table that serves as the focal point of cargo-system power until Saturday afternoon; the enforcement of laws and the adjudication of disputes in Santa Teresa are in the hands of the centurions.

After this bundle has been handed over to the centurions, an image of the crucified Jesus Christ is taken out of the sacristy to be tied to the apostles' cross and covered with a black and purple shroud. This same image of Hesu Kristu Tavástara was earlier carried by one of the "owls" during the Festival of the Deceased, but here it is tied to the apostles' large crucifixion cross with the same black horse-hair rope that was also used in that earlier festival. Another of these distinctive horse-hair ropes is placed at the foot of the cross. This rope is used later in the day by the apostles to tie the large crucifixion cross to each of their waists in turn in the same way that one of the "owls" earlier tied the smaller image to his waist during the Festival of the Deceased. Similarly, the black and purple shroud that covers this image on the crucifixion cross during Holy Week is used in the Festival of the Deceased to cover the flower image of Tayaxuk+, Our Deceased Grandfather. These connections between Holy Week and the Festival of the Deceased point to the approaching re-emergence of the older Tavástara aspect of Hesu Kristu Tavástara from behind the younger Sáutari/Tyaru aspect that dominates the New Year's, Pachitas, and Holy Week festivals. This eventual re-emergence is brought about by the crucifixion of Hesu Kristu Tavástara, which in Santa Teresa sets the stage for an all-night vigil.

To complete this crucifixion a small procession is undertaken within the protected confines of the church. This internal procession focuses on the festival's second figure of Jesus Christ, a smaller image of Hesu Kristu Tavástara that serves as a counterpoint to the image tied to the apostles' cross. This smaller image (which is always carefully hidden) is carried out of the sacristy by the senior of the two centurions, who embraces the image to his chest in the same way that maize bundles are embraced at descent-group mitote ceremonies. During the procession this centurion is covered with a four-posted tapestry held by mayordomos, and is engulfed in smoke from incense-burners held by tenanchis. The captain of the urraca dancers sounds a wooden clacker (referred to in Náyari as a *taravi'ira*, or "rainmaker"). He is preceded by three red-robed boys and followed by a group of women. They in turn are flanked by two men carrying the xandaru flag and lance and by pairs of men carrying bows and arrows, rifles, and machetes.

The senior centurion moves around the church on his knees as blankets are thrown down so that he never touches the ground. The procession circles counterclockwise towards the apostles' cross. There the centurion lights the two candles that will burn through the night at the base of the cross. These candles are located on the same woven mat that held the food that was offered to Tayaxuk+ during the Festival of the Deceased. The procession then continues towards the tall mountain-like altar. There the centurion climbs up the steep stairway on his knees, pausing to light the candles that border both sides of this stairway. At the top, the centurion places the smaller image that he has carried around the church into a decorated box. Following this symbolic crucifixion, members of the procession take the opportunity to "visit" and make offerings to both of the figures of Hesu Kristu Tavástara. Before long, however, the old apostles and a few mayordomos and tenanchis are left alone to guard the church against the devils outside.

Prior to entering the church in the morning, the centurions lead the devils to the south side of the church. There the centurions begin the day by supervising the painted young men as they run in their distinctive back-and-forth pattern just outside the gate that separates them from the plaza. But once the centurions enter the church, groups of devils take the opportunity to extend their patrol to the entire town surrounding the plaza. They head off in noisy groups in order to establish their own dominance over day-to-day affairs. A "voluntary contribution" of liquor or cigarettes is demanded from each of the shops in town, and then they are ordered shut. Additionally, the use of any conveyance is outlawed by the devils, who are known to drag people off of their horses or out of their trucks. Occasionally, they will kidnap outsiders who have come to the festival at this time. They paint the unfortunate visitors and prod them to dance and run with them for the next two days and nights (and, if they "eat the banana," for the next five years). The devils particularly relish their power over women. They prohibit all bathing or laundering, and women who wear their hair in braids (which are prohibited) become the targets of dirty songs and instructive love taps from the devils' wooden sabers.

After the centurions have set the stage for Hesu Kristu Tavástara's last night, however, they leave the church and again mount their horses and round up the dispersed groups of devils in order to invade the plaza. Each devil grabs a long reed from the senior centurion's house, and then the group runs in two lines back to the south side of the church. From this former graveyard the centurions supervise the opening of the gate that protects the town's central plaza, and each then leads a single-file line of devils as they invade, holding a saber in one hand and a tall reed "lance" in the other. This group makes one half of a counterclockwise circuit of the plaza before crossing through the center of the plaza and laying their "lances" on either side of the church. The devils are then released to dance, sing, and saber-fight with each other in the plaza. Inside the church, the apostles offer copal smoke to their crucifixion cross as a pair of men guard the door with bows and arrows against the devils outside.

The dramatic entrance of the devils into the plaza takes place shortly after the placement of the dual image of Hesu Kristu Tavástara on the crucifixion cross and mountain-like altar, which accounts for the most common name for the devils in Spanish—judíos, "Jews" or "Judases" who pursue Jesus Christ. Eventually, the apostles leave the church and join with these judíos to celebrate a chaotic "last supper" in the courthouse.

The beginning of this meal is signaled by the leaning of the centurion's cavalryman's cross diagonally in front of the flowered cross of the courthouse authorities. It takes the same place behind the courthouse table as the xandaru flag during Lent, emphasizing that during Holy Week these centurions are the legitimate traditional authorities in Santa Teresa. The focus of this meal is not the centurions or the judíos/devils, however, but the elderly apostles who otherwise remain within the church and so stand at the pure moral center of the festival. Indeed, during this meal, each of the twelve apostles wears a crown of thorns that seems to identify him as the elderly aspect of the crucified Hesu Kristu Tavástara. This elderly aspect is in turn opposed to the youthful and vigorously masculine Sáutari/tyaru aspect that the judíos represent.

The foods that are given to the apostles also refer to this festival's place within the whole year-long festival cycle. These special foods are squash, fish, painted hard-boiled eggs, century-plant syrup, and bananas. The squash is stored from the end of the rainy season, and seems to point towards the return of the wet season. The fish is served in broth, which refers back to the beef broth that should be given to the young boys during the Little Bulls ceremony. Fish also connotes the Catholic prohibition against eating meat during Lent, and reinforces the notion that adult men must fast. The eggs have a twofold signification. First, the paint of the eggs refers to the colorful dyes that were tossed over the pachiteros to complete their festival. Second, the eggs themselves refer to a chick that is carried in the final procession of Good Friday. This chick in turn refers to the roosters that are sacrificed for Santiago's Festival, which follows Holy Week during the stormiest part of the rainy season.

In a strange twist, the century-plant syrup (Spanish: *miel*) also refers to Santiago's Festival. A number of people commented to me during my years of participation in the festival that in crucifying Hesu Kristu Tavástara, "the wrong brother is killed." That is, the devils kill themselves by killing the two-sided earth-bound character called San Miguel Sáutari, which allows San Miguel Sáutari's "clean" elder brother—San Miguel Xúrave—to return as the rains during Santiago's Festival. Here the status of San Miguel Xúrave as the *older* brother of Sáutari is his marked characteristic. In this way, San Miguel Xúrave is conflated with Santiago, who is called Tayaxú (Our Grandfather), the character that ultimately departs at the end of the rainy season during the Festival of the Deceased as Tayaxuk+ (Our Deceased Grandfather). Interestingly, in the local dialect, Tereseños pronounce San Miguel Xúrave's name as "San Miel"; his name is even spelled like that on the small wooden pallet that is used to carry this particular winged saint in processions. Like the eggs that will symbolically grow into roosters, then, the century-plant syrup that is exchanged during this festival also refers to the forthcoming Santiago's Festival, in which "San Miel" appears as an aspect of the ancestor rains.

More directly, however, this syrup also refers to the paint of the devils, who use it to cover their bodies with black ash. Peeled bananas are served in this syrup; this presentation of one of the prototypical symbols of masculine authority seems to emphasize the relationship of the sticky, painted devils to the austere (but weak) elders of the courthouse. Like syrup on the bananas, the devils completely engulf the courthouse, plaza, and town. This symbolism is extended when handfuls of bananas are tossed from the courthouse to the crowd of devils. The devils clamor for these treats, literally consuming this symbol of courthouse authority ("eating the banana") as they roam freely about the plaza.

Following this "last supper" in which the apostles, centurions, and judíos all receive food, the day's procession gets under way. The apostles are also the focus of this procession, in that they trade off carrying the large and heavy black-and-white-painted apostles' cross, which is strapped to their waists in turn with the horse-hair rope. In addition to this large cross, the procession includes all the saints of the church, which are carried on the heads of the mayordomos and tenanchis on small wooden pallets. As the procession leaves the church, it is flanked by devils who have picked up the "lances" earlier placed to the sides of the entrance to the church. These young men are compelled into formation by the centurion-horsemen, who charge through them delivering blows with a horsewhip and the broad side of a sword. In this way they are assembled into two single-file lines extending from the front of the church. The procession emerges from the church between these two single-file lines. As it turns right to circle the plaza in a counterclockwise direction, the devils arch their reed lances over the procession to provide a type of canopy. People say that these reeds (haká) symbolically "rain" on the procession as it travels around the town. The taravi'ira, the "rainmaker," is also sounded to begin the procession, but then is left on the stone cross in front of the church, where the liquor that serves as the prize in a race that follows this procession will soon be placed.

This first procession of the Holy Week Festival stops at each of the wooden crosses within the plaza and then leaves the plaza through its eastern gate. It then stops at each of the wooden crosses that mark the outer path encircling the town as the assembled group follows this path in a counterclockwise direction. At each of these crosses the apostle carrying the large crucifixion cross curtsies briefly, and so symbolically transfers the figure of the crucified Hesu Kristu Tavástara from the apostles' painted cross onto each of the other crosses that surround the plaza and the town as a whole. After stopping in this way at each of the crosses, the procession eventually returns to the church, where the saints are replaced. The apostles' cross is again placed near the door, and the devils leave their lances on either side of the church door.

After this procession, near sunset, the centurions lead a race around the same course that was earlier followed by the crucified Hesu Kristu Tavástara, but in the opposite direction. They charge out of the plaza through the west gate with the devils in hot pursuit. The liquor and cigarettes placed on the church's stone cross are prizes for the devils who manage to beat the mounted centurions around the outside path and then around the inside of the plaza. Few succeed in this difficult trial, but in this fashion the centurions are able to convince the self-centered devils to complete their ceremonial work of patrolling the crosses where the crucified Hesu Kristu Tavástara is now located.

After this race has been completed, the devils are again released to drink and fight in the former graveyard on the south side of the church. Meanwhile, the apostles return to their own cross within the church to again begin the offerings of smoke that they will continue through the night within earshot of the rowdy devils outside. This ceremonial vigil, however, is interrupted at midnight by devils who invade the church in order to torment the old apostles.

During the apostles' night-long vigil, the bows and arrows, machetes, and old rifles are in the same positions at the base of the altar where they were left following the earlier symbolic crucifixion of Hesu Kristu Tavástara inside the church. At midnight a few captains again enter the church from outside and take up these defensive weapons against the increasingly aggressive devils. These devils eventually disrupt the vigil undertaken by the apostles, but they also make sure that the apostles are awake, taunting them for their inability to "fast from dreams." Like all behaviors associated with the devils, this taunting is characteristically crude. They drop their pants in lewd displays, or rub rotting animals in the faces of the sleepy apostles. Others jump around the church, yelling out in unison "Apostulu '+ra'ara!" a reference to the supposed desire of these old men to return to their wives' beds rather than complete their ceremonial work. Eventually the apostles tire of this abuse, and they take up incense-burners and use the smoke to repel the devils. The devils react to this smoke by dramatically coughing and grasping at their chests as if the smoke were a type of poison. Once they leave, the church is quiet for the rest of the night as the apostles wait for the dawn, like they would at a mitote ceremony.

On Friday the devils add red paint to their earlier black and white, which tends to accentuate the blood that has dried on their various saber wounds. The centurion's cavalryman's cross is also accented with red, a reference to the death of Hesu Kristu Tavástara that occurs on this day. This death is symbolized during a procession within the church like the procession through which Hesu Kristu Tavástara was crucified the day before. It begins in the morning and is structured almost identically to the procession of the previous day. Now, however, three more boys accompany the boys wearing red robes, and these three boys carry nails, the freshly cut braid from a young girl, and a chick. In the context of Santa Teresa's Holy Week Festival, the nails represent those that would be pulled out of a cross to remove the dead body of a crucified man. The braid refers to the vigorously masculine authority of the devils, who outlaw the wearing of such braids during the festival. Lastly, the chick refers to the roosters of Santiago's Festival, and thus to the notion that the "elder brother" aspect of Hesu Kristu Tavástara is not really killed, but reappears during that later festival as Santiago.

In addition to these differences, Friday's procession inside the church moves in a clockwise rather than counterclockwise direction, an indication of completion. Now, instead of lighting candles, the senior centurion uses a red flower to snuff out each of the candles that edges the Holy Week altar's stairway leading to the smaller figure of Hesu Kristu Tavástara. At the apostles' cross he then uses the same red flower to put out the two candles that have been burning through the night next to the crucified image of Hesu Kristu Tavástara. The procession then returns to the sacristy where the smaller image of Hesu Kristu Tavástara and all of the other ritual paraphernalia are returned to their storage places. The mountain-like altar upon which the smaller image of Hesu Kristu Tavástara was placed is also broken down, and the wooden framework is returned to the mezzanine above the door of the church. In the process, a coin-studded cloth that decorated the box holding the image of Hesu Kristu Tavástara on top of that altar is brought down to be used on the small wooden pallet that will serve as the *Santo Entierro* (Spanish: Holy Sepulcher).

At this moment the doors are opened and the devils who have been milling about outside stream in to join the rest of the people in the church, everyone grabbing pieces of the green foliage that decorated the altar. This foliage is said to help fruit trees grow, and so (like the crepe paper that decorates the hats of the devils, which is also hung in fruit trees) it is taken to particular homes. The devils, however, will find another use for this foliage, and so they tuck it into the waistbands of their rolled-up pants. After the altar is entirely disassembled, the apostles then supervise the construction of the pallet of the Holy Sepulcher.

This small pallet is initially painted on Wednesday along with the apostles' crucifixion cross, and it shares the black-and-white motif of that cross. To finish its preparation, a clean white cloth is first laid upon this painted wooden pallet and some split reeds are arched over the top. Other split-reed spikes are made to extend straight upward from six holes that hold the ends of these arches. These reed spikes are used to secure six stacks of flattened disk-shaped pieces of cotton. The coin-studded cloth veil that was used to cover the opening of the box that held the smaller figure of Hesu Kristu Tavástara on top of the altar is then laid on the pallet so that its coins and multicolored ribbons hang over the pallet's forward edge. With these preparations completed, the pallet is ready to receive the image of the crucified Hesu Kristu Tavástara.

This image is untied from the apostles' cross and is laid onto its sepulcher, where it is then covered with five black rebozos that are hung over the split-reed arches. These rebozos refer back to the similar ones that were used during the ceremonial birth of Hesu Kristu Tavástara during the Christmas Festival. Finally, the whole platform is covered with the purple and black burial shroud that was earlier used to cover the figure of the crucified Hesu Kristu Tavástara (and even earlier covered the figure of Tayaxuk+ during the Festival of the Deceased). Once it is completed, this pallet remains in the church until it is carried in a procession later in the day.

Before this Holy Sepulcher is taken out of the church, however, an earlier procession centered on the grieving parents of Hesu Kristu Tavástara—Joseph and Dolores (who share a single box in Santa Teresa's church)—circles the town. This procession is structured like the previous day's procession, except that the group splits up as they leave the church. Half of the group follows Joseph and the other half follows Dolores as they leave out of opposite gates in the plaza. They then proceed in opposite directions around the path that surrounds the town, curtsying at each of the crosses. After completing circles in opposing directions, and so visiting for the last time each of the crosses upon which their crucified son Hesu Kristu Tavástara was symbolically placed during the previous day's procession, they again meet in the plaza and enter the church as one group to complete the procession.

Once this procession has ended, the devils again lay their reed "lances" on either side of the church's entrance and begin a "war" at each of the outer crosses. In doing this they also begin the bizarre, backward behavior that they will continue the following day. Their war starts as they break into two groups, following centurions in opposite directions out of the plaza and towards the crosses that stand closest to the plaza. At these crosses a pair of younger devils is selected, and a pair of older captains forces them to bend over. These captains tear pieces of the banana-leaf foliage that the devils have earlier pulled from the Holy Week altar from their waistbands and use it as paper to write secret communiqués. Using a stick, the captains pretend to load their "pens" with excrement from the bent-over devils. They concentrate intently as they use these pens to write on the banana leaves, and then fold up these messages and shove them into the mouths of the devils. These "spies" are then ordered to protect their messages as they run a reconnaissance mission around the town, which they do by running together with the folded banana leaves in their mouths. However, when these spies reach the respective opposing group, they are captured, and their colorful hats are removed and held by that "army's" opposing centurion. They are then sent on their way around the town, eventually to arrive back at their own army, which has been sending spies out from each of the crosses that they have been passing. When the devil-messengers arrive they remove the leaves from their mouths, bend over again, and pretend to defecate the messages as they pass them backward to the captains between their legs. These messages are opened with great flamboyance, and the captains try to top each other with their humorously scatological creativity in "reading" them to the assembled group of devils. This process of sending out spies and receiving back communiqués continues until the two armies meet in a field near the three crosses that mark the northern point of the circular path that they have been following. As discussed below, the battle between these two armies reinforces the connection between the devils and Hesu Kristu Tavástara.

Combat begins as the centurions line up the devils opposite each other. A captain then steps forward from each side to issue opposing challenges in Spanish like those heard in past wars in the area: "Who goes there?" (¿Quién vive?). "A Chihuahuan!" (¡Chihuahueño!). "Who goes there?" (¿Quién vive?). "An agrarian revolutionary!" (¡Agrarista!). The centurions then give a signal, and the opposing groups move towards each other with their sabers raised. As they meet each other, one group is compelled by the captains to lie down, defeated in war. These devils are symbolically cut into pieces with the sabers of the opposing army, but are then soon revived by a character called the *Chucho*.

The Chucho is a boy of the same age as the monarco of the Pachitas Festival, but dressed like a devil. In his youthful innocence he seems to represent the Sáutari aspect of Hesu Kristu Tavástara within the group of devilish judíos. His name—Spanish slang for "Jesus"—also helps to connect him to Hesu Kristu Tavástara. During the battle this young boy plays on this identification with one aspect of Hesu Kristu Tavástara to resurrect each of the devils with his little saber (a "sword" like the one carried by San Miguel in Catholic iconography). But although the Chucho revives each of the casualties, many of them still seem to carry the effects of their symbolic death. They wander around in a daze "curing" each other as if they were ritual healers or carefully examining the strange faces, bodies, and clothing of the observers who have come to see the spectacle. Others engage in languid cow-dung fights, their comical battle seeming to take place on some mystical plane. This brief ritual death seems to foreshadow the coming self-sacrifice of their lustful, devilish selves, even as it mocks that destiny. The centurions end this comic spectacle by charging through the disorderly group before galloping out of sight. When they return, their costumes have been switched so that the cross-carrying junior centurion becomes the hat-wearing and sword-carrying senior centurion. This switch in the middle of the devils' "war" is another sign of growing political and moral reversal in the town brought about by the death of Hesu Kristu Tavástara.

With the centurions back among them, the two armies then continue past each other, sending out spies and receiving back messages until they meet at another field on the opposite side of town where the battle is repeated, ending their war. Once this second battle is completed the devils enter the plaza from the opposite gate from which they left several hours earlier. The culminating procession of Holy Week takes place after this war.

Like the earlier procession with Joseph and Dolores, this one is also structured like those of the previous day, but now the Holy Sepulcher—the symbol of the dead Hesu Kristu Tavástara—is the focus. All of the saints, as well as the apostles' cross (now carried horizontally), are carried behind this shroud-covered platform. Like the earlier processions, this one also pauses at each of the twelve crosses that stand around the town, symbolically connecting them with the image of the deceased (rather than crucified) Hesu Kristu Tavástara. This procession also ends back in the church, at which point the apostles and other church officers become passive spectators in the symbolic overthrow of their world.

As night falls, the judíos/devils briefly return to the plaza before a house-to-house search for the sandals of *El Nazareno*, a Judas character who is said to be "the saint" of the judíos. This pursuit of El Nazareno is carried out by two groups of devils, who follow their respective centurions in opposite directions along the same path that was earlier followed by the "owls" of the Festival of the Deceased and then by the pachiteros preceding Lent. This trail leads the devils through each of the Náyari houses of Santa Teresa, connecting the members of these houses with the character whose sexual "dirtiness" is soon revealed to be an outrageously magnified version of that of the devils. At each of the houses a captain calls out that they have come from "Santa Rosalena" and that they are looking for El Nazareno. The people within the house respond that he is not there, but that they have his sandals, and so they hand out a piece of cooked maize dough in the shape of a footprint to the centurion, who hides it away in his shoulder bag. Occasionally during these visits, the devils will make mocking reference to the Urraca dancers, who sometimes visit particular houses as part of saint's day festivals. As in the case with those dancers, the devils put on performances in order to win the favor of the householders. But instead of doing beautifully choreographed matachine dances, the devils do dances meant to resemble the wild animals that are characteristic of Santa Rosalena, that is, the wild lands "outside" (tyat+ki) from which they are said to come. Their lewd dances are meant to represent the movements of turtles, snakes, mountain lions, and other animals, and they demand payment in alcohol and cigarettes, rather than in the form of the pure chocolate, coffee, and pastries that the Urraca dancers request. The devils proceed in this way from house to house through the night, continuing the lewd mockery of church ceremonies that is characteristic of their own "saint's" day, the final day of the Holy Week Festival.

*

On Saturday of Holy Week—the final day of the Holy Week Festival in Santa Teresa—people say that "everything is inside out" (Spanish: *todo al revés*). In a general sense, this statement refers to all the upsetting interruptions of daily life that the Holy Week Festival causes, including the closing of shops and the imposition of arbitrary "laws" by the devils, as well as the political and legal interruption that is marked by the transfer of the courthouse officers' staffs-of-office to the centurions within the church. But in a more specific sense, this statement refers to the "inside-out" behavior of the devils themselves throughout this final day of the Holy Week Festival. Significantly, this behavior is associated with "la gloria," the moment when the heart of Hesu Kristu Tavástara is said to ascend to heaven after the long journey through the world of people that began at the time of the Festival of the Deceased. On the Saturday of Holy Week, then, one half of the year-long Day-of-the-Dead/Holy-Week cycle comes to an end with the killing of "the other brother." From this death, "Our Older Brother" (San Miguel Xúrave) then emerges during the rainy season. Unlike his younger brother who commits "sins" on earth, San Miguel Xúrave appears as the rains and so remains disembodied and distant from the concerns of people.

On Saturday of Holy Week, the devils' "inside-out" behavior is focused on a final procession. This procession is meant as a burlesque of the somber processions of the previous days, and scandalously ridicules their seriousness as the devils thumb their noses at the death of Hesu Kristu Tavástara. The lazy and drunken preparations for this procession begin well after sunrise at the house of the senior centurion. There the devils again paint themselves black and white, but now they substitute multicolored dye for the red paint that they wore the previous day. This dye, like their multicolored crepe-paper hats, refers back to the Pachitas Festival. However, in the context of this inside-out procession this reference becomes malevolent; the innocent sexuality of the pachiteros is replaced by the morbid lustfulness of the devils. To finish off their costumes, the devils now wear their rolled-up pants inside-out and backwards, a reference to

the similar clothing that is used to cover the grotesquely sexualized figures of El Nazareno and his "wife," who finally appear as the focus of this
procession after the devils' night-long pursuit.

These two images are the same human size and shape as the flowery
figure of Tayaxuk+ that was earlier made during the Festival of the Deceased, but they are made of dry straw. Like the clothing of the devils, the
Tereseño-style clothing of these straw figures is put on backwards and
inside-out. The closest affinity between El Nazareno (and his wife) and
the devils, however, is signified by the hugely distended genitals that are
attached to these figures. These genitals are modeled out of a century-
plant flower-spike and leaf, respectively, and are fastened by the devils in
their appropriate positions on each of the straw figures. The devils identify closely with these figures and try to top each other in their sexual attention to them. One may pantomime the masturbation of El Nazareno,
which causes another to feign copulation with the "wife," which causes
another to drink the "semen" from El Nazareno's agave penis as if it were
fine tequila, and so on.

Once these two straw figures have been dressed and fitted with their
genitals, each is then placed on the back of a burro. Such burros are nota-
ble for their long black penises, which are similar in shape to El Nazareno's century-plant penis (and to the sabers carried by the devils) and
in color to the black paint that is a distinctive feature of the devils. Pairs
of devils seated facing each other are placed on more of these shaky-
legged burros and with strong blows the beasts are compelled to move
forward. The remaining devils surround these unfortunate animals with
their reed "lances" and the mounted devils begin to sing. Rather than using the hand-printed hymnals of the elderly singers in the earlier processions of Holy Week, however, the devils sing from pieces of century plant
that have been cut to resemble books. Instead of singing the mysterious
songs of the church, they sing, "Perdido ha Cristo Jesús"—backwards Spanish for "Jesus Christ has lost." The depravity of this public spectacle
clearly suits the vulgar devils, but also represents a moral low point that
relates both to the death of Hesu Kristu Tavástara and to the absence of
civil authority under the elders of the town.

This motley procession, with the grossly sexualized figures of El Nazareno and his wife as its focus, eventually arrives at the plaza, where it makes a counterclockwise circuit around the crosses. After this circuit has been completed, the straw figures are removed from their burros and are deposited in the same spot near the church where sweepings and old flowers are dumped during the year. The reed lances carried by the devils are laid on either side of this dumping ground, just as they had earlier been laid on either side of the entrance to the church.

After El Nazareno and his wife have taken their places, the devils are forced by their centurions to sit on the ground facing each other in two single-file lines extending out into the plaza from the front of the church. They form a long, narrow corridor to the opening of the church as they sit at a type of obscene attention, sabers held upright between their legs like the century-plant phalluses of their "saint"—El Nazareno. The centurions dismount, and with five selected devils they charge down this passageway, storming the church. Inside the church, the centurions and devils kneel below the slightly raised space occupied by the church's pantheon and rap the wooden plank that edges this space five times with the butts of their upright sabers as a message to the saints above them. Outside, all of the devils who are seated in the plaza also thump their saber-erections five times in the dirt, signaling the completion of the grisly job of killing Hesu Kristu Tavástara that was passed on to them from the pachiteros.

Suddenly, the centurions with their devils are expelled from the church, seemingly thrown back by some kind of strong, repulsive force. They all roll out the door as the bells sound and rockets explode in the air. People report that these rockets announce the Glory, the moment when the heart of Hesu Kristu Tavástara rises to heaven. This moment also marks the end of the whole ceremonial cycle of which this festival is a part, which will then begin again with the coming rainy season (and so the emergence of "the other brother").

To mark this transition, the devils turn against their centurions, who, acting as if they were in a panic, brush themselves off outside the church and run together in a counterclockwise direction around the inside of the

plaza. At each of the crosses one of the centurions fights through a gaunt-
let of devils, while the other knocks over the cross. The centurions then
mount their horses and try to leave the devils behind as they charge off
in a counterclockwise direction to the crosses marking the outer path
around the town, where they fell each of these crosses in a similar manner. During this chase, the courthouse authorities take the opportunity
to cross the plaza into the church where they retrieve their bundled staffs-
of-office and bring them back to the courthouse. Next to them a violinist begins to play and someone dances on a wooden foot-drum called in
Spanish a *tarima*, which is associated with the civil offices of the cargo
system. Daily order has been restored in the courthouse and the cargo-
system officers are once again the legitimate authorities of the town of
Santa Teresa. Correspondingly, the centurions lose their authority and
promptly fall prisoners to the devils.

When the group of centurions and devils arrives back in the plaza, the
frustrated devils pull both of the centurions from their horses, interrog-
ating them over and over again as they push them from cross to cross inside the plaza. They seem to confuse Hesu Kristu Tavástara (who was earlier placed symbolically on those crosses) and the sexualized Judas
character, saying in Náyari, "Where is El Nazareno?" (*onyi h+renye + nazareno?*). The centurions feign ignorance, and the devils take the distinctive hat that the centurion received from the malinche and replace it with
one of their own crepe-paper decorated hats. Meanwhile, other devils
close off the gates that serve as entrances to the plaza in order to trap the
centurions inside. The centurions are also given sabers and bottles of liquor in order to trick them into joining the devils and revealing the location of El Nazareno. The centurions play along, dancing and fighting
good-naturedly with the devils, and then suddenly make a break. They
use the commotion created by the mass of devils in the plaza as a distrac-
tion, and escape through the crowd to hide.

Eventually the centurions are found, and the devils drag them to a
wooden framework in the center of the plaza. There they are symbolically hanged as their new crepe-paper hats are strung up. But the centurions escape five times, each time hiding farther away and struggling

harder against the devils who drag them back towards the plaza. Finally, on the fifth escape, a pair of boys is recruited to act as bloodhounds to sniff out the centurions once and for all. They sniff along the edges of the plaza, drawn particularly to the skirts of women who are seated there observing the spectacle. These women break into hysterical laughter as the boys root inside the folds of their long dresses. Eventually, however, this is exactly where these boys find the centurions, who have slyly hidden under the skirts of two different women in the confusion of the hunt.

These centurions, now defeated, lead the devils across the plaza to the figures of El Nazareno and his wife, and offer them to the devils. The devils relish what seems to be their culminating moment of power, but this power only draws them deeper into the immoral world of their "saint." They celebrate this immorality with a final symbolic inversion, a nadir of outrageous "backwardness" that marks their final and absolute low point and so leads to their redemption as the festival comes to a close.

A pair of devils is selected to receive the cloths and genitals of El Nazareno and his wife. The devil playing El Nazareno immediately grabs hold of his long century-plant penis and starts brandishing it at his "spouse," who takes her huge century-plant vulva and runs off to hide with her "sisters," the women who are sitting around the plaza. El Nazareno gives chase, slamming his penis against the walls and shoving its juicy end into the faces of the women that he passes. He finally catches up with his wife, who briefly feigns modesty before spreading her legs wide to reveal the fruit of her husband's desires. This pair continues around the plaza humping each other to the roaring laughter of the crowd, the final outrage of a grotesquely violent and sexual festival.

This culminating "backwardness," however, also exhausts the devils. As the festival comes to an end, they proceed to tear the leftover straw figures of El Nazareno and his wife into pieces, ripping out their own "dirtiness" in the process. This straw is taken to the center of the plaza, where it is lit on fire. The reeds that served as lances are dragged through this fire and leaned against the raised framework that was earlier used to hang the centurions, and all the devils warm their feet and jump through the fire, "in order to remove our sins" (Spanish: *para quitar nuestros pe-*

cados). The sinful "devil" within each of the young men also seems to be exorcised in this fire, burned out in order to reveal a renewed sense of austere strength. At this point people say, "The festival is over" (Spanish: *ya se acabó la fiesta*).

As the fire dies down, all the young men who portrayed the devils are called to the courthouse, where a speech is delivered by an elder. He tells them that the festival has definitely concluded and that they should go and bathe in the creek where they first painted themselves at the beginning of the festival. At this point in the festival the devils are also periodically asked to begin the job of re-roofing one of the community buildings that surrounds the plaza by tearing down its old straw thatch (as they previously tore apart the straw El Nazareno and his wife). This communal labor symbolizes the authority that has now been fully returned to the courthouse officials. Moreover, it also points out the role that these young men play in providing unbridled vitality and energy to the old men of the courthouse, whose "strength" in fasting is too often weak. In their confused anarchy, the devils also clean out the "dirtiness" of these all-too-human traditional authorities.

In summary, the ceremonies of the Day-of-the-Dead/Holy-Week cycle in Santa Teresa should be understood in terms of their relation to a particular spoken narrative. This context provides meanings that allow a ceremonial participant (or an interested outsider) to interpret the symbols that are mobilized within the Holy Week Festival, as it also links the fate of those individual participants with the moral and political lessons that are played out in that forum. Perhaps the most interesting character to emerge out of the whole symbolic narrative created by the juxtaposition of this ceremonial cycle to Don Goyo's text is "Jesus Christ," the character referred to as Hesu Kristu Tavástara by Tereseños. At the time of the Festival of the Deceased, he seems to be a child of the deceased ancestors, a token that is passed from them to the living courthouse authorities as the rainy season ends. But as the ceremonial cycle unfolds, so does the figure of Hesu Kristu Tavástara. After he is born onto the earth during the

Christmas Festival he becomes enmeshed in the world of humans. This earthly existence is initially symbolized through the figure of San Miguel Sáutari, the innocently sexual "flower-cutter." However, as the sexuality of Sáutari and the humans among whom he travels remains undiminished, Sáutari also changes, and a more deeply embedded aspect of this character is revealed—the figure of the lustful "devil" that serves as a counterpoint to Sáutari's innocence.

During Holy Week this "devil," embodied by the judíos, turns the world upside down. In doing so, the dirty part of the embedded Sáutari character kills himself in his own sexual frenzy so that "the other brother" might appear. The young men who portray the devils are meant to identify with Sáutari, and like him they should pass through their sinfulness in order to eventually sacrifice this part of themselves as they take on the bodily restraint that is required of courthouse authorities. This sacrifice—at the moment of "the Glory"—both returns Sáutari to his mother and releases the elderly aspect of Tavástara as Xúrave the Elder Brother to begin his own brief journey, passing over the earth as the pure rains. "The heart of Hesu Kristu Tavástara becomes the Morning Star," people in Santa Teresa say, "but that is also a lesson that we will be dying that way."

For the cargo officers of Santa Teresa, this lesson provides them with a particular moral standpoint, a clear position as legitimate traditional authorities in relation to the male youths (and women) of the ranches. Although during the course of the Day-of-the-Dead/Holy-Week Festival cycle the cargo-system authorities of Santa Teresa are represented as weak and lazy (through the banana-stools that serve as their "thrones"), it also becomes clear that they are far better than the unrestrained young men who portray the devils. They, more than anyone else in the community, must at least attempt to provide an example of purposeful restraint. They must abandon their own impulsive wishes in order to focus on the ceremonies that they have received from generations of deceased community-level ceremonial elders. These unifying ceremonies include not only the Day-of-the-Dead/Holy-Week cycle, but also the pair of community mitote ceremonies that serve to reproduce the sense of hierarchical inclusiveness upon which the legitimacy of these offices is based. As in the Day-of-the-Dead/Holy-Week cycle, these community mitote ceremonies mobilize sets of symbols that position cargo-system officers (but particularly ceremonial elders, consejeros, and governors) as the unitary, "higher" authorities over all of the other maize-bundle-group elders and their respective descent-group members and territories. This whole set of "customs," then, provides a distinctive place for cargo-system officers as the legitimate traditional authorities in Santa Teresa.

Although explained in some detail here, this point—that respect for local authorities is based on the ceremonies and festivals—would have been completely obvious to Náyari people in Santa Teresa during the time of my fieldwork. But even as Tereseños were aware of the unifying political possibilities implicit in their ceremonial traditions, they were equally cognizant of the fact that this costumbre had reached a crisis point because of the violence that threatened to overtake it. Perhaps less well understood, however, were the specific historical processes that had led to this crisis point. After all, neither drinking nor violence was new to Santa Teresa during the time of my fieldwork. Indeed, both were institutionalized as part of Santa Teresa's Holy Week Festival. Why, then, had drunkenness and violence had such a profound effect on the ability of Tereseños to successfully continue their ceremonial traditions and so live together? Tereseños asked me, "Why are we killing each other?"

In the following chapters I take up this question directly, and argue that a historical analysis of local ceremonial traditions in terms of regional and national political changes provides the key to answering it. Specifically, I trace the gradual erosion of the relationship between descent-group and cargo-system ceremonies in the context of larger historical changes that affected the region following the Lozada Rebellion of the nineteenth century. With this analysis, the particular importance of recent violence becomes clear: beyond the misery and suffering that it caused at a personal level, it also acted as a wedge aimed at the most critical point of a long-simmering political contradiction—the contradiction between local, ceremonially based traditional authority and forms of political power linked to unevenly expanding municipal and national governments.

6

The Politics of Tereseño Ceremonialism
in Historical Perspective (PART 2)

We no longer do these festivals like our ancestors,
who passed them down to us.

FELIPE RAMOS

NÁYARI/VECINO STRUGGLES, 1873–1965

The exact history of the emergence of Santa Teresa's integrated descent-group and community-level costumbre may never be known. Was the elaboration of this ceremonially reproduced symbolic discourse the result of a gradual evolution? Or did a unified council of indigenous elders issue explicit directives? What seems certain, however, is that elements of mitote ceremonialism and Catholic-derived ceremonialism were recombined in symbolically important ways as part of a single public ceremonial tradition centered at politically autonomous and sovereign towns (Warner 1998). The "toritos," for example, were elaborated upon and moved from the mission-derived matachines dance (Rodríguez 1996: 108) to take their place as part of a distinct ceremony with very clear links to Holy Week. Likewise, the malinche and monarco (who may themselves have begun as members of the town's matachines dance group; see Jáuregui and Bonfiglioli 1996) also became associated with

Holy Week in ways that built on the previously carnivalesque (but strictly pre-Lenten) character of the Pachitas Festival. Additionally, the Festival of the Deceased was also tied to Christmas and Holy Week in ways that no missionary or priest could have found acceptable. To a lesser extent, mitote ceremonialism also changed during this period. The centrally important chánaka pole, for example, may have originated as a maypole of the type that is commonly associated with Catholic-introduced matachines dances (Rodríguez 1996: 19). Similarly, during the time of my fieldwork pachiteros brought an image of Guadalupe from the church to the community parched maize mitote ceremony and danced and played their distinctive music as part of that ceremony. Even at maize-bundle-group mitote ceremonies, flowers, arches, crossing motions, and other symbols refer to the community-level cargo system and its Day-of-the-Dead/Holy-Week cycle.

This reconstituted public ceremonial tradition provided a foundation for local men to act as the legitimate traditional political authorities of Cora towns within Manuel Lozada's nineteenth-century military confederation. By the end of the nineteenth century, however, federal troops under Porfirio Díaz had pacified most of the region, and the Sierra del Nayar was administered by newly appointed Vecino church and government officials as part of the Mexican Republic. During this period these Vecinos began to represent themselves as the natural leaders of the region in opposition to the Náyari officials appointed through the integrated community-level costumbres that had developed during the earlier part of that century (and perhaps before). As a result, the post-Lozada pacification of the Sierra del Nayar also began a long series of political struggles for control of these communities between local Náyarite and newly arriving (or returning) Vecino settlers and merchants.

Both Lumholtz and Preuss offer comments that indicate the state of interethnic relations between Náyarite and Vecinos in the Sierra del Nayar during the Porfirian period at the end of the nineteenth century. For example, Lumholtz noted that Santa Teresa was frequented by Vecino traders (Lumholtz 1902: 505) and had a literate "prefect," presumably a Vecino, as well as a Vecino schoolteacher who had worked in the town for several years. Later, as Lumholtz left the town, the Náyari alcalde of Santa Teresa gave him a message "to ask the Mexican Government to let them keep their old customs, which he had heard they were going to prohibit." He also asked Lumholtz to use his influence to "prevent the whites [Vecinos] from settling in the vicinity, since they were eager to get at the big forests" (Lumholtz 1902: 496).

In Jesús María, Lumholtz noted the presence of twenty Vecinos "counting the children" (Lumholtz 1902: 503), all of whom were poor and living in the convent of the church, which was attended by a secular priest from the mostly Vecino town of San Juan Peyotán. At that time, these Vecinos had no lands of their own and instead rented agricultural plots and worked as peons for the Náyarite of Jesús María. By 1906, however, Preuss (1998b: 127) noted that the Vecino population in Jesús María, "the regional seat of the government and the church," had risen to 100 compared to the Náyari population of 1500 inhabitants, but he did not discuss the social relations between these two groups. Other documents make it clear that in the years following the Lozada period, Vecino traders and ranchers, now allied with the few secular priests (themselves Vecinos) who replaced Franciscan missionaries in the area as a result of the Juárez reforms of 1867 (Rojas 1993: 142), increasingly expanded their presence and influence in the region. This documentary record, from small mission and community archives in Santa Teresa, is in no way complete. But by comparing the family names mentioned in these documents with those of people still living in the Sierra del Nayar, a general sense of the struggles between the Náyarite and Vecinos during this period emerges. In this chapter, I cite these records from typed copies made during my fieldwork in Santa Teresa.

The most compelling issue to emerge from documents dating to the Porfirian period at the end of the nineteenth century in the Sierra del Nayar deals with the legal recognition of land claims. For example, a copy of a document signed December 18, 1889 (which I was not able to copy), describes in detail the territorial boundaries of Santa Teresa. This document seems to have been contracted by local officials in Santa Teresa in response to an unknown *compañía deslindadora* (Spanish: surveying company) that was operating in the region at that time. Beatriz Rojas points out that these surveying companies, which won legal title to huge expanses of "unoccupied lands" (Spanish: *terrenos baldíos*) in Mexico under the agrarian laws of Porfirio Díaz, drew up maps in Tepic that showed "the intention of taking over all of the Cora country" (Rojas 1993: 150). In the Sierra del Nayar such large-scale expropriation did not take place, but the above-cited document seems to have been drafted in response to the threat that these companies represented. As in the Huichol country that Rojas discusses, these companies allied themselves with regional Vecinos "who entered little by little with pretexts and false friendships" (Rojas 1993: 150) in order to draw up privately contracted maps to be used as de facto legal titles consolidating stolen lands.

A number of documents were also drafted by individual Náyarite at the same time for the purpose of creating their own legal deeds to particular lands within the community limits of Santa Teresa. For example, on June 5, 1901, Norberto Flores signed a document that was meant to establish his ownership of a "plot that is on the north side of this same plaza whose property is acknowledged by inheritance from his deceased father Tomás Flores" (p. 1). Similarly, at three o'clock in the afternoon on August 6, 1900, Venancio Campos signed a document claiming that he had lost the property titles of his deceased parents Bacilio Campos and Juana Ramos Ortiz. His newly created deed described the boundaries of his small plot in careful detail: "It is located on the stream that runs from north to south next to the plots that pertain to Gumercindo Santos and Tomás Salazar, and its borders lie on the other side of the above-mentioned stream having an extension in that direction of 93.2 meters and on the west and east having an extension of 13.9 meters and on the north 64 meters and on the south 47 meters, an area that includes the house in which he lives and 15 apple trees and 3 peach trees" (p. 2). A number of other inheritance documents from this same period are equally detailed in their accounting of lands, fruit trees, and other property. In every case these documents seem to have been drawn up in response to perceived threats against specific lands and properties in Santa Teresa made by Vecinos settling in the area during the Porfirian period.

A variety of other documents provide a basis for the fear of Vecino expansion expressed to Lumholtz by the Náyari alcalde of Santa Teresa in 1898. For example, in 1895 the teacher Melitón Comparan, whose wife Lumholtz (1902: 491) described as a "Mexican [Vecino], who apparently took her lot very contentedly 'among these people whom no one ever knows,' as she expressed it," is recorded as taking charge of a grammar school in Santa Teresa. By 1905 Santa Teresa's "National School number 39" is recorded as having been in continuous operation, presumably still under the authority of a Vecino teacher.

The sale of livestock also helps to account for the increasing presence of Vecinos in Santa Teresa during the Porfirian period. At least two Vecino cattle traders, Amador Madera from Valparaiso, Zacatecas, and Secundino Soliz from Acaponeta, Nayarit, are recorded as dealing in livestock with the Cora Juan Salazar in 1895 (p. 5). Much more livestock trading must have been taking place, but unfortunately this is the only document mentioning the cattle trade that remains in Santa Teresa's archives from the Porfirian period.

Like the previously mentioned inheritance documents, this document was drafted by the *juez de paz* (Spanish: civil judge), to whom Lumholtz referred as the "prefect" of Santa Teresa. During the Porfirian period, this judge in Santa Teresa was subordinate to a Vecino official in Jesús María who was appointed directly by Mexican president Porfirio Díaz to be in charge of the "Political Sub-Prefecture of the Sierra." In 1905 this office was held by the Vecino José María Arellano, with another Vecino named Camilo M. Martinez serving as his secretary (p. 2). At the time, these Vecino officials claimed complete political authority over the traditional officeholders who were appointed as part of the costumbre that Lumholtz and Preuss both observed during this period.

A document located in the mission archives of Santa Teresa also shows that the attitudes of secular priests, whom Lumholtz reported had protected Vecinos around the church in Jesús María, seem to have allied them with regional Vecino cattle merchants and politicians against the Náyarite. For example, on page 102 of his "inventory, inspection and register" the priest Manuel Estragues writes of his inspection of Jesús María during

Holy Week in 1884: "This tribe finds itself within absolute religious ignorance, observing various remnants of pagan practices and poor imitations of gentilism, many of which I could observe in the Holy Week that
just ended. These wretches practice various ceremonies that seem more
like jokes or comic imitations of everything that the Holy Church practices on these solemn days. Most repugnant to human morals are certain
obscene actions that in their nakedness they observe in public places
without any other costume or mask than to paint themselves over their
entire body."

This document also reflects the Vecinos' attitude towards the Náyari
political authorities who received their offices through the practice of
their costumbre. For example, on page 91 of this document Estragues
writes of the many questions put to him by the authorities of Santa Teresa:
"The governors, that is what the civil judges are called, are known to
confer and ask a thousand questions of the priest, all of which touch on
cases of public law and justice." A decade later Lumholtz (1902: 490–
491) had a similar reaction to the persistent questioning directed to him
by Tereseño authorities: "Anything coming from Mexico impresses these
people deeply . . . the Indians could not hear the documents read over
often enough." For Lumholtz, as well as for the priest Estragues, this
grave interest represented some type of naive foolishness typical of "Indians." But for Náyari authorities of the time, the documents brandished by
Lumholtz, Estragues, and the new Vecino authorities of the region must
have seemed like the first signs of an ominous new legalistic mode of political power that harkened back to the colonial period. It is not surprising, then, that these traditional officeholders might have exhibited a certain dubiousness towards the self-important Vecinos who used these
documents as justification to settle the region during the Porfirian period.

Vecino settlement of the Sierra del Nayar continued without break
through the Mexican Revolution and into the Cristero Wars that
emerged in reaction to post-revolutionary reforms aimed at neutralizing
the power of the church in Mexico. However, documents from Santa Teresa suggest that a number of local Náyari families also allied themselves

with Vecinos representing the post-revolutionary national government during that time. Indeed, people in Santa Teresa pointed out to me that it was precisely in this period—after the end of the Mexican Revolution and during the Cristero Wars—that contemporary divisions during the period of my fieldwork between Tereseños who supported the post-revolutionary government and those who opposed (or ignored) it began.

In Santa Teresa, I often heard stories of "*la revolución*" told at night around the hearth or open fire. It was difficult to know whether "the revolution" of which older people spoke referred to any clearly delimited period, or whether they were instead collapsing together the several decades of banditry and war that engulfed the Sierra del Nayar during the Cristero Wars, the Mexican Revolution, and even earlier conflicts. Such stories, however, do offer some clues that help shed light on the little-known history of the Sierra del Nayar during this turbulent period. Braulio Salazar, for example, was born in 1910 and claims to remember the Mexican Revolution. He told me of how his father fought with Pancho Villa at Zacatecas, eventually returning from that battle with a rifle and a mule, only to be killed by another band of Villistas near the town of San Miguel Zapote. Perhaps Salazar's father fought with the Vecino Rafael Buelna, who had established a Villista military headquarters in the Náyari town of Jesús María during this period, and who from there "dominated a large part of this area of the Sierra Madre" (Rojas 1993: 164). Or perhaps Buelna and his men killed Salazar's father and his band. It is difficult to know, but Rojas (1993: 164) is surely close to the mark when she writes that "at this level Villism and banditry were nearly the same thing." Other stories told around the fire corroborate documents found in Santa Teresa's archives, and clearly show that this banditry continued in the Sierra del Nayar well after the post-revolutionary government in Mexico City pacified central Mexico in 1920.

Many of the stories I heard told of a final battle during the revolution fought against Cristero (or post-Cristero) "bandits" (Spanish: *bandidos* or *malditos*). According to Braulio Salazar, for example, Santa Teresa and all of the other Náyari communities supported the post-revolutionary government during this period. In return, the new federal government supplied these Náyari communities with arms to defend themselves against the Cristeros who roamed the region. Salazar, himself a cold-blooded man who once bragged to me of hanging a cattle thief, eventually joined Santa Teresa's government-sponsored Rural Defense Brigade (Spanish: *la defensa*). He described the bandits he fought as groups of gunmen composed of Tepehuans from the towns of San Francisco Ocotán and Santa María Ocotán and Vecinos from the town of Huazamota. A document in the community archives of Santa Teresa dated February 15, 1939, indicates something of the tension that existed between these bandits and government-sponsored Rural Defense Brigades in the Sierra del Nayar at that time. In it a Vecino named Martín Nieves, who was acting as the local judge in Santa Teresa, addresses the "Governor of the Tepehuan tribe in San Francisco Ocotán": "In this headquarters I communicate to you in your present office and make manifest that you maintain in peace the Vecinos of the headquarters under your authority and that you do not get mixed up in affairs that do not concern you, and that you keep quiet and do not tell lies so that none are told to you. We here know full well and have good reason to believe that you all are ready to attack and kill us. Here there is no one in opposition [to the government], nor are there any rebels. In any case, here we are [ready to fight you]" (p. 13). Maximilio Morales Hernández told me that the battle to which this document refers was eventually fought at a ranch called Las Cruces, near the mountain called Cerro Paloma that serves as a de facto boundary between the lands of Santa Teresa and those of San Francisco Ocotán. During that battle a small force of between twenty and thirty Tereseños defeated a much larger group of Tepehuans and Vecinos, forcing them to turn away from Santa Teresa and down the river towards Huazamota. According to Ygnacio Orozco, who is himself a Vecino from that neighboring town, Huazamota was divided at that time between those who supported the post-revolutionary government represented there by Tiburcio Muñoz, and others who followed the former Villista Florencio Estrada as rebels. When Estrada and the rest of his group were defeated at Las Cruces, they proceeded to burn all of the towns from San Pedro Jícora to San Juan Peyotán along the Jesús María River. From there they climbed into the mountains to the east where government forces eventually caught up with them at the ranch of Tierras Coloradas outside the town of Santa Lucía de la Sierra. My friend Amadeo Flores's father participated in that battle, and described to him the dead that lay scattered over the ground after the rebels were defeated by forces loyal to the post-revolutionary government.

But if in telling stories of the revolution people focus on the defeat of these bandits, and so on their own unity against aggressive outsiders, other Tereseños also point out that it was precisely during this period that the ongoing division in Santa Teresa between pro- and anti-government factions began. By 1920 the government that some Tereseños supported was headed by the Vecino military leader (Spanish: *jefe de armas*) Mariano Mejía, who presumably took over the military headquarters at Jesús María in the wake of the constitutionalist capture of that position (Rojas 1993: 163). Initially Mejía seems to have headed one of the "small bands of Villistas" (Rojas 1993: 164) that operated in the area during the Mexican Revolution. By 1920, however, he both represented the post-revolutionary government and armed the Rural Defense Brigades that had been established in each of the Náyari towns of the Sierra del Nayar.

Mejía's Vecino-based administration in Jesús María also defended the interests of the Vecino cattle merchants and ranchers who increasingly operated in the region. The scale of this regional cattle trade is attested by documents in Santa Teresa's archives. In what is surely an incomplete record, between 1920 and 1923 at least 548 heads of cattle are recorded as being bought from Santa Teresa alone. The buyers of these cattle were nearly all Vecinos, with last names like Meir, Sisneros, Ruiz, Garay, Durán, and Muñoz. Most of the vendors of this livestock in Santa Teresa were Náyarite, with last names like (in descending order of importance) Salazar, Morales, Ortiz, Soto, Aguilar, Noriega, Valencia, Flores, Zepeda, Galindo, and Espinosa. A number of Vecinos, however, are also recorded as selling cattle and living in Santa Teresa at the time. These included Casimiro and Regino Blanco, Pablo Mitrí, Rogelio Escobedo, and, most importantly, José Medina. Medina was referred to in 1920 as "a native and vecino [Spanish: *originario y Vecino*] of this place who has always dedicated himself to commerce" (p. 8). A number of his sons eventually became important Vecino leaders in Santa Teresa during the time of my fieldwork. Like José Medina, other resident Vecino cattle traders in Santa Teresa seem to have taken advantage of the support offered by Mariano Mejía's regional military government and its dependent local Rural Defense Brigade to settle in Santa Teresa and to consolidate their spheres of commercial influence. Documents also show, however, that the Rural Defense Brigade and allied local officials generated an opposing faction of Tereseños who refused to submit to the authority of this faction, and who used the costumbre as a platform to challenge their legitimacy.

In 1920 Santa Teresa's Rural Defense Brigade was under the authority of a resident Vecino named Julio Orozco, a Huazamotecan. By at least 1932, however, a local Tereseño man named Estanislau Valencia had been appointed by Vecino authorities in Jesús María as Santa Teresa's *jefe de la defensa* (Spanish: Rural Defense Brigade chief), a position that he occupied until his violent death in 1942. During this period Estanislau Valencia and a group of other Tereseños not only supervised the distribution of arms for use in defense of the community against "bandits," but also served as the eyes, ears, and throats of Jesús María's Vecino leaders in Santa Teresa. Although no records remain to explain the specific events that led Vecino leaders in Jesús María to name Estanislau Valencia as the military leader of Santa Teresa's Rural Defense Brigade, it is tempting to see a connection between his appointment and a killing that occurred in 1932.

On March 18 of that year the auxiliary judge of Santa Teresa was taken to a house that had burned in the ranch of Tepeistes, about ten kilometers from the center of Santa Teresa. There he encountered "a burned straw-thatched house, and in its rubble the remains of a human cadaver with its abdomen entirely burned that in life was called Manuel Ortiz Santos" (p. 1). In the weeks following this discovery the brothers Loreto and Florentino Salazar were accused of murdering Manuel Ortiz because he was a *hechicero* (Spanish: sorcerer): "[Loreto Salazar] had been informed that Manuel Ortiz wanted to hurt him, that is to curse him, and that among he and his brother Florentino and other persons they had thought to take his life because he was a bad man and that in any case no one in the town liked him and that he was good for nothing" (p. 11). Both of these brothers, however, eventually presented alibis, and the blame was placed on a man named Manuel Campos who, along with Miguel and Tadeo Ortiz (Manuel's brothers), confessed to beating Manuel Ortiz to death before burning the house and fleeing (p. 11). It is unclear whether this crime and the sorcery accusations that followed it reflect a more widespread political instability in Santa Teresa. Still, documents clearly show that by the following year Estanislau Valencia and the judge who worked with him were attempting to crack down on a perceived disorder in the community.

Shortly after the New Year's Festival on January 20, 1933, for example, a document attests to the confiscation and burning—"on higher authority" (Spanish: *por órdenes superiores*)—of some liquor that a pair of Vecinos were selling in Santa Teresa. Then, on April 12, the Jesús María–appointed judge signed a document along with Estanislau Valencia as leader of the Rural Defense Brigade warning the centurions to avoid the drunkenness and disorder that seem to have characterized the town's Holy Week festivals in the previous years: "To Mr. Florentino Salazar and Mr. Wenseslau Noriega, leaders of the Holy Week Festival [Spanish: *judea*] in this place. I order that in the festival that is celebrated beginning from today to Saturday that you should avoid scandals without allowing the presence of any liquor in these days, nor that the boys in school paint themselves, advising you that if you do not complete the above-expressed orders you both will be responsible for the disorder that is committed and you will be punished according to that crime, which I communicate to you both for your information and for legal purposes" (p. 10). Later documents note that Estanislau Valencia and the judges who were working with him carried out a number of orders from Jesús María concerning recruitment for roadwork (p. 12), divorce settlements (p. 14), and the mandatory attendance of Náyari children at the new federal schools that had been reopened in Santa Teresa and Jesús María. Of these actions, this latter issue of mandatory attendance at the post-revolutionary government's federal schools, particularly the boarding school that was established in Jesús María, became a key point of opposition between those Tereseños who supported the government and those who did not.

The first Tereseño student to attend the post-revolutionary boarding school in Jesús María was Florentino Salazar (presumably the son of the centurion and suspect in the above-mentioned murder case). Salazar, now a quiet old man and a consejero, remembered that he was taken to the boarding school in Jesús María in 1934. He and all the rest of the Ná-yari students there were locked into the school at night for fear that they might flee. From the national government's perspective, such harsh measures were required "in order to incorporate into the national soul all of the indigenous tribes of the country, removing them through education from the state of backwardness and ignorance in which they have lived up to the present date" (p. 11). After a few years in the school, Florentino had proved his faithfulness and was given permission to return to Santa Teresa to visit his parents. His parents, however, refused to let him return to Jesús María. Instead, they fled the town with their son to avoid the teacher who came after him, and Florentino never returned to the school. The only other Tereseño to attend the boarding school in Jesús María during those years was Manuel Morales Rojas, who lasted only a single year there before his parents forced him to quit. According to both Florentino Salazar and Manuel Morales, their own and other parents saw this boarding school as an unwanted imposition by Vecino authorities in Jesús María, who were gradually eroding the rights of Náyarite like themselves in Santa Teresa.

Tereseños also resisted sending their children to a small day school located in the plaza of Santa Teresa, a task that was made easier by the lack of professionalism of the teachers who were recruited for that cold and isolated mountain post. In 1933, for example, a document was written to register a complaint that the teacher in Santa Teresa "does not dedicate himself to work, or to teaching the classes that he is supposed to give, . . . [and instead] he dedicates himself to his commercial enterprise" (p. 10). Despite this official protest, most Náyarite in Santa Teresa during this period did not seem to have put much pressure on this teacher to fulfill his duties, a fact that is attested by the widespread truancy of the period.

During this period, for example, the Vecino municipal commissioner Fidel Garay Parra of Jesús María wrote to the judges in Santa Teresa, ordering them to put a halt to the persistent truancy of Náyari children in Santa Teresa: "You would be served to order the family heads to without any pretext at all take their children to the school of that place, giving an accounting to this office of having completed this order. And if some family head does not follow through, then you should also provide an account of that person in order to determine subsequent proceedings" (p. 12). Later, on December 3, 1940, a new teacher named Severiano López Guevara issued similar threats against persistent Náyari truancy: "To the Governor of the Cora Tribe. Given that the work of harvest-time is now over, and parents still do not send their children to the school, which makes them subject to fine according to law, permit me to manifest to you that if you do not oblige the fathers and mothers of these families without any exception whatsoever to send their boys and girls to the School, I will communicate that fact to the Municipal President in Jesús María for him to order that which is most convenient, imposing a punishment for disobedience" (p. 14). Only five months later this teacher, who complained to his superiors of his "total desperation" (p. 14) at being stationed in the isolated town, abandoned his post in disgust. However, his letter to the authorities of Santa Teresa points out most parents' clear opposition to forced schooling in the years following the establishment of the postrevolutionary government in the region.

For a number of families in Santa Teresa, this opposition to the influence of the government and its representatives in Santa Teresa ran much deeper. The most notorious member of this group of Tereseños in opposition to the pro-government faction represented by Estanislau Valencia was a man named Cresenciano Morales, a maize-bundle-group elder whose mitote ceremony is now celebrated by his nephew Felipe Morales Morales. In 1938, for example, the auxiliary judge in Santa Teresa received a note from the Vecino municipal commissioner in Jesús María advising him that "some armed individuals headed by Cresenciano Morales are wandering around here, and they declared various issues against the town [of Santa Teresa]" (p. 12). Cresenciano Morales's group also included a number of men who were active in the community ceremonies of Santa Teresa's cargo system, and who opposed the other Tereseños who sought to represent the community based on their access to weapons and political authority from Jesús María.

People who lived through the period describe tensions between these groups as coming to a head during a particularly drunken and disorderly Holy Week Festival in the 1930s. As Manuel Morales Rojas explained, instead of concluding that festival on Saturday, the devils attacked Estanislau Valencia and other members of his Rural Defense Brigade. This group, Morales said, was particularly angry because of Valencia's involvement in a scheme with Vecino officials in Jesús María. In addition to requiring Tereseño students to attend their new boarding school, Valencia allowed Vecino officials to purchase logs from Santa Teresa's pine forest at its border with Jesús María for use as ceiling beams in that school's roof. For Tereseños opposed to Valencia and his Vecino allies, this logging, even on such a small scale, represented a threat to Santa Teresa's territorial integrity and one more incident of treason by Valencia against his own people. The symbolic reversals associated with Santa Teresa's Holy Week Festival provided the opportunity to try to eliminate Estanislau Valencia once and for all.

Estanislau Valencia and members of his Rural Defense Brigade were captured by the devils and dragged to the courthouse where they were to be jailed and perhaps executed by the cargo-system officers who had just taken over from the centurions. But as he was being jailed Valencia managed to get hold of a knife. In the struggle he was stabbed deeply in the stomach, leaving his intestines exposed. Government officials soon heard of this rebellion, and sent soldiers from Jesús María, the Mesa del Nayar, and San Francisco. These soldiers freed Valencia and his men, and took into custody the cargo-system governors who seemed to have been involved in planning the attack. These governors were initially jailed in Jesús María while Estanislau Valencia was taken overland to Tepic to undergo surgery for his wound. This surgery was successful and Valencia returned to supervise the execution of the former governors who had been returned to his custody. In the wake of this conflict, whole families fled their homes, and the Tereseño supporters of the Vecino government in Jesús María regained control of Santa Teresa's courthouse to fill its traditional cargo offices.

The people who fled Santa Teresa joined with Cresenciano Morales's group in the town of Saycota on the San Pedro River, pointedly taking the symbols of the traditional courthouse officers with them. A document written on August 27, 1939, sought the peaceful return of these people, or at least the return of the symbols of office that the Náyarite who sought to represent the government suddenly lacked: "To the judge and governor of Saycota. Item. I communicate to you that you should make the greatest commitment in saying to all of the persons who left this place that they should come and live in their houses and that they should no longer walk around outside of their lands because here they have every type of guarantee [of safety]. We also request that you endeavor to send the staffs-of-office of the Governor and of the Judge if those officials themselves cannot come right away. In any case, the staffs-of-office should be sent as soon as possible because we need them here immediately, and also the lance" (p. 13). Many of these exiles, along with the staffs-of-office and the lance, seem to have returned to Santa Teresa from Saycota in the months after this letter was sent, but tensions remained. These seemed on the verge of flaring up again in 1942, when Estanislau Valencia, the longtime leader of Santa Teresa's Rural Defense Brigade, was killed.

According to a document written shortly after the event, both Estanislau Valencia and Zenon Morales, that year's cargo-system governor and a longtime ally of Valencia's, were killed in a melee at the conclusion of the Santiago Festival: "At about five in the afternoon they killed the citizen leader of the Rural Defense Brigade Estanislau Valencia Morales about five meters from the door of the courthouse. Mr. Valencia was patrolling the area and had apprehended a subject who is a native of Dolores [near Saycota], and struggling arm-to-arm with said individual a soldier of the Rural Defense Brigade fired a shot to defend the commandant, instead hitting him five or six centimeters from the right ear, causing him to fall dead" (p. 15). Prisciliano Rivera Mejía, the Vecino municipal president of Jesús María (and nephew of former Vecino military leader Mariano Mejía), downplayed the political relevance of this killing, issuing orders that all appropriate paperwork be completed and that the guilty parties be apprehended and sent under guard to Jesús María "to avoid confusion that results from a lack of authentic news when foolish people, without any basis in fact, spread rumors or propaganda concerning the recent bloody events that occurred in Santa Teresa, which were in fact a result of a vulgar dispute among drunks, as it might be prejudicial to the tranquility of the inhabitants of this municipality" (p. 14). Perhaps the Vecino municipal president was correct to see the killing of Estanislau Valencia as a simple "dispute among drunks," because Vecino influence in Santa Teresa continued unabated in subsequent years. A group of Tereseño men drawn from the same limited group of families that had occupied the courthouse prior to the killings—men who were marginally literate and familiar with the conventions of writing government documents—continued to be appointed to the local offices of governor and judge. Thus, they continued to control the staffs-of-office and lance used in the costumbre, as well as the rubber stamps (Spanish: *sellos*) used to mark official correspondence and government directives.

By 1942 these rubber stamps carried the seal of the newly proclaimed municipality of El Nayar, and Jesús María was also referred to in official correspondence and on maps as "El Nayar," the capital of the new municipality of the same name. The ongoing influence of Tereseños faithful to the Vecino political authorities in El Nayar is demonstrated by the names of the leading political authorities in Santa Teresa between 1943 and 1952, the years immediately following the killing of Estanislau Valencia. During this period a few members of only five families (Ramos, Salazar, Flores, Carillo, and Ortiz) held most of the government-authorized offices in Santa Teresa, and these men proved to be amenable to the continued influence of Vecinos in the political and economic affairs of Santa Teresa.

During this time, for example, a small-scale tin mine was opened under the ownership of the Vecino José Ascensión Escobedo in the ranch of Abispas (p. 20). Also, a serious correspondence was begun with the Vecino Tiburcio Muñoz of Huazamota concerning the desires of William Elton Brock and Thomas H. Frothingham to begin a lumber operation in Santa Teresa. A number of surveyors had begun to map the region. They worked under the auspices of the Indigenous Affairs Department (Spanish: *departamento de asuntos indígenas*) as part of the Adolfo López Mateos Brigade (Spanish: *brigada Adolfo López Mateos*), which Salomón Nahmad (1981: 6)—an anthropologist who once headed a federal Indian agency in El Nayar—later called "an official tool for legally dispossessing the Indians of their legitimately owned lands." "Official" maps and legal titles to community lands proliferated and came to be used in shadowy attempts to obtain timber concessions from local authorities. As a result of these developments the local judges in Santa Teresa—appointed by Vecino municipal authorities in Jesús María—again found their legitimacy challenged by Tereseños whose opposition to the policies of Vecino municipal officials in Jesús María marginalized them from local offices connected to the municipal government.

A letter written on December 5, 1960, from Serafín de la Torre Muñoz, the Vecino municipal president of Jesús María, to Prudencio Medina, the Vecino livestock inspector of Santa Teresa, makes clear the inherent conflict between officials appointed in Jesús María and those appointed based on their practice of the costumbre: "My office has the good fortune of commissioning you to focus the attention of all of the citizens of that town in order to appoint as representative of this municipality a person who will act as Municipal Authority during the year of 1961. Of course, this person should be a person of good conduct and a progressive, for the benefit of that town. As soon as this commission of naming the First Judge is completed, you would be served to communicate with this office. Thanking you in advance and reiterating our close bonds . . ." (pp. 25–26). As this letter points out, in Santa Teresa only "progressives" were suitable candidates for local municipal office. Those Náyarite who opposed the mandatory schooling that was meant to educate away their "backwardness," or who opposed the development of their mineral and timber resources and the increasing control of local political affairs by Vecinos and the group of Tereseños who were allied with them, were kept from municipally approved political offices. At the same time, however, the costumbre through which local officials received their offices continued during this period, creating a growing rift between the externally appointed officials (particularly the judge) who represented the government, and all the other locally appointed officials who derived their legitimacy from the practice of public ceremonies.

The commissioning of Prudencio Medina to arbitrate the appointment of the following year's "progressive" civil judge in 1961 seems to have led to a culminating break between the pro- and anti-government factions that had been moving apart during the 1940s and 1950s. In that year a notice was sent on June 2 from the Vecino municipal president Francisco Daniel E. Torres of Jesús María—presumably based on a decision by Prudencio Medina—that the judge who had been appointed by the council of elders (whose name does not show up in these documents but presumably was a member of the anti-government faction and not a "progressive") should immediately turn his office over to a government-supported Tereseño named Mercurio Flores (p. 27). Later that month Flores sent word to the municipal president that he and Prudencio Medina were in control of the courthouse, and that he would begin the registration of children in order to force them to attend school, but also noted that he was unable to begin these activities "because the people are not in agreement" and because "the problems here have still not ended" (p. 27).

As in the earlier killing of Estanislau Valencia, these "problems" seem to have come to a head during the Festival of Santiago. During that festival a man named Everardo Ortiz was arrested by Mercurio Flores and the "progressives" who stood with him. The following day, however, a number of armed men on horseback returned to free the jailed man. After forcibly removing Ortiz from the local jail, they rode off to plan their revenge for the arrest, a threat that Flores took very seriously in a letter sent to Jesús María on July 29:

[After freeing Everardo Ortiz] they went to a place called Rancho Viejo where they are meeting and planning on assassinating all that are with me, as well as the livestock officials who are also with me [i.e., the Vecino Prudencio Medina and another unnamed official]. They want to kill us all. It is a large band, very well armed. Everything that I say is true, for which reason I ask you whether there are guarantees of governmental support [in Jesús María], because they say they have guarantees of support from Tepic and that they are waiting for people from all of the other towns to help them because they are not in agreement with the recent change of authorities. They have been waiting a long time to take over and then just send a dispatch to the state government, so this matter is of the utmost importance. (p. 27)

Events continued to be very unstable into September, when Mercurio Flores wrote another letter stating that Tercerio Salazar, who had been appointed governor of Santa Teresa that year, had also abandoned the town and had joined with the faction that had earlier been meeting in Rancho Viejo: "To the Municipal President of Jesús María. I am making known for your information that the governor is not in this place and there is information that he is wandering among the towns stirring up people to come here. To do what, we do not know. According to them, they do not want any kind of arrangements [with the Vecino government]. It is the same old problem, and it will continue until no one does anything that they do not agree to. Some say that they have gone all the way to Tepic to gossip against us and we are awaiting their return to find out the result. They are sticking to the same line; they continue with their objections" (p. 28). By October, however, any fear that the state government might intervene on the side of the ousted, traditionally appointed officers had passed, and the support that Flores had hoped for was forthcoming; the Vecino municipal president himself arrived in Santa Teresa, along with the Náyari governor of Jesús María (a man whom Fernando Benítez [1973: 27] characterized as a "renegade Cora, married to a Vecina"). Together these officials from the municipal capital were able to call a general assembly in which Tercerio Salazar was officially removed from his office and the second governor, Pedro Aguilar, was put in his place (p. 28).

In the wake of this move, killings continued, but the political relevance of these killings was no longer the same. Since the Porfirian period,

Vecinos and Náyarite had struggled to represent "the government" in the Sierra del Nayar, but by the early 1960s the shape of that government was changing. In years past, Vecinos—because of their knowledge of writing and legal procedures during times of peace, and because of their ability to marshal weapons and troops during times of war—saw themselves as the natural political leaders of the region, a progressive force in a backward country. Tereseño officials initially depended on these Vecinos in Jesús María for guns to defend themselves against "bandits," even as their own local legitimacy was at the same time based on the ceremonies that had been developed into an integrated costumbre during the nineteenth century. Opposition to this group of pro-government Tereseños emerged after the pacification of the region, when Vecino officials in the newly named municipal capital of El Nayar continued to expect the political allegiance of local authorities in Santa Teresa, even as these Vecino officials advocated policies (like mandatory schooling, Vecino settlement of Santa Teresa itself, and the development of mining and timber operations) that alienated large segments of Santa Teresa's Náyari population. As a result of this opposition, community festivals became battlegrounds between Vecino-appointed authorities with their Tereseño supporters and the other Tereseños who had been marginalized from local political representation.

By the early 1960s, however, the old struggle between Vecinos and Náyarite was complicated by a series of changes in the region. At the forefront of these changes was the arrival of a national governmental agency —the Instituto Nacional Indigenista (INI)—whose goal was to finally open Santa Teresa and the other Náyari communities of the Sierra del Nayar to modernizing economic development. To do this, political officials at both the local and the municipal levels, whether Náyari or Vecino, were simply bypassed, and change was promoted "by decree" (Rojas 1993: 195). As a result, local authorities in Santa Teresa became increasingly irrelevant to the changes going on around them and community festivals became a forum for chaotic violence that splintered previous pro- and anti-government factions.

FROM THE INSTITUTO NACIONAL INDIGENISTA TO THE FEDERAL ARMY IN SANTA TERESA, 1966–1987

Applied programs of directed cultural change aimed at Indian communities in Mexico began in the 1920s. These programs were initially promoted by progress-minded Mexican anthropologists and were proclaimed as post-revolutionary government policy by Mexican president Plutarco Elías Calles in his "Cry of Guadalajara." For Calles, *indigenismo*, the forced assimilation of isolated indigenous people into the economy and culture of Mexico, was fundamental to his larger project of "forging the fatherland" (Gamio 1916). Not surprisingly, this project was also profoundly paternalistic. The paternalism implied by this "historical identification of indigenism with Mexican nationalism" (Hewitt de Alcántara 1987: 53) continued in the policies promoted by the regional coordinating center of the Instituto Nacional Indigenista that was established in 1960 to assimilate Coras, Huichols, and Tepehuans of the Sierra del Nayar region.

Despite the heavy-handedness of Mexican indigenism, for many Tereseños the forcefulness of the new INI administration, with its promise of a direct "executive power" (Spanish: *poder ejecutivo*) emblazoned on its official seal, initially seemed to promise a break from the previous century's factional struggles between Náyarite and Vecinos. This break from previous factionalism was foreshadowed by the new political strategy taken by Tereseños opposed to Prudencio Medina's appointment to the local courthouse in 1961. Rather than again fleeing to Saycota in order to engage in sporadic skirmishes during Santa Teresa's community festivals, the anti-government faction sent a delegation to Tepic. There they sought out higher-level authorities that might defend them from arrogant exercise of power by regional Vecinos and their supporters.

By 1966 Salomón Nahmad Sitton, the new director of INI in Tepic and himself an applied anthropologist working in the tradition of Gamio, had begun a program of judicial and political reforms. These reforms were meant to resolve the nagging violence and factionalism that stood in the way of economic development in Santa Teresa and the rest of the region.

A document written by Tereseño authorities on February 14, 1966, expressed hope that a new INI-sponsored political commission might resolve tensions in the area, particularly between authorities in Santa Teresa and the groups who had fled to the area around Saycota and Dolores over the previous years:

> To the Auxiliary Judge of Dolores. By means of the present note I am making known to you that we are still waiting for the commission that I have requested in order to have a general assembly to deal with all of the issues and anomalies that are present in these towns as a result of the many problems among ourselves. For this reason, I am trying for the second time to come to some kind of agreement with some of the inhabitants that make up your town about all of the problems that exist between us. And because the county seat [Spanish: *cabecera*] has recommended that I do all of this for the well-being of our towns so that we can stop having these difficulties, I am waiting for you to come as soon as possible and talk to us and to understand us, and to put to rest all of the gossip and to forget the past.

But despite the hope for a common understanding under the new political umbrella represented by INI, this program of legal and political reforms foreshadowed a new era of divisive conflict in Santa Teresa.

Far from "forgetting the past" and "coming to some kind of agreement" as the authorities of Santa Teresa had hoped, the new "cultural promoter" (Spanish: *promotor cultural*) who was appointed to carry out INI's projects in Santa Teresa instead began to send dispatches to Nahmad Sitton in Tepic. Based on gossip and hearsay, he identified supposed perpetrators of a number of the homicides that had gone unresolved in previous years—a list of seventeen presumed killers—and then urged that the judicial police be sent to arrest the fugitives (pp. 30–31). In response, the authorities in Santa Teresa sent their own dispatches. They agreed to help find the parties guilty of beating and hanging a twelve-year-old boy, but also argued that the older murder cases were best forgotten, "as it is impossible to know the particular causes and circumstances of those happenings" (pp. 29–30). The new promoter, however, continued his personal campaign of reform by decree.

The authorities in Santa Teresa responded to these dispatches by seeking the promoter's removal, but they had little immediate success. Despite the wide variety of complaints registered against this official—that he appropriated the typewriter used by the local authorities to make his own official communications and that he had ignored higher orders to move to a new job in the neighboring settlement of Santa Gertrudis (now Linda Vista) (p. 30)—they were able to get rid of him only after they sent a final letter charging him with improprieties in the local school. "To speak more clearly," they wrote, "he likes men and is a fag" (Spanish: *joto*) (p. 64). As a result of this accusation, the first INI-sponsored cultural promoter to Santa Teresa was removed from his post, an action that caused him to write a final rejoinder to the authorities in Santa Teresa:

> To the Municipal Commissioner, August 6, 1970 . . . this dry season I will no longer come to your community, just as you all wished. For everyone's information, I am now completely detached from that community, and I only want to thank you for the few days of hospitality that you gave me, and to say that I appreciate that nothing happened to me, as you all would have had it. You only saw the bad in me, lying about me in order to force my withdrawal. To your disgrace I blame no one, because I know who were the promoters of all this ill will. . . . Now I only want to show my appreciation for all the good that you did me while I was with you, and to point out to you that I left you with a new school and a new electrical plant and with a [government-subsidized] CONASUPO shop. . . . I beg your pardon for all of this, if they also should be considered my fault. . . . (p. 36)

But if the authorities in Santa Teresa managed to have the first cultural promoter of the new INI administration removed, they were not able to stop the larger plans of that federal agency. Indeed, these developments rapidly eclipsed the political reforms that at least some Tereseños had hoped might be accomplished under the INI umbrella.

INI's initial development plans in Santa Teresa centered on an airstrip that was built beginning in 1966. Prior to the clearing of that dirt airstrip, all commerce between Santa Teresa and the surrounding regional capitals was conducted by mule or burro, and most of this commerce was based on the bartering of livestock for essential supplies like steel tools or cloth. After the clearing of this airstrip, however, building materials and bulk supplies could be flown in. As the former INI promoter's sarcastic letter points out, these materials were used to build a diesel-powered electrical generator, to rebuild the old schoolhouse on the north side of the plaza, and to stock a government-subsidized food shop (CONA-SUPO). Particular individuals also took immediate advantage of the air-strip, contracting pilots to fly in bulk maize to sell at a profit (p. 34). Moreover, this airstrip was also used to supply the Franciscan mission that Father Silvestre Rodríguez—the first missionary to work in the newly proclaimed Prelate of El Nayar—was building at the time (Anonymous 1971).

In addition to providing easy access to Santa Teresa, the new airstrip was meant to serve larger goals within the government-sponsored development process. Specifically, its construction was to provide the first of a series of federally sponsored jobs and cash payments for the development of a local capitalist economy. After the airstrip was constructed, steel picks and wheelbarrows were flown in and distributed to workmen, who were paid wages to build a new road that would ultimately connect Santa Teresa with the rest of Mexico. The segment of this road for which Tere-seño workmen were responsible took several years to complete and re-mained unconnected with the rest of the road being built from the re-gional capitals of Ruiz and Zacatecas for well over a decade. However, since the road was considered a "social-function road" (Spanish: *carretera de función social*), its short-term uselessness did not concern INI officials (Cárdenas de la Peña 1988: 165). According to INI, wages were as impor-tant as the road-building itself because they would stimulate investments in shops and improved agricultural techniques, both of which were lack-ing in Santa Teresa in the 1960s. The airstrip and the road, then, were the linchpins of all of the other development plans being implemented by the federal government in Santa Teresa during this period.

The local authorities of Santa Teresa had approved none of these plans. Instead, according to Manuel Morales Rojas, the former boarding-school student who served as secretary for the local authorities, engineers simply flew into town, recruited him to find them a house, and began to distribute tools and money. Both local Vecinos and their Tereseño allies who controlled the courthouse at the time initially spoke out against these plans. They argued that the town's cooperation with the project would constitute a tacit agreement (Spanish: *compromiso*) that would later be used by wealthy federal government officials to disenfranchise local people. Nonetheless, the engineers persevered. They were both well armed and supported by the INI bureaucracy in Tepic and Mexico City. Moreover, in Santa Teresa, laborers who stood to benefit from the projects also defended them. But as work progressed, the presence of INI jobs and money opened a new political rift in the old (but always uneasy) alliance between local Vecinos and their Tereseño supporters with far-reaching consequences.

Although the engineers and technicians sent to Santa Teresa were part of an organization ostensibly concerned with indigenous people, all of them were Spanish-speaking Mexicans who were entirely unfamiliar with the local scene. Their natural allies were not local Náyari people, but Vecinos. These Vecinos complained about INI's plans at public meetings in the town, but documents also make clear that once the INI-sponsored projects began, these same Vecinos used their influence to put themselves in charge. A number of important Tereseños who had been organized as a food cooperative by the new Franciscan missionary, for example, protested against Candelario González, the Vecino manager of the CONASUPO. They claimed that he spent all of his time "selling liquor, playing cards, and creating scandals" (p. 39). This behavior, however, did not endanger his post. On the contrary, the following year his sister, who had run the CONASUPO shop in the neighboring town of Mesa del Nayar until she was run out by local people there, joined him in Santa Teresa. Together they were later charged with robbing Santa Teresa's CONASUPO of more than 16,000 pesos (p. 71a). By 1976 CONASUPO officials had finally fired them, although González eventually received another post at the federally funded local forestry center before opening a private shop of his own. These two Vecino shopkeepers were replaced, however, by a close relative, so the Vecino operation of this important local food shop continued to be a thorn in the side of their former Tereseño supporters.

Plan HUICOT, a large development project subsequently promoted by INI and funded by a grant from UNESCO (Rojas 1993: 195), offered even more lucrative prizes for local Vecinos. The president of Mexico, Luis Echeverría Alvarez, announced this development initiative in Santa Teresa in 1970 as part of a visit to the town. During this visit, which the Náyarite of the region were urged to attend in their "old-style clothes" (Spanish: *trapos originales*) (p. 34), the Mexican president promised a new school, new homes, a basketball court, and tractors to plow the flat prairies that surround Santa Teresa. The first of these tractors arrived by airplane in 1972 (p. 73) and was soon under the control of Magdeleno Medina, a brother of Prudencio. According to complaints that were issued by Santa Teresa's authorities the following year, this local Vecino quickly ruined the tractor by using it to run errands without changing the oil or filters (p. 71a). Medina's response to these charges was to drink heavily and stagger around town yelling, "The authorities have no right to judge crimes in this community" (p. 71), an assertion that must have seemed annoyingly accurate to the Tereseños who had battled among themselves for control of the symbols and ceremonies of their traditional offices.

Throughout this period, INI administrators bypassed these traditional officers and instead presented development plans to the few literate Tereseño men whom they promoted to serve as the "presidents" (*presidentes*) and "commissioners" (*comisarios*) of local "committees" (*comités*). These committees—the "oversight committee" (*comité de vigilancia*) and the "communal properties committee" (*comité de bienes comunales*)—were supposed to represent Mexico's agrarian reform bureaucracy at the local level, but in reality they were little more than vehicles that allowed INI officials to gather the signatures and seals that were required to authorize their development programs. Names to fill these "committees"—which seem to have met rarely and which were not consulted in planning— appear to have been selected at random among the population attending town meetings. The "presidents" and "commissioners" tended to be either bilingual teachers of poor character or ambitious pretenders to local political power. These younger men, along with the municipal commissioner (a judge appointed from Jesús María), drafted a number of complaints about the new INI administrators. They also, however, signed the documents that were presented to them, in many cases using their INI-appointed positions to contest with Vecinos for control of the projects that were flooding into the town.

The pro-government Tereseño authorities were clearly antagonized by the behavior of local Vecinos (the authorities wrote in 1973 that the Vecinos "live here among us, but do not respect us" [p. 71a]), but a number of ambitious Tereseño appointees also made claims on INI projects. More tractors, for example, were sent to the community to be used in a cooperative plowing project, but they all ended up in the hands of former presidents and commissioners. At the same time, the one cinder-block house that was eventually built by the government next to the new basketball court was appropriated by a man who had earlier been accused of systematically murdering his enemies in his position as the town's police chief (Spanish: *comandante*) (p. 38). Even the smaller INI projects were fair game for privatization by other prominent Tereseños. Two sewing machines, for example, were flown in to be used in a women's cooperative, but these were soon taken by the wife of the former Holy-Week centurion Leocadio Aguilar, who considered them her own personal property. Later Aguilar himself was charged with taking mules that were assigned to the CONASUPO shop, also claiming that they were his own personal property (p. 57). Similarly, when a project to make furniture out of dead trees stalled for lack of a market, the woodworking tools were usurped, and the project came to a halt (p. 50).

All of these small projects were either taken over by individuals or neglected entirely and thus allowed to fail. In 1967, for example, fancy roosters and bulls were brought to Santa Teresa to improve local breeds, but they died immediately because of neglect (p. 70a). Later, four Swiss milk cows were also flown into the town, but these also died (p. 71a). Fifty rolls of barbed-wire fencing were delivered, but then disappeared (p. 71a). A number of ponds were excavated to be used for raising tilapia fish, but the fish died and the ponds were never restocked (p. 71a). In all of these cases INI officials blamed local authorities for their lack of oversight and direction, even as they themselves administered the paperwork and named the opportunistic "partners" (Spanish: *socios*) who were supposed to be in charge of the ill-conceived projects. Despite their problems, however, these projects continued to be promoted by a variety of federal agencies.

As failures accumulated, Tereseños holding traditional offices expressed bitter resentment towards the development projects and their administrators. At the federal health service clinic that opened in 1972, for example, things were no better than at the INI-sponsored agricultural projects. In that year a physician named Arturo Bustamante Fernández arrived to complete the year-long period of free social service that is required of doctors in Mexico (as Tereseños say, "to practice on us"), but the authorities in Santa Teresa wanted him replaced before the year was out. The following year two nurses were sent, but they were afraid to be alone in Santa Teresa and so hid inside the clinic, which, in any case, had very few supplies. When local authorities protested the incompetence of the nurses, they left (p. 72a). Only a year after the completion of the clinic itself, its roof was reported to be leaking and its walls were falling in.

The new school that began under INI supervision in 1968 turned out to be another debacle. Like at the previous schools in Santa Teresa, attendance at this one was legally mandatory for all children but was resisted by most Tereseños. With the active presence of INI officials in Santa Teresa and Jesús María, however, enforcement of mandatory schooling was more vigorous than in the past. In 1974, after the completion of a boarding school in Santa Teresa, local police were dispatched to seize truants (p. 72). In 1976 a long list of household heads were fined for failing to send their children to school, but 44 children were also noted as already in full-time attendance. As in years past, however, the teachers who were employed at the school, now Náyari-speaking "bilingual teachers" (Spanish: *maestros bilingües*), were of very poor quality.

Perhaps the most notorious of these young teachers was Hipolito Morales, a man still infamous in Santa Teresa during the time of my fieldwork for his long and violent drinking binges. During his tenure as a teacher in Santa Teresa, he was charged with stealing 2,400 pesos from the Franciscan mission (p. 71a). Ygnacio Flores had a similarly checkered reputation and was eventually arrested for choking a woman after she advised him to quit drinking during a festival (p. 73a). Fernando Morales, the son of secretary Manuel Morales Rojas, admitted to me that he also spent most of his time as a teacher drunk. Finally, a young man from the Mesa del Nayar (p. 74), whom Benítez (1973: 30) described as being at the age of twelve "a lively boy, . . . who applies himself to his studies," was a decade later drawing complaints from local officials for his persistent drunkenness while serving as a teacher in Santa Teresa (p. 74). But despite the irresponsibility of the teachers employed at the school, truancy fines had their intended effect, and 1984 recorded 176 students in attendance at the poorly managed institution.

Rather than teaching students skills to improve their lives, however, the school seemed to produce delinquents. Instead of farming and ranching with their families, these children now spent their time playing in gender-segregated age grades in the new town center. Many migrated away from the school to the new basketball court, the ceremonial plaza, and the shops that had sprung up around town. They ran errands, worked odd jobs, begged for food from shopkeepers, spied, gossiped, and periodically got into more serious trouble. A document written on July 29, 1974, for example, complains that a short-wave radio at the clinic had begun to malfunction because "some children threw mud into the tank of the electrical energy plant" (p. 42). As documents like this one show, the school, far from promoting the common good of Santa Teresa's indigenous people, served mostly to concentrate unsupervised children in the new town, creating another source of disorder for local authorities to deal with.

By the 1970s, however, unsupervised children were the least of the concerns of the traditional authorities in Santa Teresa. People were moving closer to Santa Teresa to take advantage of INI projects and the new shops, as well as to avoid leaving their children overnight in the unsupervised boarding school (p. 72), but in Santa Teresa these newcomers found a town in disarray. Vecinos ran key institutions like the CONASUPO shop while local Tereseño officials had seemingly lost their judicial and political authority to the INI administrators, who required officials' seals on each of the new development projects but who ignored their complaints and petitions. The injured and sick crouched outside the understaffed clinic, and Tereseño schoolchildren ran loose among the newly constructed government buildings.

An additional result of the completion of the new airstrip was the availability of liquor and beer every day of the year, and many men joined the Náyari schoolteachers in taking advantage of this reliable supply to drink steadily. Indeed, despite all of the other factionalism and disorder produced by INI's development projects, this new availability of liquor had perhaps the most devastating effects of all. During my stays in Santa Teresa, for example, people recalled that in the 1970s and early 1980s a two-engined DC-3 airplane would make continuous flights from the state capital of Tepic stocked with cases of beer and liquor. People paid for this beer and liquor with their new wages as well as with livestock, impoverishing a number of families. Some local people attempted to start informal cantinas. They used schoolchildren and INI wheelbarrows to carry bottles of liquor and cases of beer from the airstrip to their houses, where they stockpiled the alcohol for sale at inflated prices after the airplane left. The immediate result of this easy access to alcohol in the newly crowded town of Santa Teresa was violence, particularly during gatherings at the community festivals whose explicit purpose was to appoint and legitimate local authorities.

In a case that is typical of the period, during the rainy-season Festival of San Miguel in 1974, two groups of Tereseño drinking companions came to blows:

> On September 30 at 10 in the morning there was an incident between Pablo Morales, Edmundo Ortiz, Santos Campos and Esteban Martínez and Andrés Flores, Catalino Morales, Ygnacio Flores and Evaristo Valencia . . . and the first mentioned above declare that Andrés and etc. are the people who started to insult the others—of course all of them were in a state of complete drunkenness—saying that they were not

men, and upon seeing that they would not respond to the insults they jumped on top of the others, hitting them and injuring Mr. Edmundo, Pablo, and Santos, and then later they responded by hitting the others until Mr. Andrés Flores remained gravely injured. . . . (p. 42)

In the aftermath of this incident, the father of Andrés Flores demanded payment from those who injured Andrés, ignoring the inclination of the authorities to blame his son for the incident. These authorities later complained of their powerlessness to control this splintering factionalism to the municipal president: "These people have acted very badly but they say they have committed no crime even though they were the ones who started the incident and then say that they are not to blame . . . and they have indeed committed crimes in this community. There are some people here who have been beaten by them, but have never charged them money for the offense, even though they want to be paid for the injuries to the son of Amadeo. And so we will just see what happens the next time they do something like this, because they will get more of their own medicine. They are the ones who always start these incidents; they get drunk just to fight" (p. 42). This drunken brawl, then, resulted in not only a simmering dispute between Tereseños authorities and the members of a particular family, but also an interrogation of the legitimacy of local authorities, who then felt that vigilantism against this group was a viable alternative.

During the following festival, however, the authorities attempted a more comprehensive solution by bringing the town's consejeros to give a session of ritual oratorical counsel in the presence of the municipal commissioner: "In the town of Santa Teresa, on the 15th of October, 1974, with all of the principales and consejeros of this Cora settlement, we declare: 1) that they have given speeches [Spanish: consejos] to all of the inhabitants of this place so that they will not create scandals during the festival, 2) that they have given permission that moderate quantities of liquor may be sold, with prior notification to this courthouse, 3) that all firearms and knives will be stored away, to avoid problems, 4) that the local police have been ordered to guard public order, and 5) that the groups of mariachi musicians will work only within the perimeter of this locality, after paying the corresponding tax." Based on an absence of subsequent legal cases, it appears that this combination of ritual oratory and municipal cooperation helped to control the liquor supply and quiet violent disputes for several years, but by 1977 the problems of drinking and violence reappeared.

During the New Year's Festival of that year (immediately after the year's new authorities were put in place), Ygnacio Flores (the teacher) caused his horse to step on a small child as he rode drunkenly around the town. After he was jailed his cousin intervened, threatening the courthouse authorities with a knife. During the same festival another man pulled a gun on the teacher Fernando Morales. Then later in the year two other serious incidents occurred: Demecio Ortiz was accused of cutting Rosalio Ortiz with a machete, and Arturo Flores Flores seriously beat Daniel Soto Pacheco (p. 73).

In response to this new wave of drunkenness and violence, municipal authorities prohibited alcohol and weapons in Santa Teresa, and state-level *judiciales* (Spanish: judicial police) were sent from Jesús María following the Holy Week Festival of 1977 to enforce the law (p. 73). However, the presence of these heavily armed police in Santa Teresa only further eroded the authority of local officials, who complained in vain about abuses suffered by Tereseños. To compound the problems, by 1980 laws against selling liquor in the municipality were overturned. Merchants in Santa Teresa were now registered to pay sales tax on liquor sales directly to municipal officials in Jesús María, rather than to local authorities in Santa Teresa as they had previously done when commercial liquor was brought in by mule for sale next to the courthouse (p. 73). These new municipal taxes actively discouraged local authorities from intervening to regulate liquor sales because municipal police from Jesús María collected these taxes, and because local authorities had no way of knowing which merchants had legitimate authorization to sell liquor. As a result, they questioned no one.

But the trip from Jesús María to Santa Teresa is a long one, and even if the municipal police officers had managed to arrive in town for each and every community festival, the few unsupervised officers would have had a hard time controlling Santa Teresa's increasingly notorious festivals. As a result, by the early 1980s, drunkenness and violence reached a new crisis point in the town. The year 1983, for example, began with another conflict between local authorities and Vecinos: "On the 20th of January, 1983 in Santa Teresa Fidel Serranos acted very badly with the people of this town. At 11 o'clock at night he cut the bridles of a number of horses and the halter of the horses owned by Angel Morales Valencia and Julio Aguilar Salazar and for that we were going to jail him, but we could not because Mr. Tereso Medina had the gall to intervene physically . . . Mr. Medina is not even from this town [i.e., he is Vecino] and this is the second time that he has committed this crime . . . for which reason we see that the Mestizos think less of us as indigenous people" (p. 49).

Although the aggressive behavior of local Vecinos was particularly maddening to Tereseño authorities, Vecinos were far from the only aggressive drunks in town at that time. On the contrary, a variety of drunken "scandals" (Spanish: *escándalos*) among Tereseños were also documented in that year: a man invited another man and his son to drinks, and ended up being beaten with firewood and carried "like a sack of flour" to a dry gulch where he was left for dead (p. 52); a man who was angry with his wife for attending her father's maize-bundle-group ceremonies without his permission got drunk and began to beat her as she sold enchiladas in the ceremonial plaza at a community festival (p. 53); and an unidentified man killed two others in cold blood (p. 74). As such violent incidents proliferated, consejos of ritual advice were no longer sufficient to restore order; local officials instead were forced to risk their own lives to physically intervene in these disputes if they hoped to maintain the peace.

In the midst of this violence, the authorities again wrote to the municipal president, indicating their growing fatalism in the face of the town's aggressive drunks: "To the Municipal President on the first of September, 1983 . . . there has recently been a great deal of drunkenness [Spanish: *borrachera*] in our town without anyone's permission, as well as various scandals and the discharging of firearms. We make this known to you so that you might decide what to do. [Hopefully you will] prohibit people from bringing liquor from Tepic [on the airplane] or see what you can do

209

so that they will no longer be bringing it, which we communicate to you before anything dangerous happens" (p. 52). However, rather than immediately outlawing liquor sales, which would have cut into the lucrative tax payments at that time flowing into the office of the municipal president in Jesús María, the municipal authorities—in consultation with INI—proposed a different plan. They promised to match a grant by INI with locally administered federal funds to help with the construction of a new courthouse in Santa Teresa, a modern building that would finally provide a place for local authorities within the hierarchical judicial administration of the nation as a whole.

To show their good faith, local Tereseños Reymundo Pacheco and Teresa Ortiz both sacrificed bulls for a ground-breaking party (p. 74). This work party, drawn by the free food, proceeded to tear down the old stone-and-thatch jail next to the courthouse that also contained a room that was used by women to cook meals during community festivals. However, the funds to build the new courthouse evaporated after the jail was destroyed. Consequently, rather than consolidating the authority of local officials as part of a larger bureaucracy, the traditional authorities were left with no secure place to isolate aggressive drunks, even if they had the inclination to risk apprehending them.

Documents also show that in that same year, in addition to pledging money for the reconstruction of Santa Teresa's courthouse, INI—whose officers in Santa Teresa had by then retreated to a large, new complex of buildings in the municipal capital—had begun a secretive program of direct annual payments to traditional authorities in Santa Teresa (and other indigenous towns in the region). Inspired by anthropological arguments of the previous decade (e.g., Cancian 1965), INI officers made these payments to help authorities pay for religious ceremonies, and thus (the argument went) increase their prestige in the face of the changes that were going on around them. These direct cash payments, termed "supports" (Spanish: *apoyos*), were paid in private to the local officials that INI saw as responsible for each of the year's community-level ceremonial festivals (p. 53). Not surprisingly, far from "supporting" the legitimacy of local authorities, these arbitrary payments—in some cases for festivals that were not even celebrated in Santa Teresa—again struck at the foundation of traditional authority in Santa Teresa. If local authorities earlier felt powerless in the face of jurisdictional conflicts, or personally intimidated by violent drunks, with these annual payments they must have become equivalent to every other corrupt Mexican politician in the eyes of many Tereseños.

Ironically, this impression was in some cases false. Documents show that during this period local authorities worked quietly to refocus attention on the importance of ceremonies. For example, they sent a letter to a neighboring town seeking the use of musicians in one of the community festivals (p. 46). They were also involved in the sale of a dried eagle to their counterparts in Jesús María (p. 49) and were in communication with Tepehuans and Huichols in order to sponsor special ceremonials and ritual deer hunts (pp. 44–45). They sent locally distilled liquor for the use of traditional authorities in neighboring towns (p. 62) and, finally, they continued to practice community-level mitote ceremonies, even specifying which feathers the people of the town should bring to the community parched maize mitote (pp. 60–61). But despite the ongoing dedication of a number of Tereseños to these ceremonial traditions, it is clear that INI's payments encouraged other authorities to stay in the courthouse just long enough to cast all of the town's ballots for the *Partido Revolucionario Institucional* (PRI), Mexico's ruling party at the time. They also simply pocketed the secret payments, which, in many cases, they must have spent on beer and liquor. To compound the outrage, general "cooperations" (Spanish: *cooperaciones*) were meanwhile being solicited from local community members who held no office themselves to pay the expense of festivals for which INI was already providing money (p. 74).

Even if the idea of supporting traditional authorities with unfunded construction projects and secret cash payments was not inherently flawed, by the early 1980s, local authorities were confronted with a new source of income that re-energized Santa Teresa's already violent cash-and-alcohol economy: opium gum and marijuana. Rumor had it during the time of my fieldwork that bilingual teachers with links to narcotics organizations in Acaponeta and Sinaloa promoted these drug crops to young men at festivals. Wherever the seeds came from, Tereseño authorities were by this time far too weak to stop the cultivation of these crops among local people, and instead passed responsibility on to municipal officials. In 1983 a document written by the local authorities in Santa Teresa reported with concern on the increasing production of drug crops in the town, but indicated no serious hope of controlling the problem: "To the Municipal President on June 9, 1983 . . . in this community some people have dedicated themselves to the sowing of evil weeds that are prohibited by law. This seems to have been going on for some time, but the authorities have only become aware of it this year. We as authorities are not in agreement with these developments because we see that all of the town is now throwing itself toward this predicament (Spanish: *compromiso*). For this reason we feel that the best thing is to report this situation to your office, so that you might decide what to do, and so that we are not implicated in this muddled situation" (p. 51). By the early 1980s local people were no longer dependent on INI salaries or the sale of livestock to fund drinking binges. Armed young men now began to show up in town with rolls of bills in their shoulder bags and a willingness to pay grossly inflated prices for beer and liquor.

The increased drinking and violence linked to this drug production in Santa Teresa forced municipal authorities to again outlaw liquor, this time as part of a more general anti-drug effort. The result was a new cycle of police intimidation repeated at an even more brutal level. The notoriously corrupt and vicious federal judicial police began intensive patrols of the town. They arrested at least three people for growing opium poppies and, presumably, tortured and robbed many others (p. 74).

In addition to patrols by the judiciales, the Mexican federal army— backed by the U.S. government—began to employ helicopters to spray herbicide on clandestine gardens, in at least one case touching off a violent conflict:

> In the town of Dolores, Municipality of Nayar on the 18th of March of the current year [1983 or 1984] a helicopter was seen flying low over the settlement of Linda Vista, seemingly engaged in its daily task of spraying herbicide. On seeing this helicopter one of the inhabitants of

this settlement shot at it with a firearm, not caring whether he caused any damage with those shots. The aircraft then gained considerable altitude, removing itself from danger. A few moments later it returned to the same place accompanied by another helicopter and members of the Federal Army. The helicopters landed near the house from which the shots were fired, and entering into the same house the soldiers fired their weapons, killing the woman of the house. They then burned the house itself. They later met up with other people whom they punished with violent beatings. We have written the current official communication to inform you of the recent happenings in our settlement . . . Auxiliary Judge of Linda Vista [annex of Santa Teresa]. (p. 53)

As this document shows, beyond simply destroying marijuana and opium fields, these airborne soldiers saw themselves as engaged in a guerrilla war, and so they began to terrorize Náyari people in and around Santa Teresa as part of their search for drug growers:

In Santa Teresa on the 24th of May, 1985 . . . a dark blue helicopter with sky blue trim landed in the town and five armed men got out. These soldiers approached the home of Mateo Valencia and seized the underaged Julia Aguilar Valencia, later holding a hand over her mouth and pouring water up her nose as they asked her the location of Apolinario, to which she answered that she did not know. They went through all of the rooms of the house without asking permission, scattering everything around as they searched. Later they grabbed three children (one ten years old, one three years old, and one less than a year old) and they demanded that the people in the house tell them the location of Apolinario as they first held the children at machine-gun point and then shot their weapons in the air. . . . [Later] they landed at the clinic where they spoke with the town's nurse named Rosa Delgado, and, accompanied by her, they then went to the house of Anastacio Ramos, where they repeated their previous actions. . . . (p. 56)

Tereseño officials protested these abuses to higher authorities, but were helpless either to stop drug production on the lands of their community or to defend their town from the military terror brought by the federal police and army.

This desperate situation soon drew the attention of Father Javier, the

Franciscan priest in residence at the time. He placed the blame for the failure to control drinking and violence on the local authorities, whom he saw as neglecting their traditional responsibilities:

> In this notice we want to volunteer to the people that we think that the festivals are destroying the costumbre. It's no longer like it was in the past, because before the people respected the *santitos* [Spanish: local saints] and did not get drunk with beer. . . . The people from outside who bring beer are destroying our costumbre. Those are the ones who make themselves rich, as well as some of the people from this town who sell beer. . . . So we ask the authorities that they prohibit the sale of beer, and to put anyone who sells beer in jail, because it's not right. It is better that the airplane brings maize, flour, sugar, and beans, as you all see that the maize at the CONASUPO does not last. For this reason it is better that you tell Velasco [the pilot] that he should bring maize, and that he not bring beer. (Mission archives)

But even if the authorities had had a secure jail in which to incarcerate the town's many beer merchants and drunks, by the end of 1984, when Father Javier wrote this letter, the events of the previous two decades must have seriously eroded the motivation of the traditional authorities to carry out the priest's laudable recommendations.

This lack of motivation, or "laziness" (*huenase*), as Tereseños put it, seems to have first settled over the community's courthouse after powerful INI officials first showed up in the town in the late 1960s. These officials undermined local authorities by doling out jobs and money to Vecinos, who then taunted local authorities with their new political autonomy and economic power. These same authorities, however, were blamed when INI's development projects failed, and when Tereseños used these projects to fund drinking binges instead of their agrarian livelihoods. When these drunks turned violent and began to physically threaten remaining authorities during community festivals, the urge to stay away from the courthouse—or even to join the unruly festival crowds in the plaza—must have been great. Moreover, the periodic appearance of heavily armed police and soldiers in the town would have made it clear to the men who served as courthouse officials that the powers that be in Mexico held traditional authorities like themselves in very low regard (even if an occasional poorly planned program was ostensibly aimed at supporting their local legitimacy). Father Javier's notion that drinking and violence in Santa Teresa was destroying the costumbre, then, must have come as no surprise to the cynical and apathetic local authorities who received his letter, but they were simply too weighted down with an accumulated "laziness" to do anything about it.

Given this lack of energy—and the failure of earlier military intervention to control the situation in Santa Teresa—the federal government of Mexico stepped up its efforts. On September 19, 1987, only twenty years after the beginnings of the earlier INI-sponsored development programs, the 86th battalion of the federal army formally occupied the town. Ironically, this battalion took as their barracks the site on the north side of the plaza that had earlier served as INI's unpopular schoolhouse. During the two and a half years that the 86th Infantry Battalion was stationed in Santa Teresa, its soldiers actively continued their guerrilla war against Tereseños. Many fields of marijuana and opium were destroyed (along with any ranch house located near those fields), and a number of Tereseños were arrested and jailed in the state capital. These soldiers, however, like the INI administrators before them, tended to seek out Vecinos for friendships and social interaction (even marrying Vecino daughters and opening shops of their own), and so their anti-drug guerrilla war tended to be fought against Tereseños alone (p. 60).

This anti-drug war created great hardships for a number of Tereseño families whose men were carried off to jail or were crippled by beatings, rendering them in either case unable to work. Because of these abuses, the 86th battalion was considered by Tereseños to be an entirely unwelcome occupying force, and the Tereseño men who had been serving as traditional authorities refused to associate themselves with these aggressive outsiders. At the same time, however, as a result of INI directives (and, perhaps, in response to pleas from Tereseño authorities to "respect the festivals that we carry out . . . and to not trod upon the origins of the Mexican Indian" [p. 59]), the soldiers were warned not to intervene in the drunken and violent festivals that were celebrated in front of their new base. Thus, in response to the army's occupation of Santa Teresa, the traditional authorities lodged what they must have known would be a futile protest with the president of Mexico (p. 59) and then joined other Tereseños in turning their attention away from the courthouse and its festivals, leaving the festivals entirely unsupervised.

Thus, in contrast to the Náyari/Vecino or pro-/anti-government struggles of the preceding decades, by the time the federal army occupied Santa Teresa in 1987, the courthouse was a prize that was no longer worth much of a fight. Although the festivals continued to be performed, their message of a struggle of yearly political and moral renewal had changed. The traditional authorities now looked more like sinful devils than austere, self-denying ancestors, more like San Miguel Sáutari than San Miguel Xúrave. Indeed, by the time I arrived in Santa Teresa the following year, the backwardness and "inside-out" behavior of the devils (like myself) hardly contrasted with daily life in the occupied town.

THE RETREAT FROM
COMMUNITY FESTIVALS, 1988–1997

In contrast to the descriptions of drinking and violence in community festivals that emerge from archival documents, the mitote ceremonies that I attended from 1988 to 1997 were pleasantly calm. Along with the others who had been invited to these mitotes away from the town's ceremonial plaza, I was given bowls of pinole with roasted century plant as well as plastic bags full of other food to take home with me. By and large, the rituals that constituted these ceremonies were carried out carefully and completely, and after people had eaten, they gathered up their blankets and bags and proceeded to walk quietly back towards their houses. Unlike at the first Holy Week Festival I attended in 1988, which ended badly for myself and many others, no one drank beer at these mitote ceremonies and any interpersonal tensions were glossed over with light joking.

The easy grace of these mitote ceremonies, however, contrasted sharply with the situation developing in and around Santa Teresa's ceremonial plaza. There the presence of the federal army alienated local authorities from the courthouse and thus from responsibility for community festivals. But the "laziness" of Tereseño authorities did not extend to the practice of their own maize-bundle-group ceremonies, or to the performance of key community mitote ceremonies. Although Father Javier saw the drinking and violence that occurred in the plaza outside of his new mission as destroying the entire costumbre of Santa Teresa, these other ceremonies continued to be performed with care and thoroughness. Indeed, as the clear-cut political division of the previous century fractured, and as these fractures were converted through drinking and violence at community festivals into myriad blood feuds, attendance at maize-bundle-group ceremonies became the only viable way for Tereseños to construct and maintain local political ties. Through these private ceremonies away from the town center of Santa Teresa, people continued to link themselves to larger "peoples" (Spanish: *gentes*), as Tereseños described them. Meanwhile, however, in Santa Teresa's plaza, the political vacuum caused by the deployment of the army drew interest from regional Vecinos.

In the first full year that the soldiers spent in Santa Teresa (1988), the familiar names of Tereseños who had previously served as authorities in the courthouse are noticeably missing from archival documents. Instead, the Vecino Prudencio Medina again stepped in to claim the courthouse, serving as comisario municipal along with only a few Tereseños. During that year he alone seems to have produced most of the few documents that remain in the archives. Documents are similarly sparse for the following year, but according to a report written by INI and archived with the rest of the community's papers, this absence of official documents also seems to reflect a more important behind-the-scenes negotiation: "In 1989 this community [Santa Teresa] saw itself threatened by the penetration of private initiative: a timber merchant who has systematically come to exploit the forests of northern Jalisco and who with the support of some people from San Juan Peyotán [presumably people associated with Candelario Gonzalez Navajas, who sold his shop in Santa Teresa and moved back to San Juan Peyotán that year] has tried to convince the communal landholders of Santa Teresa to sell their timber." As this document points out, Prudencio Medina and a few Tereseños attempted to use the military occupation of Santa Teresa as an opportunity to push through the sale of the community's timber to a private contractor for their own gain. Indeed, this power grab seems to have been so startling to federal government officials (or at least INI officials) planning for the region that it resulted in the removal of the Vecino-supported army battalion from Santa Teresa's plaza and the elaboration of a new round of federally sponsored development programs.

Because of the threat to Santa Teresa's timber (and, according to others, because the soldiers committed a last outrage by murdering a former Tereseño governor), the soldiers were ordered removed from Santa Teresa's plaza in February 1990 and were redeployed to their main base at Acaponeta. Shortly thereafter, a new set of Tereseño authorities were drawn to the courthouse by the promise of more INI "supports," this time for as much as US $2,000 per festival. With such huge payments on the table, these officials promptly signed documents committing themselves to another round of development projects, this time timber-related, under the auspices of INI (p. 76).

These new development projects, all aimed at creating a small-scale timber cooperative to undercut the plans of the private timber contractor, were another huge failure. A truck-mounted band saw never worked properly, and replacement blades were nearly impossible to obtain. A solar-powered wood-drying "oven" that was built on the side of a hill next to Santa Teresa's plaza was never completed. New woodworking tools (like the old ones) were appropriated by individuals. Finally, a three-ton truck that was meant to carry finished furniture to market became the focus of a bitter struggle among the socios who had signed themselves up to work on the projects. This new INI-sponsored failure, however, surprised no one that I talked to at the time, even the INI engineers in charge of the projects. As for the newly recruited authorities, beyond collecting their new INI checks, the Tereseño men who returned to the courthouse showed little willingness to intervene in these development projects, or in the renewed drinking and violence that continued to characterize the town's festivals.

To compound problems for these already-reluctant traditional authorities, after the army's departure municipal officials in Jesús María liberalized liquor laws in Santa Teresa for the first time since the beginning of army operations in the region years earlier, taxing beer at the rate of 10,000 pesos a carton (US $3). During my fieldwork I estimated that about 2,830 cartons of beer were purchased from local merchants during a single year, so this tax represented a significant source of income to municipal officials (US $8,490 per year from Santa Teresa alone).

This heavy drinking, in turn, led to new disputes and violence,* and in response, municipal officials again dispatched judicial police. I wrote about the frightening tactics of these police in my 1994 fieldnotes:

> While the people were gathering to see the stools be turned over to the new cargo holders the Judicial Police came into the plaza . . . it seems that the judiciales were called up on the radio at the clinic. They arrived heavily armed with machine-guns and side-arms and were wearing their characteristic baseball hats and T-shirts, both of which carry the design of a snarling tiger. These are aggressive paramilitary police and people were startled. "They're really tough" [Spanish: *son muy bravos*] more than one person assured me. . . . Not to overstate the case, but had even one drunk pulled a gun, it may well have caused a bloodbath, considering the number of people that would have found themselves in the line of fire. The judiciales checked men's shoulder bags, and even tried to find needle tracks on my own arms, ankles, and be-

---

*In a very rough (and presumably low) estimate based on cases recorded by the *síndico municipal* (Spanish: municipal police chief) of Jesús María, 27 men in Santa Teresa were convicted of homicide and 17 men were convicted of assault (including rapes) between September 1988 and October 1994. Given a population of 2,000 in Santa Teresa, this puts the annual murder rate, based on convictions alone, at 225 per 100,000 as compared to the 1981 murder rate of 17.7 per 100,000 in Mexico as a whole (United Nations 1985: Table 31, cited in Greenberg 1989). In the months prior to the killing of Antonio Morales Morales in 1994, Tereseños were killing each other at the rate of 1,400 per 100,000, almost 80 times higher than the murder rate in Mexico as a whole.

hind my ears. Eventually they grabbed four young men who had been fighting, and two of these boys were chained to the roll-bar of the judiciales' pick-up, where they spent the long ride to Jesús María—torture itself. (pp. 118a–119a)

In cases like this one, prisoners were normally ransomed from the beds of the judicial police's white pickup trucks. If cash was immediately forthcoming, such boys might be released for a few hundred thousand pesos (US $100), the price that I twice paid to free the sons of a friend. But if no money was produced, the prisoners would be transported to Jesús María, where they were held on the threat of transfer to the state capital, which would only increase the price of their release. In other words, the judicial police found it worth their while to occasionally appear at Santa Teresa's festivals following the army's removal for this lucrative reason alone. Otherwise, they left local authorities without help to control ongoing drinking and violence.

The increased availability of alcohol was also facilitated by the flourishing new Vecino shops that opened in town as a result of the completion of the Ruiz-Zacatecas dirt road, a project begun twenty years earlier. Immediately upon completion of this road, pickup trucks and lorries began to appear in Santa Teresa driven by Vecinos from Huejuquilla, Jalisco. These truckers quickly established contracts with other Vecinos in Santa Teresa who traced their ancestry to Huejuquilla. The completion of the road thus allowed these Vecinos to undercut the airplane-dependent supply line of the Tereseño-run shops in the town (see Table 2). The Vecino shop owned by Pedro García grew rapidly and became the focus of much of the commerce in the town. García, an even-tempered man who went out of his way to be polite to Tereseños, hardly fit the stereotype of a crass and aggressive Mexican *cacique* (Spanish: strongman). Nonetheless, his economic power made it nearly impossible for Tereseño authorities to enforce local laws against him. One former official was explicit regarding this point. "Look," he said, "I don't want to make any enemies . . . I may need credit to buy maize from Don Pedro just like anyone else." Other Vecinos, however, were also quick to point to García's special status, demanding equal treatment under the law and so over-

TABLE 2 *Shopkeepers in Santa Teresa in Order of Importance (with Ethnicity)*

1983*	
Candelario Gonzalez	Vecino
Gerónimo Ortiz	Tereseño
Cruz Soto	Tereseño
Blanco Ortiz	Tereseño
Manuel Morales	Tereseño
Florencio Noriega	Tereseño
Calixtro Noriega	Tereseño
Santos Morales	Tereseño
1993†	
Pedro García	Vecino (from near Guadalajara)
Candida Zúñiga	Vecino (from Acaponeta)
Demetrio Corona	Vecino
"Torres"	Vecino (former soldier)
"Fidel"	Vecino (former soldier)
Rafael Ramos	Tereseño
Irma Corona	Vecino
Magdeleno Medina	Vecino
Isabela Medina	Vecino
Magdalenillo Medina	Vecino
José Medina	Vecino
"Eulogio"	Cora bilingual teacher from Jesús María

*Based on list of tax payments; community archives, p. 74.
†From fieldnotes; community archives, p. 73a.

whelming the already weakened abilities of the local authorities to act against them.

As a result of their new economic power, the Vecino shopkeepers of Santa Teresa expanded their relatively well-made homes and shops, taking more and more space for themselves and their families in Santa Teresa's town center and increasingly defining the conduct of day-to-day life there. The diesel generator initially constructed by INI in the 1960s, for example, was usurped, and a number of shopkeepers took advantage of its electricity to string bare light bulbs outside of their shops and to open small movie houses showing violent action-adventure videos on city-bought television sets. As the influence of these Vecinos grew, land in the town center was fenced, rose gardens were planted, and a nearby (sacred) spring was tapped in order to provide the new Vecino commercial center of Santa Teresa with a reliable water supply. This Vecino consolidation of the town center stranded Santa Teresa's ceremonial plaza within a ring of new shops and older government buildings, separating this plaza from the outlying ranches of the large majority of Tereseños.

Although community festivals continued to be practiced in the plaza, anyone with hopes of reasserting control of these ceremonies in the wake of the army's departure had to confront the new social reality of day-to-day Vecino control of the town. Ironically, a document signed in 1992 by a number of leading Tereseño men, in which they state their common desire to "rescue" their ceremonies, clearly points out the difficulty of following through on this wish: "It was amply established among everyone at this meeting that the costumbres are no longer practiced as they were left to us by our ancestors. But a resolution was also passed among all of the Consejos de Ancianos of the participating communities that from here forward the costumbres will be rescued by following the example of the elders who still know them, and so there will be more respect of the costumbre, not allowing anyone who is outside of this costumbre to sign official papers, because it is not a game" (p. 61). Despite the feeling of common purpose expressed by this document, it was written not in Santa Teresa's courthouse, but in a small "auxiliary courthouse" (Spanish: *juzgado auxiliar*) in the neighboring annex of Rancho Viejo, located about five miles across the prairie from Santa Teresa. In a secret meeting away from the town center, then, all of the leading Tereseños could agree on their common desire to save the costumbre, but actually intervening in the violent ceremonial festivals carried out in Santa Teresa's encircled ceremonial plaza was a much more complicated task. Nonetheless, in at least three different ways, they tried.

Perhaps the most difficult festival to control was the Holy Week Festival, in which hundreds of devils invade the plaza in what should be a display of their own sinfulness in relation to the austere and self-denying authorities. By the late 1980s, however, the devils had instead come to represent just one extreme instantiation of the pervasive drunkenness and violence that characterized Santa Teresa. During the Holy Week Festival of 1993 (my last year as a devil in that festival), for example, I wrote about that drunkenness and violence in my fieldnotes: "On Holy Thursday at the Centurion's house there were plenty of drunks, nearly everybody had a bottle. I got painted and before long Oscar had hit me with his saber, causing my hand to bleed. Later Raúl would tell me that there was a steady stream of injuries at the clinic, and that this year seemed even worse than last, despite all the talk of trying to keep order. . . . We were given a consejo by an anciano, but no one listened. . . . The authorities watched the festival gravely and seemed worried as the judíos drank and danced. . . . Every once in awhile there was a commotion in the plaza as blood pumped out of this or that head-wound. I was drunk, too, so things became unclear."

Later I asked Don Goyo what went wrong at the festival. His explanation pointed to the difficulties that the authorities faced in attempting to control violent disputes without an effective local police presence or jail:

It is very difficult when something bad happens. The governors should want to consult with the community elder. So that he can plead with the people. So that nothing bad will happen. He, the governor, is in charge of that. That he speak with the elder. He is always in charge of that. Another matter is that they should put things right. The consejeros are the ones to do that, depending on the problem a person has. They should arrange it. The governors should also speak to the person. The governors are with the consejeros. They also give advice to all of us people. That the people should keep quiet. That the people do not go around saying things. For that purpose they are put in their offices. They put things right, all of the elders. Those that are there in the courthouse.

Here Don Goyo presented the first strategy that community elders and cargo officers used: a two-faceted approach of persuasive public oratory

along with the "arrangement" of monetary fines and even short-term in-
carceration ("to put things right"). From his perspective, this would
allow traditional authorities to first avoid and then settle disputes. But as
my own experience in these festivals shows, Don Goyo's strategy was un-
successful in molding public behavior given the changed social context of
the town. Oratory and advice were ignored or forgotten in the drunken
chaos of the festival, and any fines were inevitably contested by pointing
to the illegitimacy of the authorities, whose neglect of the ceremonial
traditions made them far "dirtier" than the boys and men injured in the
plaza.

Unlike Don Goyo, whose approach to judicial issues harkened back to
a time when traditional authorities claimed more autonomy and power in
relation to Vecinos and higher-level bureaucracies, other Tereseños argued to me that drinking and violence had simply gotten a bit out of hand.
For them, a second strategy of reforming the festivals was a more realistic
path for regaining control. Of particular concern were the groups of ran-
chero musicians that were increasingly drawn to Santa Teresa by the completion of the new road and the promise of free-flowing cash. These musicians were paid by drunks to provide them with ballads recounting the
lives of peasants who have become famous *narcotraficantes* (Spanish: narcotics traffickers) and murderers, the perfect soundtrack for a wild festival in a poor, drug-growing region. As one woman put it, "It's like an
illness, men hear that music and they need to drink." Indeed, the new
Vecino shopkeepers used this music-induced "illness" to their explicit
advantage, sheltering itinerant musical groups during their stays in town
in order to draw customers to expensive *borracheras* (Spanish: drunken
parties) outside their shops and away from the ceremonies in the plaza.
Domingo Morales Hernández observed, "it's like there are two costumbres now." The first costumbre pertained to the ancestral traditions of the
courthouse and plaza, while the second "costumbre" pertained to the
new Vecino town that had grown up just outside.

In response to this overwhelmingly popular second "costumbre,"
reform-minded authorities tried to subordinate these borracheras as a
lesser part of what they considered to be the more important and inclu-

sive traditional customs. Bands of musicians, for example, were occasionally summoned to the courthouse prior to the beginning of ceremonial festivals, where they were told to play for a prescribed number of days. Rather than attempting to impose any hard-and-fast laws, which they were in any case unable to enforce, these authorities hoped that the musicians would settle innocuously into a more appropriate place within the festivals. Similarly, instead of prohibiting the sale of beer and liquor across the board, authorities asked Vecino merchants to sell only after the principal ceremonies had been completed, and to voluntarily cease their sales once the elders had called the festival to a close. "After all," the merchants and authorities happily agreed, "this is a mountain town, and one needs a little bit of liquor, just for the cold." As the night air descended, however, these agreements seemed always to evaporate. Almost inevitably, men became unglued by music and drink, and blood was drawn.

In the wake of such failures to control borracheras, purely ritual solutions provided the third strategy for preserving the integrated costumbre of Santa Teresa. For example, a Franciscan priest temporarily stationed in the town was asked to intervene after a series of murders. He erected a thick wooden cross at the spot where a man bled to death during a drunken festival, and then held a special mass in which he counseled the assembled crowd against drinking and violence. After this priest left town, however, the cross fell apart, and the drunken killings continued. Later a Huichol shaman was hired to carry out a curing ritual for the town. He diagnosed a blockage that made the saints of the church unreceptive to the prayers of the town's inhabitants. To cure this blockage, he snatched a prayer arrow out of thin air during a midnight curing ritual in the town's church. Many people told me that they believed that this ritual might have healed the town of its "dirtiness," but the senior governor that year never paid the shaman his promised fee, diluting the cure's effectiveness.

In marked contrast to those hoping to "rescue" the festivals were those who simply tried to avoid coming to town as much as possible. For them, as I was told again and again, the festivals were *pura borrachera* (Spanish: a complete drunken mess), and so they no longer attended them. Indeed, during the time of my fieldwork, two former Tereseños re-jected Santa Teresa's costumbre entirely, replacing it in their own lives with a type of born-again Christianity preached locally by a Canadian evangelist named Miguel Zelenitsky (Coyle 1998). A former Pachitas singer and centurion, for example, stopped attending all of Santa Teresa's ceremonies, including those of his brother, the ceremonial elder of his (former) maize-bundle group. Similarly, his son, who might have been expected to move into an office in the town's courthouse, became a lay preacher who began a regular series of Sunday meetings for the other hal-lelujahs (slang for born-again Christians) in the town. Most important among these committed Christians—who numbered about fifty during the time of my fieldwork—was a former governor and maize-bundle-group elder, Manuel Aguilar Cerros. Upon his conversion, this ceremo-nial elder is rumored to have dispersed his white ceremonial maize into the rest of his seed maize and to have thrown a small statue of Santiago that he had kept in his home into a nearby stream.

Like Zelenitsky, these converts argued that the costumbre was used by the devil to enslave the souls of the Coras who practiced them. A pam-phlet distributed by Zelenitsky spelled out this sentiment and tied it to the drunkenness and violence of the festivals: "In the festivals it is pure evil. For most people they are nothing more than an excuse to get drunk, to the extent that women and at times children get drunk. People fight until they draw blood, and I have also seen people die of gunshots. All of this is proof that the festivals are not from God. Today the greater part of your tribe is enslaved to sin and vice, and do not want to obey God. They love dirt more than cleanliness, lies more than the truth" (Zelenitsky 1990: 6–7). Similarly, when I asked a recent convert why he had aban-doned the costumbre, he responded with a question that referred back to Zelenitsky's above-cited argument. "Which would you yourself rather drink from," he asked me, "a clean glass of water, or water clouded with mud?" From this convert's perspective, the costumbre was entirely dirty and could not be redeemed. His only option was to throw out all of the muddied water.

This extreme reaction to the drinking and violence that began to over-take Santa Teresa's community festivals in the 1970s did not typify the disposition of the wider Tereseño population. Rather, they simply shifted their attention away from the community festivals to focus on the costumbre of their own maize-bundle-group mitote ceremonies and, to a lesser extent, on community-level mitote ceremonies. These private maize-bundle-group ceremonies—celebrated away from Santa Teresa's enclaved ceremonial plaza—allowed Tereseños to construct small "peoples," which provided support and defense in an increasingly violent town.

The Flores family was particularly strong in this regard. Criticized by Tereseño authorities in the 1970s for "only getting drunk in order to fight," during the time of my fieldwork the Floreses controlled large expanses of pasture and farmland and celebrated elaborate maize-bundle-group ceremonies. In my fieldnotes I wrote about a conflict in town in which members of this maize-bundle group came to the defense of one of their own:

Cruz Flores was brought before the *juzgado* [Spanish: courthouse] for failure to pay for an animal that he had supposedly stolen. He was drunk, of course, and the authorities tied him inside the casa de los governadores, as they do with all prisoners [since the jail was demol-ished] for fear that they will escape. In this case, however, they didn't tie him up good enough, because he jumped out of a hole in the thatched roof and made for . . . Flores Territory. When I caught up to the assembled group the two comandantes were dragging him back, but then the Flores boys reached them. . . . Other Flores boys jumped on top of them: Chelo, Ubaldo, who else? Others allied with the Flo-res stood to one side, ready to jump in: Martimiano Morales, Nicho Flores, Rogelio Ortiz. Things were beginning to look ugly. Andrés grabbed at one of the commandant's pistols, which he carried loaded in his belt, and it looked like people would be killed. The commandant flushed and wildly shouted out, "LEAVE THAT PISTOL ALONE YOU SON-OF-A-BITCH." At this point the gravity of the situation seemed to strike everyone, and the comandantes were able to drag

Cruz back. . . . Andrés stayed out of sight for a few hours, but to demonstrate his attitude toward the authorities he and Chelo were later spotted drinking by Demetrio's shop, seeming to invite a confrontation that never came. (p. 121e)

After this incident, members of Amadeo Flores's maize-bundle group complained to me that Cruz Soto, the senior comandante, capriciously harassed them, using his authority to even the score on an old grudge. Cruz Soto argued that he was simply trying to complete his obligation as comandante. As a result of this dispute, however, he shortly thereafter abandoned the unpopular office that he had recently entered and retreated back to his ranch in fear of further retaliations as a result of his action against one of the Flores maize-bundle group.

Earlier that same year (1994) one of the participants in this fight, Martimiano Morales, avoided the hamstrung local authorities entirely. He went all the way to Jesús María to file an official declaration concerning another drunken dispute that threatened to escalate into a blood feud between the members of his own "people" and another group in the neighboring town of San Blasito: "Martimiano Morales states and declares that at 10 o'clock on July 25 [during the Festival of Santiago] Felipe Campos threatened me verbally. I asked him what he wanted with me, and he questioned whether I was a man or not, and I told him that I was. He invited me to go outside of town in order to shoot a few bullets at each other, and that if I didn't show up then he would be waiting in San Blasito, Municipality of Acaponeta, where he has his gente, to which I mentioned that I also have my own gente, who are known killers . . ." (síndico municipal archives). In cases such as these, maize-bundle groups were particularly important for personal defense. Without a "people," an individual was defenseless in a fight, and would have to back down from threats, weakening his local political and economic position more generally. Conversely, as the member of a large and coherent maize-bundle group, a person could actively assert himself, defending his own interests in the absence of any legitimate overarching political or legal authorities in the town. Indeed, in at least one case, a local ceremonial elder used his position as the leader of a particular maize-bundle-group "people" to shame-lessly promote himself and his sons.

For Timoteo Ramos Salazar, maize-bundle-group ceremonies served as a stepping stone in attempts to gain wider political power. His maize-bundle group became very strong in and around the district of Rancho Viejo, where a number of Tereseños had moved in the wake of the Vecino takeover of Santa Teresa. Timoteo had only a few children, but on meeting Náyari newcomers to Rancho Viejo he points out distant and con-trived kin relations and so draws these isolated households towards his own well-established maize-bundle-group ceremonies. Timoteo used his local position to claim offices for himself in Santa Teresa's courthouse (with Prudencio Medina in 1988), to take over one of the tractors pur-chased by INI, and to travel widely in Mexico making secret deals as a "representative" (Spanish: *representante*) and "leader" (Spanish: *líder*) of Santa Teresa as a whole. As a result of these deals he received a paid local government position, and each of his two sons received paid offices in Je-sús María. This self-promotion antagonized much of the rest of the com-munity of Santa Teresa, but his position as an important ceremonial elder also provided him with a large "people" that he used to intimidate smaller groups as he grabbed government contracts and promoted him-self to outside government officials.

Much more common than this dramatically self-serving use of maize-bundle-group ceremonies to gain wider power was the simpler strategy of consolidating closely related groups of people around a specific house-hold. The members of such maize-bundle groups were less concerned with expanding their political power and position within Santa Teresa's community-level political vacuum than they were with defending them-selves and their lands in a violent and fragmented town. They were less concerned with representing the community as a whole than they were with consolidating their day-to-day control over particular territories within that community. The Flores family, the Pachecos, the Zepedas, the Ortiz family, the Noriegas, the Salazars, and the Morales family have all responded to the recent breakdown of older Vecino/anti-Vecino political factions into blood-feuding maize-bundle groups not by grabbing power, but by retreating to their own costumbres.

The male relatives of a pair of maize-bundle groups (both named Morales) at a ranch outside of Santa Teresa provide a good example. These two groups traded marriageable women for a number of years, which drew the two groups closely together. As a result of their combined strength, households associated with these closely related groups spread into the territory of a neighboring maize-bundle group, whose younger brothers abandoned their oldest brother (the ceremonial elder of that group) and moved closer to the town of Santa Teresa. Unaffiliated households like that of this isolated ceremonial elder could not hope to resist such territorial expansion because they faced intimidation or physical attacks by members of the larger maize-bundle group. In this case, the neighboring maize-bundle-group elder was forced to acquiesce, even inviting members of the expanding maize-bundle groups to his maize-bundle-group ceremonies in the hope that some accommodation might be reached.

Similarly, upon the death of the weakened old ceremonial elder Felipe Soto, the mitote ceremony that had been under his control was reinvigorated by his sons, who expanded the power of his maize-bundle group through their renewed attention to his mitote ceremonies. Prior to his death Felipe Soto had been most concerned with meeting his own limited needs, and so his mitote ceremonies were small. But after his death Gregorio Soto and his younger brothers began to hold more elaborate mitote ceremonies in which quantities of food were provided to formerly estranged maize-bundle-group members. Potential conflicts with these younger brothers—who claimed their deceased father's homestead— were ameliorated because Gregorio Soto built a separate nearby homestead at which he began to hold the group's mitote ceremonies, while his brothers continued to give him access to the orchard and plowlands at his deceased father's ranch. Indeed, together these brothers and their families were able to control almost the entire mesa of flat cultivable land that surrounded these two ranches, and were also able to successfully defend a large herd of cattle and pasture against thieves and neighboring maize-bundle groups.

Like the Morales family and the Sotos, most people in Santa Teresa during the time of my fieldwork believed the performance of maize-bundle-group mitote ceremonies offered advantages that could not be matched in the town's disorderly and chaotic festivals. These mitote ceremonies helped to build relatively unified groups that gave members a "people" who defended them against arrogant assaults or capricious exercises of power. They also helped to consolidate the control of lands in the absence of any type of locally recognized legal title or legitimate local authority. For such men, supervising community ceremonial festivals and defending abstract Tereseño interests (like prohibitions against producing drug crops), while at the same time serving as local delegates of corrupt and incompetent municipal and national governments, was simply not worth it. Instead, they retreated to their own costumbres, where the performance of private ceremonies ironically helped to perpetuate the violent divisions that characterized daily life in Santa Teresa at the time.

Paradoxically, however, even as these maize-bundle-group mitote ceremonies constituted distinct and potentially violent Tereseño "peoples," the retreat to a maize-bundle-group costumbre also offered hope for the resolution of some of the disputes and blood feuding that divided Tereseños. Although Tereseños sought to avoid cargo-system offices during the time of my fieldwork, when convinced to serve, they focused their sincerest efforts more on the community mitote cycle than on the town's festivals. Just as the general Tereseño population retreated from community ceremonies to their own maize-bundle-group ceremonies, the remaining cargo-system authorities retreated from the Day-of-the-Dead/Holy-Week cycle to the more private community mitote cycle celebrated away from the town's ceremonial plaza. Of these community-level mitote ceremonies, attention was focused on the parched maize mitote ceremony, the most symbolically potent and unifying ceremony that I witnessed in Santa Teresa.

This ceremony is celebrated soon after the new courthouse authorities enter their offices, before the drinking and violence associated with the long Pachitas/Holy Week season wears down their enthusiasm (and their "laziness" catches up with them). At this point in the year, the senior authorities can still muster the will to fast, as they do at their own maize-bundle-group mitote ceremonies. Indeed, to fulfill their obligation to this ceremony, each year they spend five bitterly cold nights maintaining a quiet and sleepless vigil next to a central ceremonial fire on an exposed flank of Kweimarutse, the sacred mountain. In the years that I attended this ceremony, this effort brought much of the violently fractured town of Santa Teresa temporarily together in a way that the Day-of-the-Dead/Holy-Week festivals did not. As night fell, members of the town's distinct maize-bundle groups arrived at the "upper plaza" and lit their own small fires around the edges of the dance plaza. Many people, perhaps hesitant to show their faces, refused to leave these private fires all night. But as the bow-drum singer began his drone and the alguaciles of the courthouse took up their flag and lance to start the dancing, many others fell in behind as they would at their own maize-bundle-group ceremonies. Here, the absence of the otherwise worrying hallelujahs was hardly noticed; in the collective dance plaza they seemed like inconsequential cultists, comparable to those who several years ago started following a nearly forgotten and laughable old man who claimed to be the Virgin of Guadalupe. As the nights wore on and the dancers continued to follow their counterclockwise path around this "highest" fire, the new town of Santa Teresa itself seemed to darken and disappear. The pachiteros—who also joined in the dancing—seemed as innocent and pure as the malinche they surrounded in a protective group. Beneath the flower-draped chánaka pole, all moved together "on top of the earth," and painful memories of men like my friend Antonio Morales Morales, killed stupidly during a festival in the town's ceremonial plaza, dropped away.

Similarly, at the subsequent community-level cicada mitote in May, the aggressive selfishness that had come to be associated with the drinking of beer and tequila in the town's festivals was also temporarily suspended. This ceremony, coming as it does after the disturbances of Holy Week, drew fewer people. Still, those who harvested and roasted the wild century plants, carefully fermenting and distilling them to produce liquor, found a different kind of drunkenness on the slopes of Kweimaru-tse than they did in Santa Teresa's ceremonial plaza. Whereas Tereseños speak of the desire for commercial alcohol as a type of illness—an infec-tion that can only be purged through several days and nights of steady drinking—the liquor distilled each year at the community-level cicada mitote remained a sacramental manifestation of the deceased ancestors. It was drunk not to be a "man," but to re-establish an umbilical-cord-like connection to the long line of Tereseños—*Náyari Kweimarútsana*—who were born onto the earth around that center mountain to die flowering into heaven.

Indeed, after the community cicada mitote concluded, the rains soon began, isolating Tereseños from one another in a sort of seasonally en-forced detente. But once the Day-of-the-Dead/Holy-Week cycle started again with the Festival of Santiago in July and then with the festivals lead-ing up to the Day-of-the-Dead Festival, the drinking and violence of the ceremonial plaza's "other costumbre" resumed. By this time, cargo-sys-tem authorities looked towards the ends of their terms of office, and again became too "lazy" to intervene in the disorderly ceremonial festivals. As a result, instead of building on the sense of legitimate traditional author-ity produced by the "higher" community mitote cycle, the unruly fes-tivals that constitute the Day-of-the-Dead/Holy-Week cycle each year weakened that legitimacy. Rather than adding its own moral and political message to the costumbre, the cycle undermined the hierarchical inclu-siveness of the community's mitote ceremonies. Thus, in Santa Teresa's enclaved ceremonial plaza, the powerful but transient ceremonially re-produced sense of collective identity again faded with the turn of the sea-sons. Individual Tereseños—confronted once more by their histories of pain and loss—retreated from the new town of Santa Teresa and back to their own costumbres and their own violently divided "peoples."

7

Conclusion

In Santa Teresa, what development anthropologist Thayer Scudder (1999: 356) calls "community unraveling" is closely tied to both local social conflicts and national and international interventions. But Scudder also argues that such "unravelings" have simultaneous effects on both local communities and the transnational political economy, leading to what Hirst and Thompson (1996: 10; reviewed by Hout 1997: 102) call the "fundamental problematicity" of globalization: the difficulty of effectively governing an unevenly globalized society. Thus, a number of scholars of globalization are coming to the conclusion of the Tereseño man who spoke to me in the wake of the killing of Antonio Morales Morales: "Today there is both too much and too little government."

Jürgen Habermas presciently addressed this issue of transnational political instability at the juncture of contradictory governing institutions long before the term "globalization" came into fashion. As he puts it (Habermas 1975: 49), "advanced capitalism creates 'new' needs that it can not satisfy." Most crucially from the perspective of Santa Teresa and much of the rest of mountainous west Mexico, it creates the need for legitimate local government even as state policies undermine the authority of traditional officials—a contradiction that Habermas (1975, passim) calls "legitimation crisis." In supervising national and international development activities, for example, the Mexican state sought to improve conditions for "the realization of capital" (Habermas 1975: 36) in Santa

Teresa. At the same time, however, the federal bureaucracy also "shift[ed] its boundaries" (Habermas 1975: 47) into local affairs. As an assertive new presence in the town, the state sought to present itself as a legitimate government through projects and institutions like Plan HUI-COT and INI. Affiliated bureaucrats involved themselves in a historically pre-existing conflict for control of the courthouse, even as state policies undermined the local officials' traditional legitimacy, which, as Habermas (1975: 47) points out, "cannot be regenerated administratively." The result was a political vacuum that presented opportunities for transnational drug cartels, who used the absence of effective judicial control to promote illegal crops. Thus, community unraveling and legitimation crisis in Santa Teresa developed as globalizing forces engaged with what June Nash (1981: 398) calls "historically preexisting institutional patterns," turning the violence of one little mountain town into a test of national and international military resolve against the drug economy.

Public ceremonies in Santa Teresa have not simply reflected these trends, but have themselves been deeply implicated in this expanding legitimation crisis. As Rappaport (1979: 177) observes, "[ritual] performance is not merely a way to express something, but is itself an aspect of that which it is expressing." When speaking to me about their ceremonies, Tereseños also emphasized this connection between ritual and history by explicitly linking the shifting performance of these traditions both with the killings of local people like Antonio Morales Morales and with their own feelings of "laziness" and "dirtiness." Indeed, they would have probably agreed with Rappaport (1979: 197, 208) that ritual "established the conventions by which [people] order themselves," and that "a liturgy's hierarchical dimension orders relations of sanctity as well as of authority, efficacy and contingency." Certainly, the ceremonies that I witnessed provided a window onto such a hierarchically and synecdochically organized world, even as the public enactment of that world shattered such images.

Ranch-level mitote ceremonies have been the foundation of Náyari hierarchical political authority since ancient times, but their relation to putatively higher-level ceremonial traditions has shifted in a movement that Eric Wolf, in his classic history of Mesoamerican civilization, calls a "continuous tension between expansion and decay" (1959: 20). In the years prior to the conquest of the Mesa del Tonatí in 1722, for example, ranch-level mitote ceremonies were practiced in close relation to a more elaborate and centralized political tradition that seems to have included human sacrifice, perhaps linking it to earlier Mesoamerican ceremonial traditions. However, after the Spanish mission program finally began in the Sierra del Nayar, this centralized ceremonialism was suppressed. Jesuits like Jacome Doye had a good deal of success in substituting their own centralizing Catholic traditions in ceremonial centers like Santa Teresa, even as other Náyarite in Santa Teresa and the rest of the Sierra del Nayar resisted introduced Catholic ceremonial traditions. They ridiculed and threatened missionaries while continuing small-scale mitote ceremonialism in the canyon lands beyond the control of the few soldiers who were assigned to the region. After a brief resurgence of centralizing indigenous ceremonialism following the removal of the Jesuits from the missions of the Sierra del Nayar, this uneasy coexistence of Catholic and indigenous ceremonialism continued until the disruption associated with the War of Independence forced most government and church officials out of the area.

The War of Independence marked the beginning of an important period in the "tension" within Tereseño public ceremonialism. In the absence of state-level political or religious authorities, the Catholic-derived ceremonialism that many Náyarite had learned from their missionaries was dis-integrated (cf. Fox 1995: 278) from its mission-period structure and re-integrated with previously outlawed mitote ceremonialism by the not-too-distant ancestors of today's living Náyarite. This newly integrated ceremonialism continued the community-level ceremonialism of the mission period, and so provided Náyari authorities in the towns of the Sierra del Nayar with a platform from which to participate in the expansionist—even nationalist—nineteenth-century rebel military confederacy of Manuel Lozada. Accounts by early explorers and ethnographers make it clear that this integrated costumbre was performed in Santa Teresa and other Náyari towns of the Sierra del Nayar by the end of the nineteenth century, and that the performance of this costumbre provided a pathway (or, better yet, a staircase) that might be followed by men as they took their positions as the legitimate overarching traditional authorities of these towns.

This unifying symbolism was still apparent during the time of my fieldwork. At that time, ranch-level mitote ceremonies constructed cognatically recruited descent groups that formed localized political structures stratified by both age and gender, with a senior male serving as the group's leader. These mitote ceremonies also positioned maize-bundle-group members both spatially (in relation to a meaningful territory) and temporally (in relation to sets of still-active deceased ancestors and ancestral deities). Community-level ceremonies, in turn, mobilized particular themes that expanded and reoriented the symbolic connotations produced in maize-bundle-group ceremonies, creating an image of overarching inclusiveness between particular descent groups and the community as a whole. The community mitote cycle produced this image by elaborating tropes (e.g., the offering of maize, collective dancing around a ceremonial fire, and the drinking of freshly distilled liquor) that in each person's life were earlier produced in maize-bundle-group ceremonies. The Catholic-derived Day-of-the-Dead/Holy-Week cycle, on the other hand, produced this sense of inclusiveness by focusing on the senior members of the community's cargo system, who were portrayed as maintaining a relatively austere "sinlessness" when compared to younger men. In both cases these ceremonial cycles—when performed properly—provided a clear place for cargo-system officers, particularly senior courthouse officers, as the legitimate traditional authorities of a hierarchically organized community.

Documents show, however, that following the Lozada period, these ceremonial traditions became a battleground within a long-term factional struggle between regional Vecinos (and their Tereseño supporters) and other Tereseños who opposed the policies of this group. These Vecinos (re)settled the area during the Porfirian period, and then armed civil defense brigades against the "bandits" who operated in the area during the Mexican Revolution and the Cristero Wars. However, as these

Vecinos and their supporters began to represent themselves as the local-level officials of sovereign municipal and national governments in Santa Teresa, many Tereseños began to question their legitimacy. This anti-Vecino faction used ceremonial festivals as a forum to fight these pretenders to local authority. When they failed to push the pro-Vecino faction out of the courthouse, many fled to a neighboring town in fear of their lives, taking the traditional symbols of office with them. This relatively clear-cut political factionalism, however, splintered after the federal agency known as INI—supported by international development organizations like UNESCO—entered into this long-standing conflict during the 1960s.

The Instituto Nacional Indigenista had long been used by the national government of Mexico as a tool to open isolated areas like the Sierra del Nayar to economic development, but in doing so it also further undermined the already shaky legitimacy of the Tereseño men who occupied Santa Teresa's courthouse. Nonetheless, INI pushed through a series of political initiatives and development projects with little or no input from the Tereseño elders who were represented as the traditional leaders of the town. Thus, as the dramatic repercussions of these initiatives and projects became evident, they also eroded the willingness of local people to put out the effort required to properly continue their ceremonial traditions. The contradictory performances required of these Tereseño men both as traditional authorities and as supposed members of municipal and national bureaucracies soon proved impossible to balance. Beer and tequila, at first paid for with livestock and wages provided by INI and then with profits from illicit drug production, became ubiquitous in the town's festivals. Rather than positioning local officials as the legitimate traditional authorities of the community, these festivals instead served to enact their corruption and "laziness," as Tereseños put it. In response to this inability of local officials to control their town, national and international military and paramilitary forces were deployed, but without the bureaucratic support that might have established a legitimate government in the area. The political effect of this escalated violence was to further undermine the legitimacy of Santa Teresa's traditional authorities, who proved incapable of defending their people against the abuses of the internationally supported federal army.

Tereseños responded to this community-level political vacuum by retreating from the "dirty" festivals celebrated in the town's central plaza. Some of these people abandoned Santa Teresa's costumbre entirely to become evangelical Christians. Many more, however, simply backed away from the "drunken mess" of the community ceremonial festivals to the more private and orderly mitote ceremonies celebrated by their own maize-bundle groups (and, to a lesser extent, to the community mitotes celebrated by the remaining community-level authorities). These descent-group mitote ceremonies helped Tereseños to build relatively reliable political affinities that allowed them to mobilize closely related "peoples" to defend themselves from future violence, and to avenge past assaults. In this way, as Tereseños abandoned festivals for their own private descent-group ceremonies, the costumbre acted as a kind of fault line dividing and fracturing the community. The ancestral ceremonial traditions that held out the promise of an inclusive territory and ancestry linking all Tereseños instead produced a series of cleavages that drove the splintered Tereseño community ever more apart.

But although the ethnohistorical perspective used to understand this situation helps to clarify the shifting "tensions" within Santa Teresa's costumbre and between Santa Teresa and the outside world, it provides no simple answer to the difficult question people asked me in the wake of the murder of Antonio Morales Morales: "Why are we always killing each other?" Rather than providing a definitive answer that might open onto a new and different future, I instead focused on the past. I showed that the knife that killed Antonio had a deep history. It was unsheathed by Prudencio Medina and Cresenciano Morales as they battled for control of Santa Teresa's courthouse, and it was sharpened to an edge during the drunken fighting that overtook Tereseño costumbre after the growth of the new town of Santa Teresa in the 1970s and 1980s. But when that knife finally slashed into Antonio's throat on the morning of September 29, 1994, Antonio's relatives and friends, like those of his attacker, were less concerned with the historical determinations represented by that weapon than with the killing itself. They withdrew, turning away from the grotesque spectacle of their relative and neighbor lying dead among the town's ceremonial dancers. In anger and fear they drifted away from the courthouse into smaller groups of people like themselves, people who share their ceremonies and who might defend or avenge them when that knife is raised again.

Eventually, I also retreated from Santa Teresa and back through the heavily militarized border at Nogales, Arizona. In newspapers, I read about even more programs to increase U.S. military spending in places like Santa Teresa. The long history of Santa Teresa presented here does allow me to make at least one clear statement about these programs: reliance on military options to resolve local social conflicts is both short-sighted and self-defeating. As long as we fail to acknowledge the complicated local histories of the places in which we intervene, our actions contribute to legitimation crises with profound effects for a wide variety of human populations connected in an unevenly globalizing world.

1. Am+na tawáusimwa mehmih tátahakura'ase, '+ xú'urya'ara '+ mwaxá.

2. Am+mu tyakura'aseh tawáusimwa, am+na weirah—hachútipwamwá ti'ikweiri.

3. Atá m+xá apu tyutyátwiwa, para mehe'eranyeh tutatih hayan tyiwáchauve.

4. Para mehmih hayan yehtyé'evehsi '+ t+ tanána, a+ nyunyataxa.

5. Para t+ke hat+tyitantyi'únyi'ira. Ha'íh h+meh héhtyetya'ase.

6. Katú x+htya'ana tyé tyit+hé'ehu'ura. Hayan tyunutya'áse.

7. Siempre tyáwau '+ h+mih '+ t+ tanana. O '+ tawáusimwa.

8. Kamehke ha'a+ tyí'ivehsi. Hayapu hachwit+tyipwa + wastari, atá '+xá '+yamwatye mah+ tyú'urityeh. '+ yuri—'+ tanana—tyah+me'e huri, '+ wáw+'ra'ra t+ se'eryaha'ara.

9. Para hamw+'+mu + tawáusimwa, hamw+'+mu putyé'evehsi '+ tanána '+t+yeh hihsé'eryahá'ara.

10. '+ Dios t+hatyátau. Hayámunu hé'emat+hyá'aru ákawi'imwa hehmatatya'amwa.

11. Hapun'+mwa putyi'iyre'enye pumu mataha'aru, 'a'upumismo putyetyatau.

12. 'a'upumismo, 'ak+ Santiago. H+ntuti'ita'ú'unyi, himih '+ tava'aka. Am+'+nyunetyáutwirehsi.

13. Para t+nyaw+ra. Kanuh+ríh ha'arámwa'are . . . Hayapu tyíse'eryahá'ara. Hayan tyutyátwiwaka.

14. Hayán t+tyíse'eryahá'ara '+ wáw+ra'ara '+ tanana héht+yá'atyi'awáx '+t+ tahatsi.

15. Hayampu néihmih tyi'awáx. Tyuxának+ra, t+híhwautyáumwa'areh.

16. Hayamu tyíhyauk+áu'ut+há'aseh'ereh t+wanána, mwehtyáunachaka yapumwapuhyú'urupi s+'ata'as+.

17. Néimih putyihautawa, 'achwit+tyípwa—k+yé, yamwatye, '+ty+ritzeh. Kapú tyit+yutyaw+.

18. Hyuveme 'a'am+natáye'ehihtanyá t+ hayú'una hihyaure'enye. Háut+hi re'ese'eré+wanana.

19. Hayápui t+hatyíwaura'ara. Hayapui t+h+hnihatsú hayan pwa'ar+.

20. Ni hatsú hayan petyá'araste, héh nanyat+tyáhamwatahéh.

21. A'+na anaké, puhihya'ara '+ t+ke hihwáuchaumwa'areh, 'ata 'a'um 'a'+n hyu'ume.

22. Después ni yeh xapw+ pwa'ar+. Puri yeh yahyuve'ere 'a'+na.

23. Puri yeh muhihye'eraka chi'itá, hayapunutzi: "Kapu yeh h+h wápw+'."

24. "'áta kiye'etze. Nyanyih wany+cháumwa'areh. Nyakeh tyit+héh. Nyakeh u'uhakanye. Nyakeh hayan wá'ar+, bueno. Áta kiyehi más tyit+ 'iytya'."

25. Mat+tsami tyityútawaka: visaru, ts+ ('+ puhákwa '+ tz+), 'ata he'eh '+ mistu.

26. 'amw+'+ma pú 'aná'aratsaka hata'í ha'+ka hunána has+yéh nehkamwát+se mu vehveh.

27. 'as+ni "niché hátyatawa." 'a'hauye siempre pu k+lehn anku'uryát+.

28. 'as+yeh, "nána, natáw+'+re." Mat+yeh ha'u watyátawaka '+ mistu.

29. 'as+yeh, "nána, mahautáhe." Matá k+ ts+ watyátawaka. Muyahautáhe.

30. 'ata hautéycha himih k+ tye'era. 'ata a'+na, bueno. Kapu tyit+ watyáw+.

31. Mat+tyámi k+ visaru. Metyatáwa 'am+ yutyeche. Metyak+ para siempre.

32. Pu n+ tye'era háw+'+re. Matahe'eh k+ turu, amupui tyityátawaka.

33. 'am+na 'ikú 'atahé kawayu. Hayapui he'enye tyitye'utawaka, hayapui 'ata 'a'+natyityútawaka.

34. Kaputyityuhé hayapuna. Hayapu nahus+ makatyihénini.

35. 'ata 'a'+na, kapu hachuyéhtye.

36. Séh ní'inira. Wapwa ní'inira. 'Anxivi ní'inira, muri metyityitáve.

37. Wákasi, twixu, chívutye, kányaxe, kawayu, muri métyityihauk+.

38. 'a+na t+ núki hayan tyé'e k+hunána t+ hayan hachu tyih' hu'ure'enye 'anxíni'inira.

39. "Hayapuna hus+' makatyiyénini. Xapununahi'eh."
40. T+nuki hayán tyehatéxa '+ tye'erá 'as+yeh, "yáwa'ariche."
41. "Patayéh tyetya'a'+ háti. Patayéh katyetyatawa ya hachú katyauwatyévi. Patayéh katyatatón. 'Anxíxika puyéh 'u'umaka pehpih katyatan."
42. Bueno, hayapu 'iyiyú'+r+. 'amumi hyuwóse 'a+na t+ke hívehsiva.
43. Mat+tyáxa t+h+: "Kapúxapui nyehimí hawauka, '+t+ kewáuchaumare. Tyesi 'a+na."
44. 'ata 'a+ina—sáutari san miguel háyamu hatawamwa 'a+k+h—'a+na '+t+ pa'ar+ puké namehtyáumware.
45. 'apu '+mwa putyiháu'+r+. Tyésiwaka h+meh. Kapu 'e'eraunyit, kapu h+rí.
46. Hayapunyu, t+pwa hayán. 'a+ himí nyutányaku'uve, 'ata t+pwa haw+'+himí nyutányaku'uve san miguel sáutari.
47. Kapa hatsu t+pwa xapui núrinyi. Mí tyamwarísima h+'+mwahu.
48. T+ hayínyi h+mwá hiyautyéxa'ax. 'am+na t+ hayényi hyutyenye.
49. Hayampu hih néimih tyihyawáx '+ tyúxanak+ra, 'ata hu muku 'apuk+ tyautyámwa hukúhitze, 'ata chwinú hámwauhautyárax+ '+ túke pu hitze, 'ata múkutsara tyeketyi wakwaka '+ hukutye.
50. 'ata 'am+na 'a'+pu heh haránachiri, '+ tyetyé '+ mwáxa twiwatyáutawaka.
51. 'ata nyeputyutye'atau, 'am+na muk+k+. 'ata yeri. 'am+t+'i' nyétyutyátau. Ya mukutyáxa.
52. 'ata 'am+na '+ tavastara t+ wasé'ere hanátwiwanéwaka.
53. Hayan tyutyityé yastyéwáta'ara, haná t+pwa wanéwaka. At+n hatza t+pwa wame'ere.
54. Kameké ham+n putyehéihka, mu tyaru. Apu '+mwá putyihau'ur+.
55. Hayapu 'a+na watáu'umwa t+'+h+h hyúm+nyu.
56. Para kapu '+ pu h+me '+ytyá tyetyihikukuvata'ara.
57. 'ata 'a+na hih yau'ura hu vástarahimi, tyutyámwatye héhnetyuhúm+ni.
58. 'at+ké t+pwa nyetyeré'enexau nyam+n.
59. Narimake méneheika, hatzu tyit+'+h+h nyau tyá'u t+'+re '+ himí, '+tzáke heka hyúchatza.
60. 'atañu t+híw+'+re népuke'e t+hítyá heh netyit+tya'átawavi k+tzi.
61. 'ata yuri, hachútipwamwaka yeh tyutyátáu '+ tavástara.
62. No más que hayanu hatzu tyétyew+'+re, ti hayani tyinataka hachupwamaka tyit+ t+ ya wa'aratau.

BIBLIOGRAPHY

Amaro Romero, Jesús

    1993 *Los Coras de Santa Teresa de El Nayar, Nayarit.* Tepic: Impresora Castellanos.

Anonymous

    1971 Historia de las misiones en la prelatura del Nayar. *Ecos misionales* 15 (4): 1–7. Zapopan: Basílica de Zapopan.

Basso, Ellen B.

    1985 *A Musical View of the Universe: Kalapalo Myth and Ritual Performance.* Philadelphia: University of Pennsylvania Press.

Bauman, Richard

    1977 *Verbal Art as Performance.* Prospect Heights, Ill.: Waveland Press.

Benítez, Fernando

    1973 *Historia de un chamán cora.* Mexico City: Ediciones ERA.

Bernard, Russell H.

    1988 *Research Methods in Cultural Anthropology.* Newbury Park, N.J.: Sage Publications.

Bloch, Maurice

    1986 *From Blessing to Violence: History and Ideology in the Circumcision Ritual of the Merina of Madagascar.* Cambridge Studies in Social Anthropology. Cambridge, Eng.: Cambridge University Press.

Borah, Woodrow

    1970 Latin America, 1610–60. In *The New Cambridge Modern History,* Vol. 4, edited by J. P. Cooper, 707–726. Cambridge, Eng.: Cambridge University Press.

Briggs, Charles

    1988 *Competence in Performance: The Creativity of Tradition in Mexicano Verbal Art.* Philadelphia: University of Pennsylvania Press.

Cancian, Frank
 1965 *Economics and Prestige in a Mayan Community: The Religious Cargo System of Zinacantán.* Stanford: Stanford University Press.

Cárdenas de la Peña, Enrique
 1988 *Sobre las nubes del Nayar: Camino rural Ruiz-Valparaíso.* Mexico City: Secretaría de Comunicaciones y Transportes and Gobierno del Estado de Nayarit.

Casad, Eugene
 1984 Cora. In *Studies in Uto-Aztecan Grammar*, edited by Ronald Langacker, 151–459. Dallas: The Summer Institute of Linguistics and the University of Texas.

Cesaire, Aimé
 1972 *Discourse on Colonialism.* New York: Monthly Press.

Chance, John K.
 1990 Changes in Twentieth-Century Mesoamerican Cargo Systems. In *Class, Politics and Popular Religion in Mexico and Central America*, edited by Lynn Stephen and James Dow, 27–42. Society for Latin American Anthropology Publication Series, Vol. 10. Washington, D.C.: American Anthropological Association.

Clifford, James
 1988 *The Predicament of Culture: Twentieth-Century Ethnography, Literature, and Art.* Cambridge, Mass.: Harvard University Press.

Coyle, Philip E.
 1997 Hapwán Chánaka ("On Top of the Earth"): The Politics and History of Public Ceremonial Tradition in Santa Teresa, Nayarit, Mexico. Ph.D. diss., University of Arizona.
 1998 The Customs of Our Ancestors: Cora Religious Conversion and Millennialism, 2000–1722. *Ethnohistory* 45 (3): 509–542.

De Palma, Anthony
 1995 Mexico's Indians Face New Conquistador: Drugs. *New York Times*, June 2.

Derrida, Jacques
 1973 *Speech and Phenomena: And Other Essays on Husserl's Theory of Signs.* Translated by David B. Allison. Evanston, Ill.: Northwestern University Press.

Durham, Deborah, and James W. Fernandez
 1991 Tropical Domains: The Figurative Struggle Over the Domains of Belonging and Apartness in Africa. In *Beyond Metaphor: The Theory of Tropes in Anthropology*, edited by James W. Fernandez, 190–212. Stanford: Stanford University Press.

Eco, Umberto

 1976 *A Theory of Semiotics*. Bloomington: Indiana University Press.

Ellison, Katherine

 1989 Dark Side of Mexico's Drug War. *San Jose Mercury News*, December
 17.

Fernandez, James W.

 1972 Persuasions and Performances: Of the Beast in Every Body and the
 Metaphors of Everyman. *Daedalus* 101 (1): 39–80.

 1986 *Persuasions and Performances: The Play of Tropes in Culture*. Bloomington:
 Indiana University Press.

 1991 Introduction: Confluents of Inquiry. In *Beyond Metaphor: The Theory of
 Tropes in Anthropology*, edited by James W. Fernandez, 1–13. Stanford:
 Stanford University Press.

Fox, Richard G.

 1992 For a Nearly New Culture History. In *Recapturing Anthropology*, edited
 by Richard G. Fox. Santa Fe: School of American Research.

 1995 Cultural Dis-Integration and the Invention of New Peace-Fares. In
 Articulating Hidden Histories: Exploring the Influence of Eric Wolf, edited
 by Jane Schneider and Rayna Rapp. Berkeley: University of California
 Press.

Fox, Robin

 1967 *Kinship and Marriage: An Anthropological Perspective*. Cambridge Studies
 in Social Anthropology No. 50. Cambridge, Eng.: Cambridge University Press.

Freidrich, Paul

 1991 Polytropy. In *Beyond Metaphor: The Theory of Tropes in Anthropology*,
 edited by James W. Fernandez, 17–55. Stanford: Stanford University
 Press.

Gamio, Manuel

 1916 *Forjando patria*. Mexico City: Porrua Hermanos.

Geertz, Clifford

 1973 *The Interpretation of Cultures*. New York: Basic Books.

Goffman, Irving

 1974 *Frame Analysis*. New York: Harper and Row.

Greenberg, James

 1981 *Santiago's Sword: Chatino Peasant Religion and Economics*. Berkeley:
 University of California Press.

 1989 *Blood Ties: Life and Violence in Rural Mexico*. Tucson: University of
 Arizona Press.

Grimes, Joseph, et al.
  1981 *El Huichol: Apuntes sobre el léxico*. Ithaca: Cornell University Department of Modern Foreign Languages.
Grimes, Joseph, and Thomas B. Hinton
  1969 The Huichol and the Cora. In *The Handbook of Middle American Indians*, Vol. 8, edited by Robert Wauchope, 792–813. Austin: University of Texas Press.
Habermas, Jürgen
  1975 *Legitimation Crisis*. Translated by Thomas McCarthy. Boston: Beacon Press.
Hers, Marie-Areti
  1992 Renovación religiosa y resistencia indígena en Nayarit: Los Coras en 1767. In *Organización y liderazgo en los movimientos populares novohispanos*, edited by Felipe Castro G. et al., 177–202. Mexico City: Universidad Nacional Autónoma de México.
Hewitt de Alcántara, Cynthia
  1984 *Anthropological Perspectives on Rural Mexico*. London: Routledge and Kegan Paul.
Hill, Jonathan
  1988 *Rethinking History and Myth: Indigenous South American Perspectives on the Past*. Urbana: University of Illinois Press.
Hinton, Thomas B.
  1964 The Cora Village: A Civil-Religious Hierarchy in Northern Mexico. In *Cultural Change and Stability: Essays in Memory of Olive Ruth Barker and George C. Barker Jr.*, edited by Ralph C. Beals, 44–62. Los Angeles: University of California Press.
  1970 Indian Acculturation in Nayarit: The Cora Response to Mestizoization. In *The Social Anthropology of Latin America: Essays in Honor of Ralph Leon Beals*, edited by Walter Goldschmidt and Harry Hoijer, 11–35. Latin American Studies, Vol. 14. Los Angeles: University of California at Los Angeles Latin American Center.
  1972 Pre-Conquest Acculturation of the Cora. *Kiva* 37: 161–168.
  1981 Cultural Visibility and the Cora. In *Themes of Indigenous Acculturation in Northwest Mexico*, edited by Thomas B. Hinton and Phil C. Weigand, 1–3. Anthropological Papers of the University of Arizona No. 38. Tucson: University of Arizona Press.
Hirst, Paul, and Grahame Thompson
  1996 *Globalization in Question: The International Economy and the Possibilities of Governance*. Cambridge, Eng.: Polity Press.

Hout, Wil

1997 Globalization and the Quest for Governance. *Mershon International Studies Review* 41: 99–106.

Iturrioz, José Luis, Paula Gómez, Xitakame Julio Ramírez, and '+r+temai Gabriel Pacheco

n.d. *Estructura fonológica y sistema ortográfico.* Vol. I of *Gramática didáctica del huichol.* Guadalajara: Universidad de Guadalajara, in press.

Jáuregui, Jesús

1997 El Recuerdo del Señor Manuel Lozada está todavía patente. In *El Tigre de Alica: Mitos e historias de Manuel Lozada*, edited by Jesús Jáuregui and Jean Meyer, 13–54. Mexico City: SEP/CONAFE.

Jáuregui, Jesús, and Carlo Bonfiglioli, eds.

1996 *Las Danzas de conquista.* Vol. 1 *México contemporáneo.* Mexico City: Consejo Nacional para la Cultura y las Artes and Fondo de Cultura Económica.

Katz, Friedrich

1976 Peasants and the Mexican Revolution in 1910. In *Forging Nations: A Comparative View of Rural Ferment and Revolt*, edited by J. Spielberg and S. Whiteford. East Lansing: Michigan State University Press.

Leach, Edmund

1965 *Political Systems of Highland Burma.* Boston: Beacon Press.

Leitch, Vincent

1983 *Deconstructive Criticism: An Advanced Introduction.* New York: Columbia University Press.

Liffman, Paul M., and Philip E. Coyle

2000 Introduction: Ritual and Historical Territoriality of the Náyari and Wixárika Peoples. *Journal of the Southwest* 42 (1): 1–8.

Lumholtz, Carl

1987 [1902] *Unknown Mexico: Explorations in the Sierra Madre and Other Regions, 1890–1898.* Vol. 1. Mineola, Minn.: Dover Books.

Magriñá Ocampo, Laura María

1999 Los Coras entre 1531 y 1722: ¿Indios de guerra o indios de paz? Licenciada thesis, Escuela Nacional de Antropología e Historia, Mexico City.

McCarty, Kieran, and Dan S. Matson

1975 Franciscan Report on the Indians of Nayarit, 1673. *Ethnohistory* 22 (3): 193–222.

Meyer, Jean

1973 Problemas campesinos y revueltas agrarias. Mexico City: Secretaría de Educación Pública.

1984 *Esperando a Lozada*. Morelia: El Colegio de Michoacán.

1988 *Nayarit: Magia en la sierra, riqueza en los valles*. Mexico City: Secretaría de Educación Pública.

1989 *El Gran Nayar*. Colección de documentos para la historia de Nayarit No. 3. Guadalajara: Centro de Estudios Mexicanos de la Embajada de Francia en México/Universidad de Guadalajara.

Monzón, Arturo

1945 Restos de clanes exogámicos entre los coras de Nayarit. Publicación No. 4. Mexico City: Escuela Nacional de Antropología.

Moore, Sally Falk

1978 *Law as Process: An Anthropological Approach*. London: Routledge and Kegan Paul.

Nahmad, Salomón

1981 Some Considerations of the Indirect and Controlled Acculturation in the Cora-Huichol Area. In *Themes of Indigenous Acculturation in Northwest Mexico*, edited by Thomas B. Hinton and Phil C. Weigand, 4–8. Anthropological Papers of the University of Arizona No. 38. Tucson: University of Arizona Press.

Nash, June

1981 Ethnographic Aspects of the World Capitalist System. *Annual Review of Anthropology* 10: 393–423.

Netting, Robert McC.

1986 *Cultural Ecology*. Prospect Heights, Ill.: Waveland Press.

1993 *Smallholders, Householders: Farm Families and the Ecology of Intensive Sustainable Agriculture*. Stanford: Stanford University Press.

Neurath, Johannes

1998 Las Fiestas de la casa grande: Ritual agrícola, iniciación y cosmovisión en una comunidad wixarika (T+apurie/Santa Catarina Cuexcomatitán). Ph.D. diss., Universidad Nacional Autónoma de México, Mexico City.

Nugent, Daniel

1993 *Spent Cartridges of Revolution: An Anthropological History of Namiquipa, Chihuahua*. Chicago: University of Chicago Press.

Ortega, José

1754 Maravillosa reducción y conquesta de la provincia de San José del Gran Nayar, nuevo reino de Toledo. In *Apostólicos afanes de la Companía de Jesús*. Reprint, Mexico City: Editorial Layac, 1944.

Peirce, Charles Saunders

1931 *Collected Papers*. Cambridge, Mass.: Harvard University Press.

Preuss, Konrad Theodor

1912 *Die Nayarit Expedition*. Leipzig: Verlag B. G. Teubner.

1998a Observaciones sobre la religión de los coras. In *Fiesta, literatura y magia en el Nayarit: Ensayos sobre coras, huicholes y mexicaneros*, edited by Jesús Jáuregui and Johannes Neurath, 105–118. Mexico City: Centro Francés de Estudios Mexicanos y Centroamericanos/Instituto Nacional Indigenista.

1998b Más información acerca de las costumbres religiosas de los coras, especialmente sobre los portadores de falos en Semana Santa. In *Fiesta, literatura y magia en el Nayarit: Ensayos sobre coras, huicholes y mexicaneros*, edited by Jesús Jáuregui and Johannes Neurath, 127–137. Mexico City: Centro Francés de Estudios Mexicanos y Centroamericanos/Instituto Nacional Indigenista.

Rappaport, Roy A.

1979 *Ecology, Meaning, and Religion*. Berkeley: North Atlantic Books.

Reina, Leticia

1980 *Las Rebeliones campesinas en México*. Mexico City: Siglo Veintiuno.

Rodríguez, Sylvia

1996 *The Matachines Dance: Ritual Symbolism and Interethnic Relations in the Upper Río Grande Valley*. Albuquerque: University of New Mexico Press.

Rojas, Beatriz

1993 *Los Huicholes en la historia*. Mexico City: Centro de Estudios Mexicanos y Centroamericanos, Colegio de Michoacán, Instituto Nacional Indigenista.

Ruiz-Cabañas I., Miguel

1989 Mexico's Changing Illicit Drug Supply Role. In *The Drug Connection in U.S.–Mexican Relations: Dimensions of U.S.–Mexican Relations*, Vol. 4, edited by Guadalupe González and Marta Tienda, 43–70. Center for U.S.–Mexican Studies. San Diego: University of California Press.

Sánchez O., J.

1980 Etnografía de la Sierra Madre Occidental: Tepehuanes y mexicaneros. Colección Científica: Etnología No. 92. Mexico City: Secretaría de Educación Pública.

Sapir, David

1977 The Anatomy of Metaphor. In *The Social Uses of Metaphor*, edited by David J. Sapir and J. C. Crocker. Philadelphia: University of Pennsylvania Press.

Schieffelin, Edward L.
   1976 *The Sorrow of the Lonely and the Burning of the Dancers.* New York:
   St. Martin's Press.
Scudder, Thayer
   1999 The Emerging Global Crisis and Development Anthropology:
   Can We Have an Impact? *Human Organization* 58 (4): 351–364.
Spicer, Edward
   1980 *The Yaquis: A Cultural History.* Tucson: University of Arizona Press.
Stoeltje, Beverly J., and Richard Bauman
   1988 The Semiotics of Folklore Performance. In *The Semiotic Web*, edited
   by Thomas A. Sebeok and Jean Umiker-Sebeok. Berlin: Mouton de
   Gruyter.
Telléz Girón, Roberto
   1987 Informe sobre la investigación folklórico-musical realizada en la
   región de los coras, estado de Nayarit, enero a mayo de 1939. In
   Investigación folklórica en México. Materiales, Vol. 2. Mexico City:
   Instituto Nacional de Bellas Artes, 177–198.
Tello, Antonio
   1891 *Libro segundo de la crónica miscelánea, en que se trata de la conquista espiri-
   tual y temporal de la santa provincia de Xalisco, en el nuevo reino de la Galicia
   y nueva vizcaya y descubrimiento del Nuevo México.* Guadalajara: Impr. de
   "La República Literia" de C. L. de Guevara.
Turner, Victor
   1967 *The Forest of Symbols: Aspects of Ndembu Ritual.* Ithaca: Cornell University Press.
   1974 *Dramas, Fields, and Metaphors: Symbolic Action in Human Society.* Ithaca:
   Cornell University Press.
United Nations, Department of Economic and Social Affairs Statistical Office.
   1985 *Demographic Yearbook.* New York: United Nations.
Warner, Richard
   1998 An Ethnohistory of the Coras of the Sierra del Nayar, 1600–1830.
   Ph.D. diss., University of California, Santa Cruz.
Weber, Max
   1961a The Types of Authority. In *Theories of Society*, Vol. 1, edited by T. Par-
   sons et al., 626–631. New York: The Free Press of Glencoe.
   1961b Legitimate Order and the Types of Authority. In *Theories of Society*,
   Vol. 1, edited by T. Parsons et al., 229–238. New York: The Free
   Press of Glencoe.

Weigand, Phil C.

1992 Consideraciones sobre la arqueología y la etnohistoria de los mexicaneros, los tecuales, los coras, los huicholes y los caxcanes de Nayarit, Jalisco y Zacatecas. In *Ensayos sobre el Gran Nayar entre coras, huicholes y tepehuanos*, edited by Phil C. Weigand, 175–214. Mexico City:
Centro de Estudios Mexicanos y Centroamericanos de la Embajada de
Francia en México/Instituto Nacional Indigenista/El Colegio de
Michoacán.

Wolf, Eric

1959 *Sons of the Shaking Earth*. Chicago: University of Chicago Press.

Zelenitsky, Miguel

1990 ¡La Costumbre! Available free from Apdo. Postal 21, Rosamorada,
Nayarit, 63630, Mexico.

INDEX

ABOUT THE AUTHOR

Philip E. Coyle is an assistant professor of anthropology at Western Carolina University in Cullowhee, North Carolina. Previously, he held a postdoctoral fellowship in the Department of Anthropology at the Smithsonian Institution's National Museum of Natural History. Recent publications include "The Customs of Our Ancestors: Cora Religious Conversion and Millennialism, 2000–1722" in *Ethnohistory* and " 'To Join the Waters': Indexing Metonymies of Territoriality in Cora Ritual," published as part of a special issue of the *Journal of the Southwest* on Náyari and Wixáritari territoriality co-edited with Paul M. Liffman. Current research interests include the ethnography of the Gran Nayar region, interpretation theory, exchange economies, farming systems research, and comparative approaches to the study of legitimation crisis.